D1501710

Volume ONE

MEASURING
EGO
DEVELOPMENT

Construction and Use of a
Sentence Completion Test

Jane Loevinger

and

Ruth Wessler

MEASURING EGO DEVELOPMENT

Volume ONE

 Jossey-Bass Inc., Publishers

615 Montgomery Street • San Francisco • 1970

MEASURING EGO DEVELOPMENT
  Volume One: Construction and Use of a Sentence Completion Test
  by Jane Loevinger and Ruth Wessler

Jossey-Bass, Inc., Publishers
615 Montgomery Street
San Francisco, California 94111

Library of Congress Catalog Card Number 71–92891

International Standard Book Number ISBN 0–87589–059–8

Manufactured in the United States of America
    Composed and printed by York Composition Company, Inc.
    Bound by Chas. H. Bohn & Co., Inc.

JACKET DESIGN BY WILLI BAUM, SAN FRANCISCO

FIRST EDITION

Code 7010

THE JOSSEY-BASS BEHAVIORAL SCIENCE SERIES

General Editors

WILLIAM E. HENRY, *University of Chicago*

NEVITT SANFORD, *Wright Institute, Berkeley*

Preface

The scoring method presented in *Measuring Ego Development* is intended for use in judging level of ego development (I-level is our code term) from written sentence completion protocols of women and girls at least twelve years old. All examples are taken verbatim from real protocols but not all from the same test form. Although there are age and sex restrictions in the use of this manual, the concept and the method are not so restricted. Trained raters find much carry-over to protocols of men and boys, and the concept appears equally applicable to younger children who are administered a similar test verbally.

Choice of ego development as the trait to be measured was not accidental or arbitrary. It is the master trait. There are, of course, other ways of describing it and other modes of access to it. Granting that, we feel that mastery of our scoring manual is not just another trick for the clinician's or research worker's bag. It is a method of deepening one's knowledge of and access to personality. With the possible exception of persons skilled in scoring another closely related test of this master trait, psychologists who intend to use it either clinically or in research should become involved in scoring protocols. It is doubtful that persons with only an abstract knowledge of the construct can obtain useful results. Learning to score the test is indispensable to appreciating the nuances of ego development; the tacit component of scoring and knowledge of the trait are identical.

Our definition of ego level in terms of all its manifestations is the strength of our method, as contrasted with those techniques that depend on a single aspect, such as interpersonal relatability, conceptual complexity, moralization of judgment, achievement motivation, or recognition of oneself as origin or pawn of destiny. But this virtue of the concept comes close to being the downfall of the inexperienced rater. The number of aspects to be kept in mind is almost impossibly large. A surprising number of sheer clerical errors occur, even when conscientious professional psychologists are the raters. Hence we recommend working in teams of no fewer than two, at least until the technique is thoroughly familiar. All research work should depend on the consensus of two or more raters, except possibly with raters of demonstrated competence.

The test is intended for group administration. Small differences in instructions and conditions have occurred during our work, in some cases on purpose, and they do not seem to be important. Most subjects spend about twenty or thirty minutes completing the form. An experienced rater can count on spending approximately twenty minutes scoring each protocol.

To master the scoring system requires from one to two months of study, not full time, if the rater immerses himself in one or at most two items per day. We strongly recommend that a person who wishes to use our system follow explicitly the training program outlined in Chapter Five and Appendices C and D, regardless of whether the particular items he uses are the same as ours. As we show in Chapter Three, the scoring system can be mastered by these exercises alone. We have made no tests on persons attempting to score without following such a set of exercises or their equivalent, and we feel that a person who uses the manual without the prescribed training has no right to claim that his ratings follow our method. Most persons can profit by checking some of their scoring with an experienced rater if one is available. Or two students studying the manual can criticize each other, which is, after all, the method we used at the beginning.

Our impression is that about a year's graduate work in psychology or its equivalent in technical training is a desirable prerequisite for manual users. The corresponding intellectual level is indispensable. No amount of intuition or sensibility can substitute for a disciplined knowledge, and no amount of technical training can make a first-class rater out of someone whose personal limitations bar him from free access to his intuition and sensibility.

In another and more vexing direction, the logic of ego theory demands that only those of relatively high ego level can become adequate scorers. Our chief access to a person's ego level is precisely that it limits what he can conceive and perceive; that limitation holds for raters as well as for subjects. However, the manual and experience can be trusted to extend one's range. In general, no ordinary groups, including professional psychologists or graduate students in psychology, include more than an occasional person higher than the conscientious level. We do not consider ourselves exceptions, yet we have learned to make independently reproducible identifications at the autonomous and integrated levels, though not as uniformly as we can at lower levels. The many solid conformists among professional psychologists do not make first-class raters.

In summary, the personal qualifications for raters are technical training and the corresponding intellectual level and a capacity for introspection together with some measure of inner freedom or access to intuition. More of one compensates for less of another in only a limited way; indeed, an overrefined conscience can be incapacitating. Unhappily, except for the technical training, which is not strictly necessary, these are the qualities one cannot judge in oneself.

Whatever merits the manual has stem largely from the diverse personalities and talents that have contributed to it. To acknowledge the contributions adequately is impossible. The method was introduced to us by the late Virginia Ives Word, who had had seven years' experience with similar data and an essentially similar construct (although it was called interpersonal integration) at Camp Elliott Naval Retraining Station, San Diego, under the direction of J. Douglas Grant, Eric Gunderson, Marguerite Warren, and others. The first scoring manual, assembled by Elizabeth Nettles, was used in an early set of studies. Nina deCharms, working at first under the direction of Kitty LaPerriere, revised the manual on the basis of those studies and of a more rigorous conception. Application of the manual to several sets of data and revision in accord with feedback from those data became the responsibility of Ruth Wessler. Carolyn Redmore assumed a large share of the burden during the latter half of the revision. Collaborators in the final revision included William L. Shumate, Jr., Augusto Blasi, and Ruth Lucas. Participating in various ways at other stages of the work were several gifted persons, not all psychologists. All made distinctive contributions to our thinking, and their services as raters were essential to the work. They included Nancy Lamb, Myron Pollack,

Joan Nicholson, James Bitter, Calvin Burnett, Betty Sue North, Barbara Fineberg, Doris Storms, Ellen Rashbaum, and Paul Wagman.

We benefited from consultations on methodological and substantive issues and from validational studies; our consultants included Edward Joseph Shoben, Darrell Bock, Fumiko Samejima, Ardie Lubin, Shirley Chater, and, over a long period of time, Virginia Turner and Claire B. Ernhart. Several graduate students in psychology at Washington University used one or another form of the test in research whose results have enriched our views. These students included Dr. Blasi, Dr. Redmore, Dr. Shumate, Mrs. Lucas, Eleanore Kenney, Ivan Sherick, Mary Ann Bednar, and Elizabeth Penick.

Our first secretary, Radah Schmidt, assumed unusual responsibilities, such as coding and decoding materials, deleting information to protect subjects' identity and to safeguard research design, and catching our various errors in the course of typing manuscripts. These duties have all devolved upon Mary Jane Todoroff. In addition, Mrs. Schmidt compiled Appendix E.

The foregoing include men and women; people at all stages of adult life; married, unmarried, and divorced persons; parents, step-parents, and grandparents; Negroes and whites; old-line Americans, immigrants, first-generation Americans, second-generation Americans, and foreigners; persons from all parts of the country; persons of various and of no religious persuasions; and so on. Although it is not usual or perhaps even socially approved to call attention to such differences, we believe we have used that variety of outlook to good advantage. A moving and significant fact is that probably everyone mentioned above can find his distinctive mark somewhere in the pages that follow. For that reason it is impossible to credit anyone adequately.

Our work has been supported successively by grants M-1213, M-5115, and MH-05115 and by Research Scientist Award 1K05 MH 00657 from the National Institute of Mental Health, Public Health Service. A small grant from Central Midwestern Regional Educational Laboratory permitted multilith publication of the prepublication version of the manual. We acknowledge also the services of Washington University Computing Facilities through National Science Foundation Grant No. G-22296.

St. Louis, Missouri   JANE LOEVINGER
February 1970   RUTH WESSLER

Contents

Preface   xi

List of Figure and Tables   xix

1. The Concept of Ego Development   1
   Stages • Ego as Frame of Reference • Meth-
   odological Difficulties

2. Construction of the Manual   14
   Quantification Strategy • History of Format •
   Rules for Constructing the Manual • Empirical
   Verification Paradigm • Samples Used

3. Evaluation of the Manual   34
   *Study of Single Women   •   Studies with Prepubli-
   cation Manual   •   Summary*

4. Manifestations of Ego Level in Sentence
   Completions   54
   *I-2: Impulsive   •   Delta: Self-Protective (Oppor-
   tunistic)   •   Delta/3: Transition from Self-Protec-
   tive to Conformist   •   I-3: Conformist   •   I-3/4:
   Transition from Conformist to Conscientious   •
   I-4: Conscientious   •   I-4/5: Transition from Con-
   scientious to Autonomous   •   I-5: Autonomous   •
   I-6: Integrated*

5. Instructions to Raters   110
   *Self-Training Program   •   Procedure for Rating
   Single Responses   •   Recording the Ratings   •
   Sources of Bias*

6. Deriving Total Protocol Ratings   126
   Ogive Rules   •   Rating a Total Protocol

APPENDICES

A. Instructions for Administering the Sentence
   Completion Test   137

B. Current Forms of the Washington University
   Sentence Completion Test for Measuring
   Ego Development   139

C. Examples and Scoring Keys for Practice
   Item Ratings   147

D. Examples and Scoring Keys for Practice
   Total Protocol Ratings   182

E.   Procedures for Preparing Written Responses
     for Research Purposes   228

F.   Some Probabilistic Considerations Concern-
     ing Extreme Ratings   234

G.   Abbreviations   237

     References   239

     Index   241

List of Tables

FIGURE

1 Distributions of Total Protocol Ratings by Age and Sex of Toronto School Children   50

TABLES

1 Some Milestones of Ego Development   10

2 Example of Manual Revision   24

3 Use of Samples in Construction and Revision of Item Manuals   27

4 TPRs in Samples Used in Manual Construction and Revision   28

xix

5   DEMOGRAPHIC VARIABLES OF SAMPLES USED IN MANUAL
    CONSTRUCTION   29

6   SOURCES OF SUBJECTS FOR SAMPLES USED IN MANUAL
    CONSTRUCTION   30

7   CORRELATIONS OF ITEM RATINGS AND ITEM WORD COUNT
    WITH TPR   36

8   SEX AND EDUCATION OF RATERS   38

9   DEMOGRAPHIC VARIABLES OF SAMPLES USED IN MANUAL
    EVALUATION   39

10 SOURCES OF SUBJECTS FOR SAMPLES USED IN MANUAL
    EVALUATION   40

11 PER CENT AGREEMENT ON I-LEVEL, BY ITEMS (36 ITEMS)   41
12 INTERRATER CORRELATION, BY ITEMS (36 ITEMS)   42

13 PER CENT AGREEMENT OF SELF-TRAINED RATERS WITH
    COMPOSITE TRAINED RATER, BY ITEMS (36 ITEMS, 100
    CASES)   43

14 CORRELATION OF SELF-TRAINED RATERS WITH COMPOSITE
    TRAINED RATER, BY ITEMS (36 ITEMS, 100 CASES)   43

15 INTERCORRELATIONS BETWEEN SUMS OF ODD AND EVEN
    ITEM RATINGS FOR RATERS 5 AND 6   44

16 PER CENT AGREEMENT AND INTERRATER CORRELATIONS
    FOR TPRs FOR TRAINED RATERS   46

17 COMPARISON OF TPR OF TRAINED AND SELF-TRAINED
    RATERS   47

18 EIGEN VALUES FOR PRINCIPAL COMPONENT ANALYSIS,
    SEALED SAMPLE   48

19 COEFFICIENT ALPHA COMPUTED FOR PRINCIPAL COMPO-
    NENT SCORES, SEALED SAMPLE   49

20 CORRELATIONS OF VARIOUS KINDS OF TOTAL SCORES FOR
    TRAINED RATERS, SEALED SAMPLE   52

21 AUTOMATIC RULES FOR ASSIGNING TOTAL PROTOCOL RAT-
    INGS TO THE OGIVE OF ITEM RATINGS   129

22 BORDERLINE RULES FOR ASSIGNING TOTAL PROTOCOL RAT-
    INGS TO THE OGIVE OF ITEM RATINGS   129

V̶olume **ONE**

MEASURING
EGO
DEVELOPMENT

Construction and Use of a
Sentence Completion Test

CHAPTER 1

The Concept of
Ego Development

The concept of ego development is not new. Students today often have the impression that the concept originated with Freud and has become the exclusive province of certain psychoanalysts and psychoanalytically trained psychologists. The truth is that Freud, on purpose, did not use the term "ego." He avoided terms of Latin origin in favor of words chosen from common speech, a preference that has been ignored by his translators. We must seek the origins of the concept without regard to exact phraseology, the I, the me, the self, or whatever term might be used, and there are surprisingly many. In this broader perspective we can see the origin of the concept in ancient Greek, Hebrew, and Hindu cultures.

Probably the greatest interest in the concept was during the early

1

years of this century, partly as a result of Darwin's discoveries, which stimulated interest in all kinds of development. One of the finest books ever written on ego development is the *Ethics* of John Dewey and James Tufts, first published in 1908 and for many years a widely used text in that standard undergraduate course, more highly patronized in that day than its counterpart would be today. No standard part of the curriculum today offers insight into ego development to any comparably large group of students. In the past standard child development courses have blurred the topic, if texts are a fair indication. They tended to study development seriatim, taking in order the various behaviors of average and not so average children. The weakness of that atheoretical approach is that all kinds of development are occurring simultaneously. Mere observation will never yield a concept such as ego development nor enable us to distinguish its signs from the signs of intellectual development, of psychosexual development, or of adjustment. Ego development is an abstraction, and abstractions must guide observation in mature sciences, as, of course, the abstractions are also guided and corrected by the observations. The shift from an atheoretical child psychology to an abstract developmental psychology is occurring on many fronts at present. Our work is part of that broader movement.

A long-standing issue in the study of ego development is whether the ego is derived from and more or less explained in terms of instinctual drives. In the early years Freud and many of his followers said yes, and it was agreement on this issue that brought certain psychoanalysts and certain behaviorists into each other's arms during the 1930s in common cause. This was the issue that had separated Freud and Adler in 1911. Adler maintained that drives were largely subordinate to the ego and that the ego strove spontaneously to develop. Freud said that to adopt Adler's view would be to give up the hard-won gains of the psychology of the unconscious. Many of the other psychoanalysts felt at the time that Freud's and Adler's views could be reconciled. Some years later Freud returned to the topic of ego development and made major theoretical contributions whose importance has not yet been adequately recognized by some of his followers, including those heralded as the "new psychoanalytic ego psychologists," much less by those who see themselves as opponents of psychoanalysis (Loevinger, 1969).

Harry Stack Sullivan rendered the concept of ego development sufficiently exact and detailed to bring it within the scope of measurement. His thinking was influenced by that of Freud and Adler, but also by that of Mead and Baldwin, whose writings Freud was not familiar with. Although deeply influenced by Freud, and although he incorporated in his thinking many of Freud's major discoveries, Sullivan objected to the surplus, mythical meaning built into many psychoanalytic terms. He particularly objected to the terms ego, superego, and id. His term for what we call the ego was the self-system. *The Interpersonal Theory of Psychiatry* (Sullivan, 1953) gives his chronicle of the development of the self-system. This book and an entirely independent one, Piaget's *Moral Judgment of the Child* (1932), are the spiritual ancestors of a cohort of ego theorists in psychology. The cohort includes Clyde Sullivan, Douglas Grant, and Marguerite Warren (Sullivan, Grant, & Grant, 1957), who call the developmental sequence interpersonal integration; Kenneth Isaacs (1956), whose term is interpersonal relatability; Robert Peck (Peck and Havighurst, 1960), whose term is character development; Lawrence Kohlberg (1964), whose term is the moralization of judgment. Probably one should also include O. J. Harvey, David Hunt, and Harold Schroder (1961), although there are some difficulties in assimilating their original conception of cognitive complexity to the foregoing group of concepts. Their current versions, not necessarily all identical, may be closer. While there are differences in the conceptions put forth by all the foregoing authors, there are also common elements. All of the conceptions project an abstract continuum that is both a normal developmental sequence and a dimension of individual differences in any given age cohort. All represent holistic views of personality, and all see behavior in terms of meaning or purposes (as opposed to concepts such as psychic energy that pervade certain psychoanalytic accounts). All are more or less concerned with impulse control and character development, with interpersonal relations, and with cognitive preoccupations, including self-concept. The inclusiveness of these concerns is our case for saying that no term less than ego development can encompass the phenomena at issue (Loevinger, 1966). Finally, although the sequence of stages is not identical from author to author, there are many recurring similarities.

We shall present only our own version of the sequence; it has, however, been borrowed from many of the foregoing and other sources. An earlier version formed the framework with which we began working with the sentence completion (SC) test. The present version has been corrected and added to by the data obtained using the SC test. After presenting a synopsis of the characteristics of the several stages, we shall relate our conception to the choice of measuring instrument. Following that section, we shall give some of the reasons why the differences among the several versions of the sequence cannot be simply and unequivocally resolved.

STAGES

In the first stage the infant constructs for himself a stable world of objects. In doing so, he separates out himself as an object in that world. Constitution of self and outer reality are necessarily correlative.

This stage can be subdivided into a presocial or autistic phase and a symbiotic phase. Sometimes the term ego development is reserved for this period alone. However, intellectual development, psychosexual development, and later adjustment all depend on successful solution of the problems of this period, as much as does ego development. Strands of development later quite distinct are very much one thing at this time. We include this period in our schema for theoretical completeness, but it is not represented in our work with the SC test.

In the next stage the child asserts his growing sense of self by the word "No." He is governed by his impulses, hence we call it the impulsive stage. The impulses affirm his sense of self, although they are curbed by the environment—by immediate rewards and punishments. Magical ideas probably prevail in place of later conceptions of causation. Punishment seems to be perceived as retaliatory and as immanent in things. Other people are perceived primarily as sources of supply. Good guys give to me, mean ones don't. There is cognitive confusion as well as cognitive simplicity, but no true complexity. Good and bad may be equated with clean and dirty.

The first step in the direction of control of impulses and hence of character development is a paradoxical one. The child becomes capable of delay when it is to his immediate advantage. We formerly called this the opportunistic stage, but our own data give more support to calling it self-protective. A more or less opportunistic hedonism appears to be secondary in prominence. Persons in this stage understand the concept of blame, but they tend to blame others, or circumstances, or some part of themselves for which they do not feel responsible. If they get in trouble, it is because they were with the wrong people. They understand that there are rules, but their own chief rule is don't get caught. Some of them are manipulative toward other people, which implies greater comprehension of motives than in the receptive-exploitive attitude of the previous stage. They are concerned with controlling and being controlled, with snaring, with domination, and with competition. Life is a zero-sum game. What you win, I lose.

Most children around school age or during the early school years progress to the next stage, conformity. More people have recognized and described this stage than any other. Here the child identifies himself with authority, his parents at first, later other adults, and then his peers. This is the period of greatest cognitive simplicity. There is a right way and a wrong way, and it is the same for everyone all the time, or for broad classes of people described in terms of demographic traits, most often gender. What is conventional and socially approved is right, particularly the behaviors that define the conventional sex roles. Rules are accepted because they are socially accepted, by whatever group defines the child's horizon. Disapproval becomes a potent sanction. There is a high value for friendliness and social niceness. Cognitive preoccupations are appearance, material things, reputation, and social acceptance and belonging. Inner states are perceived only in their most banal version (sad, happy, glad, angry, love and understanding), contrasting with an almost physiological version of inner life at lower levels (sick, upset, mad, excited) and a richly differentiated inner life at higher levels. People and one's own self are perceived in terms of social group classifications. Individual differences are scarcely perceived. The way things or people are and the way they ought to be are not sharply separated. Hence we have the phenomenon that people describe themselves and others in socially acceptable or, as psychologists like to say, socially desirable terms. People at the conformist stage constitute either a majority or a large minority in almost any social group.

The next stage is the conscientious one. The transition between the conformist and the conscientious stages is marked by heightened consciousness of self and of inner feelings. This transition appears to be modal for students during the first two years of college. A related aspect of the transition is perception of multiple possibilities in situations. Rules are seen to have exceptions or to hold only in certain contingencies. Once such complexities or proto-complexities are admitted, they continue to hold for higher stages.

At the conscientious stage inner states and individual differences are described in vivid and differentiated terms. One feels guilty not primarily when one has broken a rule, but when one has hurt another person. Motives and consequences are more important than rules per se. Long-term goals and ideals are characteristic: ought is clearly different from is. Psychological causation is perceived or conceived. Individuals at this level, and even more often at higher levels, refer spontaneously to psychological development in themselves and others, something that almost never occurs at lower levels.

The conscientious person is reflective. He describes himself and others in terms of reflexive traits. Of the reflexive traits, only self-consciousness and self-confidence appear below the conscientious level (and in the case of self-confidence, the reflexive reference is perhaps spurious). The conscientious person is truly self-critical, but not totally rejecting of self, as are some subjects at the lowest levels, as well as depressed people at any level. He is aware of choices; he strives for goals; he is concerned with living up to ideals and with improving himself. The moral imperative remains, but it is no longer just a matter of doing right and avoiding wrong. There are questions of priorities and appropriateness. Moral issues are separated from conventional rules and from esthetic standards or preferences, this being one aspect of the greater conceptual complexity at this level. Achievement is important, and it is measured by one's own inner standards rather than being primarily a matter of competition or social approval, as it is at lower levels.

The transition from the conscientious to the autonomous stage is marked by a heightened sense of individuality and a concern for emotional dependence. The problem of dependence-independence is recurrent throughout ego development. What characterizes this transitional stage is the awareness that even when one is no longer physically and financially dependent on others, one remains emotionally dependent. Relations with other people, which have been becoming deeper and more intensive as the person grew from the conformist to the conscientious stage, are seen as partly antagonistic to the striving for achievement and the sometimes excessive moralism and excessive sense of responsibility for self and others at the conscientious level. The moralism of lower stages begins to be replaced by an awareness of inner conflict. At this stage, however, the conflict, for example, over marriage versus career for a woman, is likely to be seen in such terms as to be only partly internal. If only society or one's husband were more helpful and accommodating, there need be no conflict. At the autonomous level one recognizes that conflict is part of the human condition.

The autonomous stage is so named partly because one recognizes other people's need for autonomy, partly because it is marked by some freeing of the person from the often excessive striving and sense of responsibility during the conscientious stage. Moral dichotomies are no longer characteristic. They are replaced by a feeling for the complexity and multifaceted character of real people and real situations. There is a deepened respect for other people and their need to find their own way and even make their own mistakes. Crucial instances are, of course, one's own children and one's own parents. Striving for achievement is partially supplanted by a seeking of self-fulfillment. In acknowledging inner conflict, the person at this level has come to accept the fact that not all problems are solvable. We do not believe that inner conflict is more characteristic of the autonomous stage than of lower stages. Rather, the autonomous person has the courage to acknowledge and to cope with conflict, rather than blotting it out or projecting it onto the environment. The autonomous person has a broader scope; he is concerned with social problems beyond his own immediate experience. He tries to be realistic and objective about himself and others.

In most social groups one will find no more than perhaps 1 per cent, and usually fewer, at our highest or integrated level. To telescope the whole sequence as a straightline growth from the lowest or impulsive to the highest or integrated level is to miss the spirit of the exposition. Only a few individuals reach the stage of transcending conflict and reconciling polarities that we call the integrated stage. Maslow (1954) has described these people as self-actualizing persons.

There is a temptation to see the successive stages of ego development as problems to be solved and to assume that the best adjusted people are those at the highest stage. This is a distortion. There are probably well-adjusted people at all stages. Certainly it seems reasonable to assume that there are well-adjusted children at all ages. Probably those who remain below the conformist level beyond childhood can be called maladjusted, and many of them are undoubtedly so even in their own eyes. Some self-protective, opportunistic persons, on the other hand, become very successful, and it is faintly presumptuous of those of us who never quite make it to call them maladjusted. Certainly it is a conformist's world, and many conformists are very happy in it, though they are not all immune to mental illness. Probably to be faithful to the realities of the case one should see the sequence as one of coping with increasingly deeper problems rather than to see it as one of the successful negotiation of solutions.

EGO AS FRAME OF REFERENCE

Let us return to our starting point, the concept of the ego. One of Alfred Adler's best known concepts is that of the "style of life," which at various times he equated with self or ego, the unity of personality, individuality, the method of facing problems, opinion about oneself and the problems of life, and the whole attitude toward life (Adler, 1956, p. 174). Adler seemed to mean all those terms to be different ways of describing a single thing or function. That is what we call the ego. This view of the ego contrasts with that to be found in some psychoanalytic writings, where the ego is spoken of as a collection of different functions, with its "synthetic function" just one among many. Adler's view was later elaborated, in somewhat different style, by Sullivan, who preferred the term self-system. The basic point has been carried still further by Fingarette (1963), who states that the search for meaning is not something the ego does but is what the ego is.

One of the most amazing things about the ego is its relative stability; it changes only slowly. In ego theory, including some psychoanalytic writings, accounting for the stability is not often seen as a major theoretical task. Simply to call the ego a structure, and then add that structures are by definition relatively stable, is a common practice but no solution. Sullivan (1953) did formulate a theory of ego stability, an anxiety-gating theory: By selective inattention, a person tends to recognize only what is in accord with his already existing self-system; thus his ego is his frame of reference. The reason is that discordant observations are anxiety producing, and a major purpose of the self-system is to avoid or minimize anxiety. (Fingarette would prefer to say that the failure to integrate an observation into one's current frame of reference is what anxiety is, rather than the cause of an emotion called anxiety. Anxiety, to Fingarette, is meaninglessness. But this is more a difference of theoretical formulation than of substance.)

A current theoretical dispute among some psychologists interested in ego development and related subjects concerns the relative importance of cognitive and affective factors in that development. This issue appears to be a relic of outworn categories of thought, for integration of observations into a coherent frame of reference is, obviously, cognitive, while anxiety is, obviously, affective. But the failure to attain a meaningful and coherent integration is precisely what generates anxiety.

Thus the search for coherent meanings in experience is the essence of the ego or of ego functioning, rather than just one among many equally important ego functions. The ego maintains its stability, its identity, and its coherence by selectively gating out observations inconsistent with its current state. (One man's coherence, however, is another man's gibberish.) Those theoretical conclusions are the foundation for use of sentence completions (SCs) as a method of measuring ego development.

The first methodological decision is that only a projective technique, a technique that requires the subject to project his own frame of reference, will suffice to measure ego development. This decision contrasts with the belief or hope that one day psychometric technology will advance to the point where objective measures will supersede projective ones. The necessity to rely on the operation of the subject's own frame of reference as a sign and measure of his ego level means that the projective techniques in use in our laboratory and several others are not holding operations or temporary expedients. Several research workers have tried to capture the variance elicited by SC tests with multiple choice forms based on observed free responses. The conclusion has always been that the nature of the task changes, and the merits of the SC test are lost.

METHODOLOGICAL DIFFICULTIES

Table 1 summarizes our current views on the substance of the successive stages. In one way or another it differs from what any of the other investigators in the field would draw up if he were to make a similar table. All of us deal with data, many of us with hundreds or even thousands of cases. Why should there be such unresolved differences?

First of all, there is no one-to-one correspondence between a given bit of behavior and its underlying disposition—in this case, ego level. No bit of behavior can be, or can be assumed to be, more than probabilistically related to ego level.

Second, all kinds of development are occurring at the same time. There is no completely error-free method of separating one strand of development from another. A particular bit of behavior may, and in general must be assumed to, reflect more than one strand of development. Ego development is conceptually distinct from intellectual development and psychosexual development, but it is bound to be correlated with them during childhood and adolescence. There is not even a guarantee of what psychometricians call local independence; that is, even for a group of constant chronological age, there may be a correlation between ego development and other strands of development. There is thus a confounding of variance that no amount of data will resolve into its component sources. If we depend entirely on empirical methods, we are at the mercy of such confounded variance; so theory must always temper our reliance on data, the more so as our data inevitably contain gaps.

Third, there is no error-free method of distinguishing probable signs of one ego level from signs of a probable correlate. As our first point declared, there are only probable signs, not certain ones. To the extent that the correlates are other developmental variables, this principle covers the same ground as the second one. There are other correlates, such as socioeconomic status, that are not developmental. There seem to be more low ego level persons at the lowest socioeconomic levels. How can we be sure whether a particular kind of behavior is displayed as a result of low ego level or the associated low economic and social level? In principle, with infinite amounts of data, one could make the distinction. In practice, with the kinds of data available, one cannot be sure.

Fourth, no behavioral task can be guaranteed to display just what one wants to know about ego level. Neither a structured test nor an unstructured test carries a guarantee. If the test is structured, the investigator is projecting his own frame of reference rather than tapping the frame of reference of his subjects, which is the very thing that reveals their ego level. If the test is unstructured, one cannot control what the subject will choose to reveal. One can become very adept at interpreting minimal signs, but there is always a chance that a person can conceal all, or will respond in such a way as to unwittingly conceal his usual ego level, in whatever sense others reveal theirs.

Fifth, every individual, in principle if not in actuality, displays behavior at more than one level. In general, every behavior sample must be assumed to be diverse with respect to level. The basic tasks of psychometrics are the translation of qualitative aspects of behavior to quantitative and the reduction of diverse observations to single scores. There is

Table 1

Some Milestones of Ego Development

Stage	Code	Impulse Control, Character Development	Interpersonal Style	Conscious Preoccupations	Cognitive Style
Presocial	I-1		Autistic		
Symbiotic			Symbiotic	Self vs. non-self	
Impulsive	I-2	Impulsive, fear of retaliation	Receiving, dependent, exploitive	Bodily feelings, especially sexual and aggressive	Stereotypy, conceptual confusion
Self-protective	Δ	Fear of being caught, externalizing blame, opportunistic	Wary, manipulative, exploitive	Self-protection, wishes, things, advantage, control	
Conformist	I-3	Conformity to external rules, shame, guilt for breaking rules	Belonging, helping, superficial niceness	Appearance, social acceptability, banal feelings, behavior	Conceptual simplicity, stereotypes, clichés

Stage	Code	Impulse Control, Character Development	Interpersonal Style	Conscious Preoccupations	Cognitive Style
Conscientious	I-4	Self-evaluated standards, self-criticism, guilt for consequences, long-term goals and ideals	Intensive, responsible, mutual, concern for communication	Differentiated feelings, motives for behavior, self-respect, achievements, traits, expression	Conceptual complexity, idea of patterning
Autonomous	I-5	Add: Coping with conflicting inner needs, toleration	Add: Respect for autonomy	Vividly conveyed feelings, integration of physiological and psychological, psychological causation of behavior, development, role conception, self-fulfillment, self in social context	Increased conceptual complexity, complex patterns, toleration for ambiguity, broad scope, objectivity
Integrated	I-6	Add: Reconciling inner conflicts, renunciation of unattainable	Add: Cherishing of individuality	Add: Identity	

NOTE.—"Add" means in addition to the description applying to the previous level.

no unique way to accomplish either task. Different psychometric procedures may lead to at least slightly different pictures of the successive stages.

Sixth, there are intrinsic difficulties in assigning behavioral signs to any developmental level, just because the underlying continuum is developmental. A sign that appears at one level in tentative or embryonic version appears at higher levels in increasingly clear and elaborated versions. In our SC work we found that a thought that appears at one level as a cliché appears in deeper, more convincing, and more complex versions at higher levels. A paradoxical aspect of this finding is that when we group a set of responses together to make a category and select the most representative response as category title, that title response will often be the very one that comes from a protocol rated a level lower.

A seventh point is that a behavioral sign may be discriminating in one direction only; thus there is an intrinsic ambiguity in assigning it to any level within those levels it applies to.

The eighth difficulty is that when we locate a sign at a given level, there are two sets of probabilities with respect to which we may compute our probability of error. The two sets generally dictate that a sign be placed at different levels. The first set is based on the total number of subjects showing a given sign, the second, on the total number of subjects at a given level. In the first case we may ask, given this sign, what is the probability that the subject comes from a given level; or, to say the same thing a different way, given this sign, what is the expected level of the subject who so responds? With respect to a given sample, this question is easily answered. The answer is, however, sharply dependent on the composition of the sample. Most samples contain only small numbers of cases at the extreme levels. Thus, one might find no sign which could be placed at the extreme levels by following this set of probabilities. One can make a strong case for placing signs only with respect to the alternative set of probabilities: given a particular ego level, what is the probability of showing this sign? Following this set of indicators exclusively does build in much error, since extreme cases will be rare in most subsequent samples. Moreover, since extreme cases are rare, decisions will often be based on numbers of cases that are absolutely small, which leaves us at the mercy of the idiosyncrasies of a few people. Again, for decisions regarding extreme levels, theory is indispensable as a supplement to data.

Finally, we must deal with the question of clinical insight as a source of knowledge about the appropriate level to class a given sign or response type. The clinician rarely thinks of his data in terms of the complex probabilities we have detailed in the above remarks. He tends to think of every bit of behavior as completely determined by the patient's particular constellation of traits and circumstances. Many signs which we force ourselves to classify, by our ground rules that call for classifying every response, a clinician would simply say do not reveal ego level. He would be right by his lights, since such responses are not unequivocal signs. Thus we see the psychometric frame of reference as radically different from the clinical frame of reference. There is also a deeper reason why the clinician's intuitive perceptions may be misleading. Every developmental level builds on and transmutes the previous one. The unconscious or preconscious components of the attitudes of one level are the corresponding attitudes of earlier levels. Precisely because the clinician has a deeper knowledge of his patient than is available on, say, a paper and pencil test, he may misjudge the level, either of a subject or of a particular sign. Hence clinical observation fails as a court of last appeal, though with proper precautions it is a valuable line of evidence additional to theory and test and experimental data.

CHAPTER 2

Construction of the Manual

Granted a notion of ego development (our current version is in Chapter One), given the responses of a subject to a sentence completion (SC) form (our present form is in Appendix B), how then shall we assign a place on the scale of ego development (I-level) to the subject? Our goal was not to train expert raters to the point of obtaining mutually reproducible results but to evolve a method, a scoring manual, and perhaps even more, a methodology of constructing scoring manuals. Equally important was that the method should yield results of substantive interest. The scoring manual should elucidate the construct of ego development.

QUANTIFICATION STRATEGY

At first it might seem that the whole idea of measurement is inapplicable to a test where every response, in principle if not actually, is different from every other. Traditionally there have been two ways of quantifying such tests. One is by counting or tabulating instances of some response attribute observable at a minimal inferential level, the other is by postulating a polar continuum and subjectively estimating where a given response falls on that continuum.

Examples of quantification by tabulation are R (number of responses), F (number of responses based on form), and C (number of responses based on color) for the Rorschach, and some measures of achievement motive for the Thematic Apperception Test (TAT). An elaboration of this measurement strategy creates sums, differences, and ratios out of the several tabulations.

An example of quantification by postulating a polar continuum is the scoring manual for the Rotter Incomplete Sentence Blank (Rotter and Rafferty, 1950). Each completion is rated for the degree of good or bad adjustment on a scale ranging from +3 through 0 to −3, with examples illustrating each level for each stem. This quantification strategy is the same as that in degree of agreement items, where the subject himself estimates where his attitude or feelings belong on the polar continuum.

The basic measurement strategy in our use of the SC test follows neither of these models, though of course we do make some tabulations. Our basic strategy is to identify qualitative differences in the successive stages of ego development. Every response is then matched against the sequence of qualitative stages and assigned to the level it most closely matches. The same milestone sequence is used as a scale for measuring a single response, a total protocol, an interview, and so on. We assume, as do Sullivan, Grant, and Grant (1957), that each person has some level of core functioning. In rating an interview or total protocol, the attempt is to estimate that level of core functioning. A single response naturally yields much less information, but we make the best estimate we can from whatever information is encoded within it. We use thirty-six items, and rarely if ever will all items in a single protocol have the same rating. Thus for any protocol there is a distribution of thirty-six item ratings. There are various ways of assigning a single total protocol rating (TPR) on the basis of the distribution of thirty-six item ratings; this is the problem of the scoring paradigm. (Given a paradigm, one must also assign values to the parameters, but that is hardly a problem.) Here then are two of the basic tasks of psychometrics: translation of qualitative into quantitative, or at least ordered, differences, and reduction of diversity, that is, translating a distribution of ratings into a single rating. The problem of the scoring paradigm will be treated in Chapter Six. In this chapter we shall describe our approach and methodology for assigning an I-level rating to a single response to a SC stem, that is, the construction of the item manuals.

We used at first only a four-point scale, corresponding to the second through fifth levels of Sullivan, Grant, and Grant (1957). We denoted them by numbers rather than by verbal labels, but they corresponded to our present levels called impulsive (I-2), conformist (I-3), conscientious (I-4), and autonomous (I-5). In the Sullivan, Grant, and Grant schema, the opportunistic and manipulative person is a species of conformist. Our experience was that the opportunistic-manipulative protocols resembled the impulsive ones more than did the conformist ones. Moreover, our acquaintance with the other relevant conceptions, both as they appear in publications and as we learned of them through informal contacts with other investigators, confirmed our own impression that the opportunistic orientation represents an earlier developmental level than the conformist orientation. A conception similar to that of Sullivan, Grant, and Grant, but having a particularly good description of the opportunistic level, is that of Isaacs (1956). He refers to this level as the Delta level, since his typology is denoted by the first six letters of the Greek alphabet, from a high level of Alpha to a low level of Zeta. Our raters have never been satisfied with the characterization of the Delta level as opportunistic. Only in the final stages of the completion of the present volume did it become clear that our own data support a characterization as self-protective and hedonistic more clearly than as opportunistic and manipulative.

We have retained the I-level designations for the four levels borrowed from Sullivan, Grant, and Grant, though we do not guarantee that those levels, as their meaning has evolved in our work, correspond exactly to the same levels as in later work of the California investigators. Similarly, we retain the designation Delta as our code term for the self-protective level. We are often asked why we do not renumber our stages consecutively. One reason is that some comparison with other investigators is preserved by keeping similar designations for similar stages. A more profound reason is that any numbering system is doomed to become obsolete as the construct evolves, and our numbers are no more than code names for the levels.

The first transitional stage that we felt we could identify and describe in its own terms is that between the conformist and conscientious stages, called I-3/4. In retrospect, the priority of that transitional stage probably comes from the density of cases in its neighborhood. Since most cases in most samples are at the conformist level, at the conscientious level, or between them, we learned to make discriminations in that vicinity, and we also felt need of discriminations there. We subsequently came to conceptualize the transition from conscientious to autonomous rather clearly, and currently are working toward an understanding of the transition from self-protective to conformist. Since most of our cases have been girls in late adolescence or women, many of them would normally be in the transition from conscientious to autonomous stages; presumably relatively few would be in transition from self-protective to conformist stage. The transition from impulsive to self-protective we use only as a compromise rating, without any independent conception of its characteristics; again, we can hardly expect to flesh out the picture until someone studies children of an age where the transition would normally occur. We have arbitrarily not used the transition from autonomous to integrated, chiefly because the number of cases is too small in that region to give us any reliable feedback on our hunches.

In the body of the manual, where we are describing scoring procedures, we shall use our code terms without further apology. In any discursive materials, however, we shall describe the various stages in words. Nothing but confusion can result from referring, as many have, to our "third stage" or "fifth level." Such terms are thoroughly ambiguous. The conformist stage might be called our third level, since we designate it as I-3, but then what is the Delta level? The conformist level is also the third whole level of our scoring procedure (I-2, Delta, I-3). But since we use the transitional stage of Delta/3, it might be called our fourth level. Or if one admits also the earliest stages, even though we do not score for them, it could be called the fourth, fifth, sixth, or seventh stage, depending on whether one counts autistic and symbiotic as two or one and on whether the Delta/3 and the I-2/Delta levels are counted. Similar confusions would occur at any other point on the continuum.

While we have been pressed to make arbitrary decisions as to these matters, the situation would not thereby be much improved. There would be no guarantee that other people would agree with us as to what the separate stages are, even persons ostensibly quoting us and referring to our work. The difficulties are not invented; there are ambiguities in the nature of the material. We make a distinction between full steps, which are shown in Table 1, and half steps, which we call transitions. These are hunches, however, and we have no data to back up those decisions. Generally speaking, a new vocabulary is needed to describe each of the full steps; that argues for the reality or nonarbitrary nature of our levels. On the other hand, other investigators draw the line between levels in such a way that our transitions become their full stages; that argues for the continuity of the underlying variable and the arbitrary nature of the stages. If future work should lead us to study large numbers of cases at either extreme, we would expect to find use for additional transitions.

In summary, we began with a four-point scale. It has evolved gradually to be a nine-point scale, or a ten-point scale if we count the transition from impulsive to self-protective, a transition that raters are permitted but not encouraged to use. We do not rule out further changes in the substance of the construct or in the fineness of discriminations.

HISTORY OF FORMAT

Our first attempt to make a scoring manual consisted of examples of responses for the several stems at each of the four levels we then used. The listing of examples for each level of each stem might be called the *exemplar* manual. Many projective tests have exemplar manuals, for example, the Rotter Incomplete Sentence Blank.

Having completed our exemplar manual, we saw immediately that it would not serve. Hence, without using it in any empirical studies, we changed it into a *categorized* manual. In the categorized manual responses within a level were grouped into sets with common content, and every such group had a title that expressed the essence or common element. Some unclassified responses were also retained. We did not fully achieve what we set out to do in this version. In some cases the same category label was used at different I-levels. This correctly conveyed the similarity in content of responses at different levels but failed to convey how the responses differed at different levels; in such cases the titles were of little use to a rater. In those instances the differences were still conveyed by the examples, however. The categorized manual was used in extensive studies.

Our third type of manual is the *rationalized* manual, presented here. We have attempted to rationalize all empirical differences among categories in terms of theory. Incidentally, because our current sample is based on much larger samples than previous versions, it has many more categories than earlier versions. In terms of format there are no instances of identical titles at different levels. In working with several versions of the rationalized manual we have discovered that, in many instances, the most useful category title is an actual response or a composite of responses to the stem, usually the most frequent responses in the category, rather than an attempt at abstracting the common elements from all responses in a category. Thus in format the rationalized manual contains elements of both the exemplar manual and the categorized manual, with many category titles being actual examples or similar to actual responses.

The rationale for the categories is contained in Chapter Four and in the remarks accompanying the thirty-six-item manual.

There was a tendency with successive revisions of the manual to accumulate more and more examples. A final step was to eliminate as many as possible, particularly those most like the category titles. An anomalous result of condensing the manual in this fashion is that many common, replicated responses do not appear at all in their verbatim form. Some of these responses are used as illustrations in Chapter Four.

RULES FOR CONSTRUCTING THE MANUAL

The task of constructing a scoring manual can be construed in various ways. Our version is defined by three ground rules: (1) rate every response except omissions; (2) stick to the level of meanings, rather than counting words or interpreting underlying motives; (3) write in simple, intelligible English, without neologisms or technical cant.

1. *Rate every response.* Rating every response is of course more difficult than rating only those responses clearly diagnostic of a given level. Some responses do not encode I-level. They are given in the same words, verbatim, over a range of levels, even from I-2 to I-6 (see Chapter One, Table 1). Thus this rule leads on the one hand to compromise ratings (usually I-3) for nondiscriminating categories of response, and on the other hand to hair-splitting distinctions where we detect a slight shade of difference between similar responses at different levels. In the latter case raters will often make mistakes, since fine distinctions are hard to make. Compromise ratings also introduce error, but automatically so. That is, where the same rating, say I-3, is given to a response occurring on an I-2 and on an I-5 protocol, it is a kind of error on both.

Why then do we rate every response? The first reason is psychometric. Every respondent in principle makes the same number of responses (for all of our current forms, thirty-six). In the Rorschach and other tests, psychologists have long been vexed by the problems introduced by varying numbers of responses; there is no completely satisfactory solution. Parenthetically, fixing on thirty-six stems, as we have done, is not entirely arbitrary. We could have used thirty or forty. Our raters feel that fewer than thirty affords insufficient information. For more than forty stems our subjects will not stand still. Henceforth in all our studies we shall use exactly thirty-six items. We may substitute better stems for some of the present ones, but psychometric properties should be minimally affected so long as the number remains constant.

By insisting on rating every response, we are continually putting our ideas to the test. Too many hypotheses are confirmed by selection of favorable instances. We never let ourselves get away with that for long. Another advantage may be less evident. By continually pushing ourselves to the limits of our insights, we have added unexpected information. There have been many instances. Simply to ridicule the test might be considered an irrelevant, nonratable response, but it regularly turns up on self-protective (Delta) protocols. Hence we learned that hostile, callous humor is an indication of the self-protective level. We originally thought that "two I-3 responses are still an I-3 response," but this is not always the case. We now believe every response should be rated as a whole. We often found categories at one level consisting of contrasting responses each of which, separately, would be rated at a lower level. On this and other evidence we learned of a sense of choice as an indication of the conscientious (I-4) level. Similarly, we learned that where the I-4 subject tends to see a choice between more or less diametric opposites, such as love and lust, the I-5 subject will in the same context see combinations of three or more contrasted and even paradoxical but not diametrically opposed ideas.

There are always some omissions in a large sample of cases. For some purposes they are arbitrarily rated I-3, but in general their identity as omissions should be retained. At times we have tried to make inferences on the basis of the content of the stem omitted, but this has not been successful. Omissions are not useful, and some effort should be made in test administration to minimize their number. We have been surprised to discover that what constitutes an omission is not altogether obvious. For example, the response "that's a question" is similar to simply replying with "?" (see Chapter Five).

2. *Stick to the level of meanings.* This is the level that Magda Arnold (1962), in relation to the TAT, calls the import. SC responses are usually brief and from our view cryptic. We deal with exactly what the subject said, and, if necessary, we try to guess what she meant. By that we do not mean unconscious motives or unexpressed intentions, but what she herself would recognize as her meaning. Deep level inferences are inadmissible in our scheme. They are not relevant to the task of rating ego level as we construe it.

On the other hand, the manual cannot be computerized. In research we use word count, but only as a kind of base rate. It is not an admissible consideration in scoring for I-level. We are often tempted to identify certain words with certain I-levels, but this is also dangerous. Nothing less than the whole response is a safe index of the subject's meaning, and we operate only within the level of discourse of meanings. This is the level at which people give account of their thoughts, actions, and motives to themselves and others. It is the universe of discourse of the most essential and irreplaceable core of psychology.

3. *Use plain English.* We have not been able to avoid slipping into abbreviations. In principle, however, all of them can be replaced by English words. The verbal equivalent of the I-levels can be found in Table 1, of all other abbreviations in Appendix G.

Technical psychological and psychoanalytic words such as *super-ego* and *defense mechanisms* are taboo in our scoring manual. Some of the clinicians who have worked on the manual prefer to think in such terms, but they have accommodated themselves to the restriction. The argument is not that those terms are indefensible in other contexts, a point on which we take no stand, but rather that we are operating on a minimal inferential level.

Although we have avoided some of the clichés of the helping professions, such as *ongoing process* and *team approach,* we have not been altogether successful at avoiding the repetitious use of some quasi-technical terms like *focus, relationship,* and barbarisms such as *conceptualize.* We have particularly leaned on the distinction between *global* and *differentiated* views; as intimately related as this distinction is to ego growth, there seemed no way to avoid overuse of the terms.

The term *role* came from common speech, was promoted to being a technical sociological term, and now has returned to wider usage with sociological connotations. Popular magazines now discourse on the feminine role. Although it has never been an entirely satisfactory term, we do use it occasionally. The ambiguity of the idea of the *feminine role* is discussed in other terms in Chapter Four.

Some additional considerations supplement the foregoing three ground rules. More an aspiration than a rule has been the attempt to justify every rating both theoretically and empirically. This is the program of construct validation of tests. Achievement of the goal is limited by the rule to rate every response. Nonetheless, as an aspiration it has given direction to the work.

Here we are close to our Scylla and Charybdis. If the categories of response are drawn too broadly, then the manual cannot discriminate meanings as well as a trained and gifted rater. If the categories are drawn too narrowly, then replication is limited, and there is danger of gerrymandering the categories to fit the data in hand. The latter course sacrifices generality. The manual will appear to be valid when reapplied to the source data, but will be appreciably less valid when applied to new samples. While the latter course, narrowly drawn categories, is unfortunate for a final version, it has advantages for a penultimate version. The prepublication manual, the immediate predecessor of the present version, was prepared for the purpose of evaluating and regrouping categories. We therefore chose to retain many fine discriminations in that version. These distinctions were retained in the present version only if (1) the categories were useful to a rater, that is, raters did not complain that they found it difficult to distinguish between the categories, and (2) the distinctions were replicated, that is, for the three new samples of protocols the distinctions between responses rated in the categories reflected distinctions among the TPRs of the protocols from which they came.

Drawing up of categories is an inescapably arbitrary element in our technique of manual construction, both the distinction of categories from each other and the decision as to which responses are included. We have an empirical test of whether a whole category is at the wrong level, but we have no test of whether better categories might be drawn or more apt examples chosen.

Since they are arbitrary, the categories serve no purpose except to aid raters in finding the appropriate I-level for a response and to channel feedback from empirical tests to improve the manual, as will be explained presently. An attempt to extract information other than I-level from the particular category within the level is specifically enjoined. We have no evidence that categories can be used that way.

An implicit assumption underlies our technique: every person, although exhibiting variability in his responses and other behavior, belongs in principle to one and only one point on the I-level scale. This is a working assumption, not subject to any kind of test except the long-range one of the fruitfulness of the whole technique. In keeping with this assumption, we have striven to keep our conception one-dimensional. Thus we exclude consideration of degree of adjustment or kind of pathology (except insofar as low ego levels can be considered a kind of pathology). We take no stand on whether certain kinds of adjustment or pathology are more likely to occur at certain levels. What is important is to have the conceptions and measures of ego level and of adjustment or pathology independent of each other. Only then can a true picture of empirical relations be ascertained.

EMPIRICAL VERIFICATION PARADIGM

The present manual results from a long program of studies, not all of which are worth reviewing here. One paradigm was used repeatedly, modified in various ways for various reasons, but always in essence as follows.

This paradigm begins with a manual in categorized, or categorized and rationalized, form. For some sample of protocols, a list of responses, identified only by code number, is typed for each stem. The responses are thereby removed from the context of their protocols (see Appendix E). Thus the rater must get his information solely from each response considered on its own. There is no possibility of reading a response dif ferently according to other responses given by the same subject or according to background knowledge concerning the subject (age, marital status), all of which is omitted. (Our raters, however, were always told the subject's sex.) Where rigorous exclusion of context effects is needed, it is even possible for the code number of a given protocol to differ from item to item in some systematic fashion not known to the raters.

For each stem, every response in the sample is given an I-level and, where possible, assigned to a category within the level (see Chapter Five) by at least two raters, each working alone. The raters rate all responses to one stem before going on to another stem. After completing the ratings for one stem, the raters confer where they differ and arrive at an agreed rating and category for each response. This is done for every stem.

Total protocols are rated by at least three raters. If the same raters are used as for item ratings, then total protocol ratings (TPRs) must be made subsequent to all item ratings, again to exclude context effects for item ratings. Each rater rates all protocols before comparing with other raters. Context considerations are admissible for TPRs, but background information other than sex is withheld. Where two raters give identical ratings and the third is one-half step off, we have used the rating of the two as an "automatic compromise." In all other cases of disagreement a compromise TPR is arrived at after the protocol has been read aloud and the three raters have discussed it.

Originally, with no manual or a skeletal one, we arrived at TPRs by trying to imagine what kind of person would have written the protocol, that is, by hypothesizing at what I-level he was mainly functioning. Increasingly as the manual has materialized we have leaned on the distribution of item ratings. Current rules are discussed in Chapter Six.

The final step is decoding. Here every response is listed in the category the raters have put it, together with the protocol number and TPR. The decoding reports are then the basis for empirical revision of the manual. Given a manual for an item with categories of response at the various I-levels, there are several kinds of decisions that can be made. Should a category be redrawn? Should new categories be formed? At what level should a category be placed? For some categories one can see at a glance from the decoding that responses corresponding to low TPRs are distinguishable from responses with medium or high TPRs. New categories are formed primarily from responses which fit no existing category. Table 2 illustrates one such instance. In the sample used to construct the prepublication manual, there was just one response which made sense only if one had assumed that the subject had misread the stem "When people are helpless . . ." as if it said, "When people are helpful. . . ." In the absence of any other clue, we gave that response a

Table 2

EXAMPLE OF MANUAL REVISION

Stem: When people are helpless

Response	Item Rating	TPR	Sample
that would be very nice of them	3	2	Form 9-62
they are nice	2	2	Sealed
they are my friend	3	2	Sealed
i feel pretty good	Δ	Δ	Sealed
is good	3	2	Sealed
you thank them	3	2	Sealed
you prease it[a]	3	2/Δ	Sealed
I am thinkful	3	3	Sealed

Code: Level 2 is impulsive.
      Level Δ is self-protective.
      Level 3 is conformist.

[a] We interpret this response as "you praise it."

conformist rating, more or less by default. In the sealed sample, used to test the manual, there were seven such responses, five of which were rated at the conformist level by the raters; however, all but one of the TPRs was below the conformist level, and four were at the lowest or impulsive level. These eight responses now constitute a new category incorporated in the manual and placed at the impulsive level.

Drawing and defining the limits of a category admittedly is arbitrary and somewhat subjective. Placement of the categories, however, is done empirically, though we have not been able to derive absolute decision rules that cover all possible instances. The decision as to what level a category should be placed in is based on the distribution of TPRs of the responses rated in that category. This distribution of TPRs can be looked at two ways, depending on what one sees as the base of the percentages. One can ask, given a response in this category, what is the probability that it came from a protocol at level X? From this viewpoint, one would be interested in the mode, the median, and the mean of the given distribution of TPRs for the category; where they all coincided, that would be the level of placement. If, however, there were many more I-3 subjects than I-2 or Delta subjects, then a type of response that is very likely to be given by an I-2 or a Delta subject and very unlikely to be given by an I-3 subject may still end up being classed at I-3. This dependence of the decision on the relative frequency of the different levels in the sample studied is intuitively wrong. In this intuitive reasoning we are using a different set of percentages: Given a protocol of level *X*, what is the probability of its having a response in this category? Rather than computing those percentages for every category, we posted the TPR distribution of the sample being used. We then compared the percentage of cases in that category at corresponding I-levels. The I-level most overrepresented in that category, as compared to the total sample, is the level where the category should be classed.

In the example given in Table 2, five of the eight responses, or 62 per cent, come from protocols rated I-2. If the responses in the category were equally likely to be given by subjects at all I-levels, we would expect only about 3 per cent, or given the small *N* in this category, say one case, to come from an I-2 protocol. Thus, we place this category at I-2. Statistical justification can be found in Appendix F.

We cannot use this reasoning when there are only a few, say four or five, responses constituting a category. Also we cannot come to a firm decision when the rule leads to alternative choices or when the advantage for placement at a given I-level rather than another is only slight. In such instances we fall back on the theory, which, after all, encodes a broad experience.

Most categories, then, are placed at the different I-levels empirically, following the reasoning outlined above. The others are placed in terms of theoretical expectations. There are no purely theoretical categories; we deal only with observed responses. The manual and the theory have evolved simultaneously by this procedure. The first categorized manual, based on a relatively small number of protocols, contained categories located primarily on the basis of theoretical expectations. As the manual underwent revisions with an increasingly large number of protocols, the placement of many categories could be confirmed or disconfirmed by our empirical test. Disconfirmation meant that not only the manual but the theory needed to be revised, especially if such a change was indicated for several stems. For instance, we had considered that the conception of oneself as a pawn of fate, lucky or unlucky, was characteristic of the impulsive (I-2) level. However, as the manual underwent several revisions, it became apparent that this conception is more typical of the self-protective (Delta) level, requiring a change in the theory to incorporate the empirical evidence.

This paradigm, our bootstrap operation, was used repeatedly to achieve the end result, the manual presented in this book. Provided only that we can do better than chance on TPRs, we can by this method steadily improve our scoring manual and encode in the manual increasingly subtle signs of the various ego levels, not discernible a priori. Even where the revised manual for a stem bears little relation to the original, the original has made a contribution. The raters have to have something to start with in order to present the manual constructors with material for revision.

SAMPLES USED

Eight samples were used at one stage or another in the manual construction. Five samples entered into the construction of the prepublication manual, which is the manual that was used in the studies reported in Chapter Three. The remaining three samples first were used in these studies, then provided data for revision upon completion of the evaluation.

Not all samples or subsamples were used to construct or to revise all item manuals due to variation in the exact SC form used in different studies. Table 3 displays the use of the various samples in the construction and revision of the individual item manuals. The individual items are listed at the left. The subtotals in each row (Subtotal N) are the total number of protocols in the combined samples used either for construction or for revision, thus the total number of responses used to construct or to revise any particular item manual. The sum at the bottom of a column represents the number of items for which the manual was constructed or revised using responses from that sample or subsample.

Table 4 contains the distributions of TPRs assigned to the various samples. These data are incomplete for the preliminary sample and therefore are not included. The TPRs for the different samples (and in some cases, subsamples) were assigned by different sets of raters at different times using different sets of rules to arrive at their ratings. Formal decision rules for assigning TPRs (see Chapter Six) were not evolved until after the samples used to construct the prepublication manual were rated. While the ratings, and thus the distributions of TPRs in these samples, would change somewhat if new ratings were done incorporating changes in the manual and present rules for arriving at TPRs, the TPRs represented in this table served as criteria for evaluating manual revisions and can be considered representative of the range of I-level in our samples.

SAMPLES USED TO CONSTRUCT THE PREPUBLICATION MANUAL

For the most part protocols in these samples were collected for other purposes and were drawn together only later to fill certain needs in the construction process. Therefore, certain information about the demographic composition of these samples is lacking. The demographic

Table 3

USE OF SAMPLES IN CONSTRUCTION AND REVISION OF ITEM MANUALS

Item Numbers	Preliminary 1 (N = 30)	Preliminary 2 (30)	Preliminary 3 (65)	Construction Samples — Single Women (204)	Supplementary 1 (130)	Supplementary 2 (70)	Professional (106)	Form 9-62 (337)	Sub-total	Revision Samples — Sealed (543)	Toronto (100)	Dec. 1967 (150)	Sub-total	Grand Total
3, 5, 6, 8, 26, 31		x	x	x	x	x	x		605	x	x	x	793	1398
9, 18	x		x	x	x		x		535	x	x	x	793	1328
21, 23	x		x	x	x	x	x		605	x		x	693	1298
17				x	x	x	x	x	847	x		x	693	1540
10, 12, 16, 19, 23, 32, 35								x	337	x	x	x	793	1130
The remaining 18 items	x		x	x	x	x	x		605	x	x	x	793	1398
Total items	22	6	28	29	29	27	29	8		36	33	36		

Note.—Item numbers refer to Form 9-62.

Table 4

TPRs in Samples Used in Manual Construction and Revision

Sample	I-level										N
	I-2	2/Δ	Δ	Δ/3	I-3	I-3/4	I-4	I-4/5	I-5	I-6	
Single Women	2		8		96	37	48	6	6	1	204
Supplementary	14	3	13	12	52	41	48	12	2	3	200
Professional			4		33	21	32	12	4		106
Form 9-62	11	6	12	7	127	83	71	17	2	1	337
Sealed	17	11	11	22	157	143	132	29	14	7	543
Toronto	4	5	11	13	20	24	17	6			100
December, 1967	3		3	3	53	54	26	6	2		150
Total	51	25	62	57	538	403	374	88	30	12	1640

Table 5

DEMOGRAPHIC VARIABLES OF SAMPLES USED IN MANUAL CONSTRUCTION

	Samples				
	Prelimi-nary[a] (N = 125)	Single Women (N = 204)	Supplemen-tary (N = 200)	Profes-sional (N = 106)	Form 9-62 (N = 337)
Age:					
11–20	9	176	81		233
21–30	30	28	64	58	76
31–40	18		33	25	12
41–50	2		8	16	8
50+			7	2	3
Unknown	66		7	5	5
Race:					
White		203	43		67
Negro		1	58	4	82
Unknown	125		99	102	188
Marital status:					
Single	8	204	47	59	260
Married	51		84	35	54
Widowed				1	3
Separated			2	2	
Divorced				5	8
Unknown	66		67	4	12
Education:					
Grade school	11		8		17
Part high school	14	53	26		123
High school	14	40	56		17
Part college	9	99	7	52	92
College	11	9			35
College+		3		51	40
Unknown	66		103	3	13

[a] For any single item, N = 95. Preliminary sample used to construct the categorized manual.

Table 6

SOURCES OF SUBJECTS FOR SAMPLES USED IN MANUAL CONSTRUCTION

Sample	Source	N	Form Used
Preliminary-1	Psychiatric inpatients	13	75-item
	Postpartum women	17	experimental
Preliminary-2	Postpartum women	30	9-item
			experimental
Preliminary-3	Postpartum women	28	BN (36 items)
	Student nurses	4	
	Junior hospital volunteers	7	
	Hospital employees	2	
	College students	24	
Single women	High school students	19	BN (36 items)
	Student nurses	65	
	Junior hospital volunteers	56	
	Hospital employees	23	
	College students	41	
Supplementary-1	Postpartum women	100	BN (36 items)
	Child guidance adolescent patients	20	
	House of detention adolescents	10	
Supplementary-2	Junior hospital volunteers	23	BN (30 items)
	Adult hospital volunteers	24	
	Psychiatric outpatients	9	
	Medical hospital patients	14	
Professional	Social work students	51	BN (36 items)
	Graduate nurses	52	
	Prospective adoptive mothers	3	
Form 9-62	Social work students	74	9-62 (36 items)
	Institutionalized delinquent adolescents	67	
	Adult hospital volunteers	2	
	Mothers of children's hospital patients	6	
	College students	93	
	Job opportunity training group	79	
	Normal adolescent group	16	

data for the five samples used for construction of the prepublication manual are summarized in Table 5, the sources of subjects in Table 6. The following is a more general description of these samples.

Preliminary Sample ($N = 125$). This sample, used primarily in the initial stages of manual construction, was composed of three subgroups: one group of thirty subjects given a seventy-five-item SC form, another group of thirty subjects given a nine-item SC form, all items being different from the previous form, and a group of sixty-five subjects given a thirty-six-item SC form which included twenty-nine items from the long form and seven items from the short form. Except for the postpartum women included in all three subsamples, all respondents were tested in groups. All women were told that they were participating in a research project at Washington University. This was the general formula for the testing of all subjects in the subsequent samples: group testing and the information that the testing was for research purposes. Though demographic data available for this sample are sketchy, included were subjects of a wide educational range, both married and single women who ranged in age from sixteen to at least forty-one years of age. As can be seen from Table 3, only ninety-five of the respondents in the preliminary sample were used to construct the manual for each item. The preliminary sample was the sole basis for constructing the categorized manual. It was given minimal weight in constructing the present version, serving mainly as a source of a few unusual responses.

Single Women Sample ($N = 204$). This sample was limited to single women between the ages of sixteen and twenty-six years and included only one Negress. The educational range was also restricted, with over 90 per cent of the subjects falling in the range of part high school to part college. All subjects were seen in groups and were given the initial thirty-six-item form, hereafter, Form BN (36 items).

Supplementary Sample ($N = 200$). The restricted nature of the single women sample for use in manual construction soon became apparent, leading to the compilation of a more varied sample of women and girls. Of these women 130 had been given the Form BN (36 items) and seventy had been administered a thirty-item form, in which one item was added and seven items from Form BN (36 items) were deleted; hereafter, we shall call that Form BN (30 items). Many of the postpartum subjects included in this sample were seen individually; otherwise the testing took place in groups. This sample included both white and Negro, both married and single women of varied educational backgrounds, ranging in age from fourteen to sixty years.

Professional Sample ($N = 106$). The purpose of this sample in the construction of the manual was to increase the representation of the higher educational levels. Practically all subjects in this sample had at least some college education and all but three were enrolled in post-graduate professional curricula. (About half were social work students, half were nurses who had completed a four-year course.) The women were both married and single and ranged in age from twenty-one to fifty years. Though information about race is missing from most of these protocols, we know that most of the subjects were white. All women were given Form BN (36 items), and except for the three prospective adoptive mothers, all were tested in groups.

Form 9-62 Sample ($N = 337$). Form 9-62 (36 items) of the SC test was derived from Form BN by replacement of seven old items with seven new ones. This led to the necessity of compiling a sample of protocols to be used to construct manuals for the new items. All available protocols using Form 9-62 but not to be included in the evaluative studies of the manual were included. The result was a sample somewhat overrepresentative of young single women, but including both white and Negro subjects and the full range of educational level. Age ranged from twelve to sixty-six years.

ADDITIONAL SAMPLES USED IN FINAL REVISION

The final revision of the manual, the version presented in Chapter Seven, was carried out using three new samples of protocols (all Form 9-62) in addition to the five samples previously described. Because the primary purpose of the new samples was to provide data for the evaluation of the prepublication manual, they will be described in detail in Chapter Three. The following is a general description of the three samples.

Sealed Sample ($N = 543$). This sample of protocols was drawn together from a wide spectrum of the community with the purpose of approximating a representative sample of protocols. It was used in the major evaluation of the prepublication manual. Subjects contributing protocols to this sample ranged in age from twelve to seventy years, in education from grade school to graduate or professional school; they were both married and single, white and Negro.

Toronto Sample ($N = 100$). Protocols in this sample came from 100 Toronto school girls aged nine to eighteen. These protocols, as well as a comparable sample of boys' protocols, were collected by Dr. E. V. Sullivan as a part of a larger study involving other measures of ego and moral development. Our interest was to study age differences in ego level as measured by the SC. Upon completion of this study these protocols were used in the final revision of thirty-three of the item manuals. Three items, Nos. 17, 21, and 33, were not administered to these subjects.

December 1967 Sample ($N = 150$). Protocols included in this sample (rated in December, 1967) were from subjects who ranged in age from eighteen to fifty-five years and who came from sources as disparate as applicants for aid to dependent children to graduate students in counseling. These protocols were drawn together to obtain I-level ratings for four distinct studies, in accord with our procedure of combining protocols from several studies so that raters are unaware of the source of any individual protocol. Data on the interrater reliability of TPR ratings of these 150 protocols are used to supplement those obtained from the sealed sample.

CHAPTER 3

Evaluation of the Manual

The major evaluative studies to be reported used the prepublication manual. Although the manual is similar to the present version, it is not identical, since we used the data from the evaluative studies to make final revisions. This is a dilemma that test makers are familiar with. Either you freeze a test in order to do evaluative and standardization studies and decline to make changes on the basis of the new data, or you use all your data to make final revisions and end by publishing a version you have not studied. The case for our present manual rests on its similarity to the prepublication manual plus the evidence that our revision process in the past has resulted in demonstrable improvement. We present first a study using the earlier categorized manual, in part to show the improvement in the prepublication manual.

STUDY OF SINGLE WOMEN

The first version of the categorized manual was given to seven raters who rated every response out of context for each of 204 protocols in a sample of unmarried women. Subsequently TPRs were given by three raters independently, largely on intuitive grounds. Criterion TPRs (hereafter, $\overline{\text{TPRs}}$) were determined by compromising all differences by discussion. On occasion staff members who had not been among the three original raters participated in the discussion, a practice we no longer follow. On the basis of this experience, involving interminable hours of discussion, often ending in an averaging process, we settled on the "automatic compromise" when the three ratings differ only by half a step. By contrast, in the study of the sealed sample, all compromising of differences for every block of fifty cases was completed in less than one hour. The decrease in compromise time results from more agreed cases as well as from greater agreement following discussion.

The seven raters differed widely in their backgrounds. Some were gifted amateurs with little formal training in psychology. One rater (the late Virginia Ives Word) had had seven years' experience using a similar construct with similar data prior to joining our project. By every criterion we applied, she was the best rater, as judged by agreement with $\overline{\text{TPR}}$. This finding was not an artifact, since she did not participate in rating total protocols. Remarkably, each of the seven raters was the best rater for at least one item, a finding which confirmed our intuitive impression that each member of the group made a unique contribution.

We noticed early that there was an appreciable relation between the length of a response and the ego level expressed in it. Indeed, the question has occasionally been raised whether we would do better to count the number of words rather than rating at all. To test this matter, for each item we correlated the number of words in the subjects' responses with their $\overline{\text{TPRs}}$. The distribution of correlations is shown in Table 7, both for the study of single women and for the sealed sample. For comparison there is also displayed the distribution of correlations of $\overline{\text{TPR}}$ with I-level ratings given to the responses to each item. For the single women the item ratings are those of the "best rater"—that is, for each item we selected the highest correlation with $\overline{\text{TPR}}$ of any of the seven sets of item ratings. Thus each correlation is computed from the ratings of a single rater, though the same rater did not produce all thirty-six correlations. The distribution of correlations of item ratings with $\overline{\text{TPR}}$ presented under sealed sample "best rater" was derived in the same way,

Table 7

CORRELATIONS OF ITEM RATINGS AND
ITEM WORD COUNT WITH TPR

Correlation	*Single Women*			*Sealed Sample*	
	Word Count	Best Rater	Word Count[a]	Best Rater	Composite Trained Rater
.10–.14	1				
.15–.19	2	1			
.20–.24	5	3	1		
.25–.29	9	7	5		
.30–.34	8	10	12		
.35–.39	10	10	10	9	5
.40–.44	1	3	6	11	14
.45–.49		2	1	10	8
.50–.54			1	5	7
.55–.59				1	1
.60–.64					1
Range	.14–.40	.18–.45	.23–.51	.35–.57	.36–.60
Median	.31	.33	.35	.44	.44

[a] The few responses with more than thirty words were counted as exactly thirty words.

except that for the sealed sample there were four raters involved, with two raters, rather than seven, rating any single item. Ratings denoted as from the "composite trained rater" were those obtained when the two raters compromised their differences. They tend to be slightly better than those of the best rater, but the medians are identical. The rise in correlations for the sealed sample as compared to the single women may be due partly to the greater variability of the sealed sample, partly to more valid variance in the $\overline{\text{TPR}}$. The combined effect of those two factors is shown in the rise in the median correlation of item word count with $\overline{\text{TPR}}$ from .31 for single women to .35 for the sealed sample. The greater rise in item-$\overline{\text{TPR}}$ correlation, from a median of .33 to a median of .44, indicates the improved validity of the scoring manual. Those data refer to the improvement of the prepublication manual over the categorized manual. Basically the same process was followed in deriving the present version from the data with the prepublication version; there were, however, fewer changes. It seems reasonable to infer that the manual presented here is at least as good as the evaluative data show the prepublication manual to be. The problem of the high correlations with word count will be discussed presently.

STUDIES WITH PREPUBLICATION MANUAL

For the remainder of the chapter we shall present studies done with the prepublication manual, chiefly with the sealed sample, but also making some use of other samples where noted.

RATERS

Ten raters were involved in these studies. Six (Raters 1, 2, 3, 4, 7, and 8) were familiar with the scoring manual and the theory of ego development, all having contributed to the construction of the manual. Two advanced graduate students (Raters 5 and 6) served as self-trained raters who, though having some familiarity with the theory, were not involved in the construction of the manual. Rater 5 had no contact with it before the initiation of this study. Rater 6 had done some rating using an early version of the manual over a period of four weeks the year before. Two undergraduates (Raters 9 and 10) also served as self-trained raters. Neither was familiar with the theory or the manual before entering the study. The training for these four raters came entirely from written materials included in the manual itself. They were not allowed to discuss with themselves or with the other staff members any theoretical or rating problems during the course of their rating task. Table 8 gives the sex and education of the ten raters.

Table 8

SEX AND EDUCATION OF RATERS

Rater	Sex	Education
Trained:		
1	M	B.A.
2	M	Graduate student
3	F	Graduate student
4	F	Ph.D.
7	F	Ph.D.
8	F	Equivalent of Ph.D.
Self-trained:		
5	F	Graduate student
6	M	Graduate student
9	F	Sophomore
10	M	Junior

NOTE.—Graduate students were Ph.D. candidates in clinical psychology who had completed internships.

SAMPLES

In the studies of the prepublication manual three different samples of protocols were used. Demographic data for these samples are presented in Table 9. The sources of subjects in each sample are listed in Table 10. A general description of each sample may be found in Chapter Two. For the major evaluation study, protocols were collected from 543 girls and women aged twelve to seventy. This is called the sealed sample, because no one who was to rate these protocols read them prior to the initiation of the evaluation, nor did anyone working on the prepublication manual read them. The sealed sample was drawn from a wide spectrum of the community to approximate a representative sample. Code numbers were assigned in a more or less random fashion so that every block of fifty cases contained cases from every source, mixed in order and proportionate to its numbers in the total sample. From these protocols a typist prepared two kinds of materials: (1) typed copies of each protocol in which all identifying information was removed, and (2) for each item, a list of all 543 responses given to that item, again, identified only by code number. (Where the response contained identifying information, the typist deleted it.) For other samples of protocols used in supplementary or additional studies, only typed copies of each protocol were prepared,

Table 9

DEMOGRAPHIC VARIABLES OF SAMPLES USED IN MANUAL EVALUATION

	Samples		
	Sealed ($N = 543$)	Toronto ($N = 100$)	Dec. 1967 ($N = 150$)
Age:			
−10		14	
11–20	172	86	67
21–30	162		24
31–40	99		10
41–50	71		3
50+	34		5
Unknown	5		41[a]
Race:			
White	364	100	76
Negro	152		34
Unknown	27		40
Marital Status:			
Single	266	100	85
Married	237		20
Widowed	13		
Separated	5		
Divorced	15		4
Unknown	7		41
Education:			
Grade school	74	65	
Part high school	115	35	
High school	85		59
Part college	133		29
College	61		22
College+	66		
Unknown	9		40

[a] 40 subjects for whom there is no information on each variable are from the applicants for aid to dependent children subsample.

Table 10

SOURCES OF SUBJECTS FOR SAMPLES USED IN MANUAL EVALUATION

Sample	Source	N	Form Used
Sealed	Mothers of children's hospital patients	126	9–62 (36 items)
	Social work school applicants	73	
	Student teachers	31	
	Mothers' club (upper-class Negroes)	45	
	Institutionalized delinquent adolescents	26	
	Enrichment summer school students	29	
	State hospital volunteers	75	
	State hospital recreation workers	5	
	Junior hospital volunteers	20	
	Student nurses	61	
	Job opportunity group	27	
	Prospective adoptive mothers	25	
Toronto	Toronto school children	100	9–62 (33 items)
Dec. 1967	Applicants for aid to dependent children	40	9–62 (36 items)
	Student nurses	59	
	University undergraduates	29	
	Graduate students in counseling	22	

again with identifying information deleted. Appendix E gives further details of the methodology. Actually, the term typist does injustice to the calibre of judgment required to prepare protocols adequately.

GENERAL RATING PROCEDURES

To obtain item ratings the rater was given a list of all responses to be rated for a given item. Using the manual for that item, he assigned to each response an I-level rating. All responses to one item were rated before he proceeded to the next item.

To obtain TPRs, each rater was given typed copies of each protocol he was to rate. Using the manual he assigned item ratings to each
of the thirty-six responses in a given protocol. He then assigned an I-level
rating (the TPR) to the protocol, assisted by scoring rules based on the
ogive of the thirty-six item ratings in conjunction with certain nonpsychometric indications of ego level (see Chapter Six). Variations and
additions to these general procedures will be noted when necessary.

RELIABILITY OF ITEM RATINGS

Four trained raters (two per item) independently assigned I-level
ratings to all 543 responses of the sealed sample to each item. Disagreed
ratings were discussed and compromised by the raters involved. The final
(agreed or compromised) ratings will be denoted as from the "composite
trained rater." The four self-trained raters each similarly rated 100 responses to each item. They did not compromise disagreements.

For each item, interrater correlations and the percentage of agreed
ratings were computed between the I-level ratings given by each pair of
self-trained raters for 100 responses and by two trained raters for all 543
responses from the sealed sample. Table 11 shows the distribution of the
per cent agreement on I-level ratings for the thirty-six items for trained
and self-trained raters. The three medians are not significantly different,
as is borne out by a median test, illustrating essentially the same degree

Table 11

PER CENT AGREEMENT ON I-LEVEL, BY ITEMS (36 ITEMS)

	Sets of Raters		
Per Cent Agreement	Trained Raters $N = 543$	Raters 5 and 6 $N = 100$	Raters 9 and 10 $N = 100$
60–64	1	1	
65–69	1	3	3
70–74	9	4	5
75–79	15	15	9
80–84	8	7	9
85–89	2	4	8
90–94		2	2
Range	60–86	63–91	65–94
Median	77	78	81

of agreement between raters, trained or self-trained. Table 12 shows the corresponding distribution for interrater correlations between I-level ratings for each of the thirty-six items. The medians are almost exactly the same, .75, .76, and .76. For these two indices of interrater reliability, then, amount of training did not make a difference.

Table 12

INTERRATER CORRELATION, BY ITEMS (36 ITEMS)

Sets of Raters

Interrater r	Trained Raters $N = 543$	Raters 5 and 6 $N = 100$	Raters 9 and 10 $N = 100$
.40–.49	1		
.50–.59	1	2	1
.60–.69	6	6	9
.70–.79	21	17	11
.80–.89	7	9	11
.90–.99		2	4
Range	.49–.88	.53–.93	.56–.93
Median	.75	.76	.76

Raters might agree with each other, however, because they both and in the same way make use of only a few of the possible I-levels. Using the rating the two trained raters agreed on as the criterion for the item ratings, the ratings of each of the four self-trained raters were tested on the two reliability indices for each item. Results are presented in Tables 13 and 14. Both in terms of per cent agreement and interrater correlation these results are comparable with those presented above, supporting the conclusion that amount of training does not affect the interrater reliability.

Considering either per cent agreement or interrater correlation, the ratings of Rater 9 were most like those of the composite trained rater. In fact, the difference among the four median correlations in Table 14 is significant ($p < .02$), with no significant difference found among the median correlations of Raters 5, 6, and 10. Thus, considering the ratings of Raters 9 and 10 as the "purest" test of the manual, since these raters had little or no background in psychology let alone the theory of ego development, we interpret the median correlation (.76) of Rater 10 with the composite trained rater to be an indication of the reliability of item ratings built into the manual. Unknown individual differences must explain the exceptional results produced by Rater 9, who had just finished her freshman year in college and had had no psychology courses.

Using as the total score for each subject in the sealed sample simply the sum of the item ratings, we computed a measure of internal

Table 13

PER CENT AGREEMENT OF SELF-TRAINED RATERS WITH COMPOSITE
TRAINED RATER, BY ITEMS (36 ITEMS, 100 CASES)

Per Cent Agreement	Rater 5	Rater 6	Rater 9	Rater 10
60–64				2
65–69	2	1	1	1
70–74	7	7	6	8
75–79	14	13	6	10
80–84	9	11	9	11
85–89	3	4	7	4
90–94	1		6	
95–99			1	
Range	67–90	69–86	67–95	60–89
Median	78	77	82	79

Table 14

CORRELATION OF SELF-TRAINED RATERS WITH COMPOSITE
TRAINED RATER, BY ITEMS (36 ITEMS, 100 CASES)

Interrater r	Rater 5	Rater 6	Rater 9	Rater 10
.40–.49				1
.50–.59		1	1	
.60–.69	8	2	3	8
.70–.79	11	16	6	14
.80–.89	17	17	18	13
.90–.99			8	
Range	.60–.89	.57–.88	.57–.98	.44–.89
Median	.78	.79	.85	.76

consistency, coefficient alpha (Cronbach, 1951), which is a generalization of the Kuder-Richardson formula 20, for each of four scores. These were the scores based on the following sets of ratings: (1) those given by the composite trained rater to each of the 543 subjects, (2) those given by the composite trained rater to the first 100 subjects, (3) and (4) those given to the same 100 subjects by Raters 5 and 6. The alphas were .91 for the composite trained rater for 543 subjects; for the subsample of 100 subjects, they were .92 for the composite trained rater, .90 and .88 for the two self-trained raters (Table 19). These correlations again are quite similar and indicate a high degree of internal consistency irrespective of degree of previous training.

A rater could achieve internal consistency at the expense of valid variance by a tendency to use extreme ratings or to rate certain words or phrases at a given I-level regardless of the context of the word or expression. To determine whether the variance in item sums is attributable to response variance or to rater variance, the sums for the odd items and for the even items were computed from the item ratings given by Raters 5 and 6, who were the only raters for whom we had the appropriate data. Table 15 presents the intercorrelations computed among these four

Table 15

INTERCORRELATIONS BETWEEN SUMS OF ODD AND EVEN
ITEM RATINGS FOR RATERS 5 AND 6

	Rater 5, Σ Odd	Rater 6, Σ Even	Rater 6, Σ Odd
Rater 5, Σ Even	.83(.91)[a]	.95	.81
Rater 5, Σ Odd		.82	.94
Rater 6, Σ Even			.78(.88)[a]

[a] Odd-even correlations corrected for length.

sums. The highest correlations are obtained when the sums are over the same items, even though the raters are different. The other four correlations, involving sums over different sets of items, do not differ according to whether the correlation involves the same rater. Thus the variance in item sums derives primarily from variation in the responding subjects rather than from variation in the raters.

RELIABILITY OF TOTAL PROTOCOL RATINGS

Each protocol in the sealed sample was assigned a TPR by each of three trained raters. Five raters were used in all possible combinations of three.

Because a large proportion of the time to rate a protocol is devoted to rating the individual items, to shorten the task of obtaining

TPRs for this study, raters were not required to rate each response in the protocols. Instead, raters were provided with the distribution of the thirty-six item ratings given by the composite trained rater to each protocol and with the ogive rules in Chapter Six for utilizing this information. Raters were, however, encouraged to use all the information in the protocol, regardless of whether it was reflected in the item ratings. They were permitted to disregard the item ratings if they believed them to be incorrect, which, on occasion, they did. After completing their ratings they compromised their disagreements by discussion, obtaining thus our criterion ratings, hereafter TPRs.

In assigning TPRs to the sealed sample protocols, each of the five trained raters was paired with every other rater in rating at least 143 protocols. Thus with five raters there were ten pairs of raters for whom each of the following indices of interrater reliability was computed, in each case over a different subsample of subjects: (1) interrater correlation between TPRs, (2) percentage of protocols agreed for TPR, (3) percentage of protocols agreed for TPR within one half step. The manual provides for half-step differences between the stages discussed in Chapter One, except for the two highest stages. Considering each stage and half step between them as one point on a scale, we have a ten-point scale. If we think of ego development as a continuum, then disagreements of half a step are inevitable for intermediate cases. Hence they are in this sense not errors, or not necessarily errors.

Table 16 summarizes the results giving the range and median for each of these three indices for both the sealed sample and the December 1967 sample. Considering first the results for the sealed sample, it can be seen that though the per cent complete agreement is somewhat low (median = 61 per cent), the median interrater correlation is .86. Only from 3 to 12 per cent of the disagreements between two raters were greater than one half step. Self-trained Raters 5 and 6 similarly each rated 150 protocols from this sample. Their indices of interrater reliabilities compare favorably with those given in Table 16 for the trained raters. For example, the correlation between TPRs assigned by the two self-trained raters was .87. The correlations between the TPRs assigned by each of the self-trained raters and the one trained rater who rated the same 150 protocols were .86 and .89 respectively.

Because each of the three trained raters who rated any given protocol in the sealed sample was provided with the same distribution of item ratings for that protocol, that is, the distribution of item ratings made by the composite trained rater, it is possible that the reliability of the TPRs was overestimated, as they are not completely independent from rater to rater. The December 1967 sample consisted of protocols from 150 females aged eighteen to fifty-five. As with the sealed sample, each protocol was assigned a TPR by each of the three raters, with a

Table 16

PER CENT AGREEMENT AND INTERRATER CORRELATIONS
FOR TPRs FOR TRAINED RATERS

	Range	Median
Per cent complete agreement:		
Sealed sample	50–72	61
December 1967 sample	53–80	71
Per cent agreement within ½ step:		
Sealed sample	88–97	94
December 1967 sample	91–100	94
Interrater correlation:		
Sealed sample	.81–.93	.86
December 1967 sample	.78–.93	.85

NOTE.—For sealed sample, there were five raters with 143 to 200 protocols in common. For December 1967 sample, there were five raters with 45 protocols in common.

total of five raters participating. There were two major differences between the procedures for the sealed sample and those for the December 1967 sample. In rating the December 1967 sample, each rater provided his own distribution of item ratings for each protocol he rated, following the general rating procedures given above. This is the more natural situation and permits two raters to derive different distributions of item ratings for the same protocol. The second difference was that self-trained Raters 5 and 6 were two of the five raters in this study. They were now considered trained, since they were permitted to discuss questions with each other and with staff members on completion of the previous study. Of course, no discussion was permitted of responses or protocols in the sample being studied until each rater had recorded his ratings. As can be seen in Table 16, essentially the same results were obtained despite the differences in raters, procedure, and sample. Each TPR given by a rater in this supplementary study was experimentally independent of that of any other rater. Thus, we can be fairly confident in presenting the median interrater correlation of .86 between ratings for the sealed sample as a good index of the interrater reliability of total protocol ratings.

There is one final comparison to make between TPRs given by trained and self-trained raters to the sealed sample. Table 17 presents the correlation of the individual TPRs of each trained rater as well as those of the self-trained raters with the criterion $\overline{TPR}$ and with the composite rater ogive score, which is an automatic I-level rating assigned

Table 17

COMPARISON OF TPR OF TRAINED AND SELF-TRAINED RATERS

Rater	N	r with Criterion $\overline{\text{TPR}}$	r with Composite Rater Ogive Score
Trained:			
2	293	.94	.90
3	350	.96	.92
4	350	.95	.94
7	343	.92	.85
8	293	.90	.86
Self-trained:			
5	100	.89	.83
6	100	.92	.93

to the composite rater's ogive for each respondent. These correlations would be expected to be high for the trained raters because each rater was one of three who contributed to the $\overline{\text{TPR}}$ and each used as a basis of his rating exactly that ogive. The correlations presented for the self-trained raters are between sets of ratings that are completely independent in terms of procedure. The self-trained raters provided their own item ratings and ogives for these 100 cases, yet their correlations with the $\overline{\text{TPR}}$ are .89 and .92, respectively. Thus, not only do they agree well with each other, but their resultant ratings correlate well with that of a team of experts, to a degree that is comparable to the trained rater who is a contributor to the $\overline{\text{TPR}}$. The same can be said for the correlations of the self-trained raters' TPRs with the composite rater ogive score. Neither rater used these ogives, yet one produced TPRs that correlate .93 with an automatic rating given these ogives and the other produced ratings that correlate lower, .83, but not much lower than some of the trained raters.

To summarize to this point, the data indicate (1) that use of the scoring manual for rating level of ego development leads to ratings that attain a high degree of interrater reliability and (2) that raters whose only training in making such ratings has come from the manual itself are capable of achieving the same degree of reliability and of producing essentially the same overall ratings as are those persons who were involved in the construction of the manual.

FACTOR STRUCTURE

In evaluating a test such as this, one naturally asks if the ratings can be considered a measure of a general factor. In order to test the hypothesis of a general factor, four sets of item ratings were each submitted to a principal component analysis by Hotelling's iterative procedure (Thomson, 1939): (1) the item ratings given by the composite trained rater to responses of 543 sealed sample subjects, (2) the same ratings for the first 100 subjects only, (3) and (4) the item ratings given by Rater 5 and Rater 6 to the responses of these same 100 respondents. In each analysis the first component accounted for over 20 per cent of the total variance, with the contribution of the second component dropping to 5.6 per cent or less. Corresponding eigen values are shown in Table 18. To determine the relation between the first components from the several analyses, each subject was assigned three scores, the first component scaled score from the trained raters' analysis ($N = 543$) and the first component scaled score from each self-trained rater's analysis. These

Table 18

EIGEN VALUES FOR PRINCIPAL COMPONENT ANALYSIS, SEALED SAMPLE

	Raters				Word Count
	Trained	Trained	5	6	
Component	$N = 543$	$N = 100$	$N = 100$	$N = 100$	$N = 543$
First	8.8	9.8	8.3	7.5	13.5
Second	1.2	2.0	2.0	2.0	1.7
Third	1.2	1.7	1.9	1.8	1.2
Number of eigen values > 1.0	7	10	12	12	5

scores correlated .96 or .97; thus the factors obtained from Rater 5, Rater 6, and the composite trained rater are closely similar.

We had hoped and more or less expected that second and third factors might appear that would reveal which kinds of items are best for measuring ego level and which kinds are tainted with other variables. Our items differ with respect to first or third person, topics raised, grammatical structure, and so on. Although we do not consider it decisive, we were unable to make any sense out of factors beyond the first one. The first factor is essentially identical with the sum of item ratings ($r = .999$). Rotation therefore did not seem appropriate. The alpha coefficient corresponding to each first factor was computed and, of course, was virtually identical with the alpha coefficient computed directly from the item ratings (Table 19).

Table 19

COEFFICIENT ALPHA COMPUTED FOR PRINCIPAL COMPONENT
SCORES, SEALED SAMPLE

	Raters				Word Count
	Trained	Trained	5	6	
Component	$N = 543$	$N = 100$	$N = 100$	$N = 100$	$N = 543$
First	.91	.92	.91	.89	.95
Second	.19	.52	.51	.51	.41
Third	.15	.42	.47	.44	.18
Computed from sum of item ratings	.91	.92	.90	.88	.95

We conclude that the first components are essentially identical regardless of the amount of training of the raters, and, beyond that, the items taken together measure a unitary dimension.

VALIDITY STUDIES

Construct validity studies can lead off in many directions, some of which we are currently pursuing. Other investigators will choose their own applications and evaluations. Completed studies have related the SC test to age and to interview ratings of I-level. The question of whether verbal fluency taints our ratings sufficiently to invalidate them is also an aspect of construct validity.

Interview. Ruth Lucas, a collaborator in the manual development, chose as a criterion measure responses to a scheduled interview. The interview, which was about one and a half hours in length, though similar to the SC test in that it calls for verbal responses, allows for a more extensive and varied sample of verbal behavior, ideas, and attitudes. Mrs. Lucas interviewed twenty-six college students, all women, ranging in age from eighteen to fifty-one years, who also completed the SC test. These protocols were assigned TPRs in the usual manner by three raters and were rated as a part of the December 1967 sample. Two raters rated the interviews for I-level independently of each other and with no knowledge of the SC responses or ratings. The correlation between the interview ratings given by the two raters was .81. The two sets of ratings correlated .58 and .61 with $\overline{\text{TPR}}$. Considering the restricted range of ego level ratings (both $\overline{\text{TPR}}$s and interview ratings spread over only five of the ten possible points on the scale), these correlations are quite respectable, to be compared, for example, with a biserial correlation of .64 between ratings of adjustment and Rotter Incomplete Sentence Blank (ISB) scores for women reported in the ISB manual (Rotter and Rafferty, 1950). As is often the case, the criterion measure, I-level based on interview, is in some ways more dubious than the test being validated. We have not agreed on rules for reducing the diversity of an interview protocol to a single TPR, for example.

Age. To test the hypothesis of age differences, we were fortunate to be provided with two samples of protocols collected by E. V. Sullivan as a part of a larger study of Toronto school children aged nine to eighteen. There were 100 protocols of girls and 101 protocols of boys. The boys' and girls' samples were rated separately. Within each sample, protocols were randomly mixed for age, with any reference to age or year in school deleted in the typing. Three raters independently rated each protocol, first by rating each item in the protocol, then assigning a TPR utilizing the ogive of their own item ratings. TPRs disagreed on were compromised by the raters involved. The raters were not able to use a manual for the boys, as none yet exists. However, all raters were highly trained in the theory and the use of our manual, and their ratings are the best we have.

Figure 1 illustrates the results, giving the cumulative frequency distributions, in terms of per cent, of TPRs at each age level for both girls and boys. The age groups were nine to ten, eleven to twelve, thirteen to fourteen, and seventeen to eighteen. The Ns in each age group were fourteen, twenty-four, twenty-seven, and thirty-five, respectively, for the girls, and thirteen, twenty-four, twenty-five, and twenty-nine, respectively, for the boys. There is no overlap between the ogive curves for the four age groups. (Obviously, the frequency distributions for the age

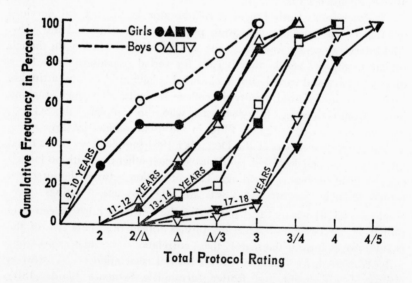

FIGURE 1. DISTRIBUTIONS OF TOTAL PROTOCOL RATINGS BY AGE AND SEX OF TORONTO SCHOOL CHILDREN (DATA OF E. V. SULLIVAN)

groups do show overlap.) There are progressive age differences at all points on the ego level scale for the cumulative distributions.

Given the small Ns involved at the various age groups, the curves for boys and girls are remarkably similar. As is to be expected by examination of the curves, a chi square test shows no significant difference in TPR at the various age groups between boys and girls. We had no prior hypothesis concerning sex differences. The hypothesis of age differences in TPR, however, is clearly supported by these data, which can be summarized by the correlations between TPR and chronological age, .74 for boys and .69 for girls.

Verbal Fluency. Since we had known ever since the early study of single women that item by item the word count correlated almost as well with $\overline{TPR}$ as the item rating, it took faith both in theory of ego level and in psychometric theory to continue working on the manual. Some correlation between TPR and word count is expected because conceptual complexity is part of what we call ego development. To exhibit conceptual complexity in a manner recognizable to raters usually requires longer responses, combining several ideas. We simply could not believe, however, that counting words was as good as taking all aspects of response into account.

Let us look at the matter psychometrically. Suppose that word count can be conceived as resulting from I-level and also from verbosity or verbal fluency. To make the psychometrics manageable, we adapt classical psychometric theory, which expands the score as a sum of true score and random error factor, by adding also a systematic error factor that represents verbosity. It has been shown (Loevinger, 1954) that such systematic error factors or distortions operate as follows: The correlation of the item with the criterion depends on the weight of the true factor in the item and not at all on whether the error factor in the item is random or systematic. For a test made up of items equally weighted with true score, the correlation with the criterion will depend on whether the error is random or systematic. Where the items all contain a common distortion factor (here, verbosity), the correlation with the criterion will be lowered. The homogeneity of the test whose items are weighted with distortion will, however, be higher than the homogeneity of a test with items similar except that the errors are random rather than systematic.

This model fits the present situation quite well. The item word count correlates almost as well with $\overline{TPR}$ as item rating, or at least it did so in early versions (Table 7). Let us look at the remaining values, testing the hypothesis that word count contains excessive distortion. Each subject in the sealed sample was assigned four scores: (1) the criterion $\overline{TPR}$, (2) an automatic rating applied to the ogive of thirty-six item ratings of the composite trained rater, (3) the sum of the thirty-six item ratings given by the composite trained rater, and (4) the total number

Table 20

CORRELATIONS OF VARIOUS KINDS OF TOTAL SCORES FOR
TRAINED RATERS, SEALED SAMPLE $(N = 543)$

	Ogive Score	Ratings Sum	Word Count Sum
Criterion $\overline{\text{TPR}}$	.93	.93	.58
Ogive score		.92	.56
Sum of item ratings		(.91)	.65
Sum of item word counts			(.95)

NOTE.—Values in parentheses are alpha coefficients.

of words used to respond to the thirty-six sentence stems. Table 20 contains the intercorrelations among these scores. Scores based on item ratings are almost interchangeable with the $\overline{\text{TPR}}$. Word count, however, attains only moderate correlations with the other scores. At the same time, the test made up of sum of word counts is more homogeneous than one made up of sum of item ratings. Parenthetically, many of the ills of personality measurement came from early workers being seduced by the high internal consistency coefficients obtainable with items heavily weighted with systematic errors, to wit, with the various response biases.

Both a priori and in terms of the data we conclude that word count is heavily weighted with distortion and not a useful measure of I-level. If this conclusion is accepted, we can then use correlation with word count as a criterion to evaluate the three other methods of finding TPRs. As Table 20 shows, a score computed by summing the item ratings correlates higher with word count than the other two scores, the automatic ogive score and the ogive score with leeway for intuitive modification (used in obtaining the $\overline{\text{TPRs}}$). We conclude that item sum is probably also somewhat weighted with the same distortion and is less good than the other two methods for obtaining TPRs. Until further evidence is obtained, we conclude that for new raters the optimal score is obtained by using the automatic ogive rules. We assume that raters highly trained in the theory and with long experience with the method will reserve the right to make judgments based also on aspects of the protocol not encoded in the distribution of item ratings.

Intelligence. The question of the relation of ego development to intelligence is more ambiguous than it may sound. Probably a wide variety of coefficients could be obtained, depending on the nature and variability of the sample concerned. What is important, of course, is that what we call ego development should not just be another name for intelligence, or that all of its valid variance should not be accountable for in terms of intelligence.

Mr. Augusto Blasi tested two groups of black sixth grade children of low socioeconomic class, fifty-nine boys and sixty-four girls. The form of the sentence completion test they were given differed slightly from the one presented in the present manual; the protocols were scored, however, by expert raters. IQs were determined by the Lorge-Thorndike Intelligence test; this test had been given as part of normal school procedure and results were obtained from the students' files. For the boys the mean IQ was 95 with a standard deviation of 12.6; for the girls the mean was 94 with a standard deviation of 12.3. Correlation between I-level and IQ was .45 for the boys and .47 for the girls.

Perhaps more important, for children at the I-2 level, the IQ range was 69 to 109 for girls, 68 to 98 for boys. For those at the I-3/4 level, which was the highest in this group, the range was 91 to 115 for girls, 87 to 119 for boys.

OTHER SCORING PARADIGMS

To take one final look at the scoring paradigm, two additional methods of scoring the test were evaluated on both the sealed and the Toronto samples. Taking the composite rater's item ratings for each of the thirty-six items in a protocol, each of the protocols in the sealed sample was scored in terms of the modal level (as Kohlberg does with his test) and the mean of highest five ratings (similar to D. E. Hunt's use of his test). The mode score produced essentially a two-point scale with 74 per cent of the subjects placed at the conformist level and 21 per cent at the conscientious level. Only six of the 543 respondents scored above or below these two levels. The score based on the mean of the highest five ratings in a protocol did slightly better in terms of variability. However, by this scoring method almost 90 per cent of the subjects would be classed at the conscientious level or above, not one below the conformist level. Applying the same two scoring schemes to the protocols in the Toronto girls sample yielded correlations with chronological age of .22 for the modal score and .32 for the mean of the highest five ratings as compared with .69 for our TPR. Thus, in terms of our instrument and our data, our scoring paradigm leads to much greater variability in measured ego level and correlates much higher with age in the crucial preadolescent-adolescent age range than do the alternatives of the mode or the highest level shown.

SUMMARY

To summarize, studies with the scoring manual have shown it to be quite reliable regardless of amount of previous training of the raters above a certain self-taught minimum. The test provides a measure of a unitary dimension that can be considered to be a developmental trait.

CHAPTER 4

Manifestations of Ego Level in Sentence Completions

Before reading the present chapter one should have a general feeling for the process of ego development and a picture of its various stages. It may be helpful to have a copy of Table 1 at hand in reading. What the present chapter aims to do is not to reveal new insights into ego development, though it may do so incidentally, but to show how the several stages are manifest in SCs for women and adolescent girls. Only those facets that appear in several items are included. Those that appear in only one or two items are noted in the scoring instructions for that item. There may be important aspects that do not appear in SCs at all or that appear but have escaped our notice. We may err in the other direction also. Themes that are statistically prevalent at a given level may in fact not represent ego level at all directly.

The format of the present chapter, relying on single completions taken out of context rather than on total protocols, fails to convey one important clue to ego development—the richness of the total protocol. Low-level protocols tend to give the same or similar answers to several items, high-level ones introduce a variety of thoughts and topics. In any event, if a given thought is expressed in virtually the same language for several items in the following account, it will never be the case that all illustrations are drawn from a single unusual protocol. Major emphasis in this chapter is on what is most common, not on what is unique, except, as noted, that at high levels uniqueness is a common element.

Many responses fit more than one category at a given level in this chapter. Naturally, this reinforces the conclusion that the several categories are indeed illustrative of a single syndrome. In general, we do not pause to point these instances out. The observation holds at every level.

One difficulty in writing down scoring rules is that ideas do not spring fullblown at one level but tend to appear in cliché form at lower levels, in fully realized form at higher levels. For many items it turned out that category titles, expressing what was common to a group of items, would be the very responses that came from lower levels. For example, the notion that women must fill "varied roles" is found in those words typically at I-4, while responses explicitly describing role differentiation are more typical of I-5. This is the kind of thing that gives an intuitive rater of long experience some advantage over a set of rules. We have tried to indicate the difficulty where it was most evident.

Another difficulty is that a theme that appears at one level in several stems may appear at a slightly higher or lower level in relation to other stems. Even an experienced rater may have difficulty keeping such differences in mind; hence we always use the item scoring manuals (Part II) except when scoring items for which we have no manual.

The purposes of the present chapter are, then: to flesh out the picture of ego development with the words of ordinary people; to serve as an introduction to the item manuals of Part II, alerting the users of our test to aspects of response governing scoring; to guide the rating of unclassified responses; and to serve in place of an item manual for new items. Since replicated responses are rare at the two highest levels, I-5 and I-6, the present chapter may provide about as much guidance as the item manuals for such ratings.

All responses are quoted verbatim, with subjects' errors of grammar, spelling, and punctuation faithfully preserved. Erasures or crossed out words are not indicated, except where part of the stem has been crossed out.

I-2: IMPULSIVE

The I-2 tends to dichotomize the world into good or bad, mean or nice, and clean or dirty. Stereotypy is the most conspicuous sign of this level. It cannot be fully illustrated here, since many I-2 protocols contain the same or almost the same completion to three or more stems.

Most men think that women—*are good*
                                      —*are bad but some are good*

A good mother—*is nice*

When my mother spanked me, I—*always bad*

Being with other people—*is nice if they don't do immoral things*
                                      —*I am very mean*

A woman should always—*keep clean*

My conscience bothers me if—*I am unpure*

In addition to the conceptual oversimplification of the dichotomies, there is often conceptual confusion in I-2 protocols. While there are various ways to interpret these peculiarly illogical responses, one way is to say that the subject has reacted to one key word in the stem. Such psychological causation as is carried by the word *because* is beyond these subjects. Causation is understood only in concrete terms.

Women are lucky because—*they can't have babies*

Men are lucky because—*there happy*
                                      —*they are cute*

What gets me into trouble is—*school*
                                      —*bills*

The worst thing about being a woman—*is drinking*
                                      —*is diseases*

Tautological responses are frequent at this level. The criterion is not echoing the words of the stem but echoing the thought.

Raising a family—*having children*
                                      —*by working and feeding them*

For a woman a career is—*very good work*

A pregnant woman—*has a baby in her*

My main problem is—*trouble*

The I-2 subject seems unaware of mutuality or reciprocity between people; for her, people are seen as sources of supply, she demands things from them, and *good* often if not always means *good to me*.

Usually she felt that sex—*is good to me because I get hot*

Whenever she was with her mother, she—*ask for things*

Women are lucky because—*they get nice things*

If my mother—*is good to me our be to you*

The I-2 subject recognizes in concrete terms the traditional responsibilities of women, but probably because of her self-centeredness and dependence, they come through as burdens.

A wife should—*keep the house clean*
     —be able to get pregant

A good mother—*is a woman who stay at home and cook, wash,*
     iron, make bed and take care of him

The worst thing about being a woman—*having babies. If you could*
     stop it be alright
     —is taking care of kids
     —is when you are marred
     and have kids who spank
     them

Frank dependence is expressed by giving going home as a solution to many problems. There is another aspect to such responses, however; trouble is located in a place rather than a situation. So other subjects at I-2 want to solve things by running away.

When they talked about sex, I—*get mad and go home*

When they avoided me—*I cried and ran to mommy*

Whenever she was with her mother, she—*always ran away*

If I can't get what I want—*I run away*

Constructive action is not the program of the I-2. If she is not given what she wants, she may turn self-destructive. Such responses often sound like those of children who try to compel others to give to them by uttering empty threats. A closely related group of responses indicates complete self-rejection and inner barrenness.

> If my mother—*died I would kill myself*
>
> Sometimes she wished that—*I was dead*
>
> The thing I like about myself is—*not much*
>
> I am—*I don't no*
>
> If I can't get what I want—*I don't want noting*

Affects are seen primarily as bodily states or impulses rather than as differentiated inner feelings. The sexual and aggressive impulsivity is described in blatant and unsocialized language.

> My mother and I—*fight sometimes*
>   —*drink*
>
> When my mother spanked me, I—*could murder her*
>
> When I am with a man—*want to shoot him*
>   —*I get hot*
>
> A woman feels good when—*she gets screwed*
>
> A pregnant woman—*is sick*

In addition to the impulses and affects that are primarily bodily states, the emotions of the I-2 include aversive and negative reactions, dysphoric moods, and positive responses so bland and vacuous as to be inappropriate in context. There is thus a limited emotional range, with all the more differentiated and abstract and cognitively shaded emotions missing.

> Being with other people—*is very nice*
>   —*gives me the creeps*
>
> A woman's body—*is a mess*
>
> When people are helpless—*they feel bad*
>
> Whenever she was with her mother, she—*cried*
>   —*feels O.K.*
>
> Raising a family—*is all right with me*
>   —*is hell!*
>
> My mother and I—*is OK sometime*

DELTA: SELF-PROTECTIVE (OPPORTUNISTIC)

The I-2 comes through on this test as vulnerable, somewhat confused, and having inadequate conception of the complexities of the world. While we have long felt that some stage had to intervene between the impulsive stage and the conformist one, our previous characterization of the intermediate stage as opportunistic has caused dissatisfaction among raters, who often felt it did not capture the essence of the transition. The more malignant signs of this stage, such as blatant opportunism, deception, and coercion, are shown by few of our respondents. Presumably they are those who have experienced what H. S. Sullivan referred to as a "malevolent transformation," but they are by no means all of the subjects at this level. Our data show that at the Delta level the subject's primary preoccupations are self-protection and staying out of trouble. She must be on guard at all times to control the situation and to control herself.

My father—*is fun but I can't tell when he is serious and I get into lots of trouble this way*

When I am nervous, I—*get in all kinds of trouble*

A good mother—*should try to teach her children to obey, and stay out of trouble*

Being with other people—*I will watch myself*

When people are helpless—*I don't like to be bothered with them*

I am—*very careful with whom I play with*

When I am with a man—*This is also none of your business*
—I be very careful

A woman should always—*be alert and on guard*
—keep one step ahead of the man
—be careful not to get a bad reputation

When they talked about sex, I—*listen, cause I wont get in trouble, also I know what I'll be doing*
The thing I like about myself is—*my ability to think fast*

A possible outcome of the Delta self-protectiveness is a manipulative and exploitive attitude toward people, as opposed to the I-2 waiting to be given to. The world is divided into those who rule and those who are ruled, those who take advantage of you and those you can get the better of. For our respondents these attitudes show most clearly in regard to the war between the sexes and possibly to the relations of parents and children. At this point self-protection merges with a second theme, a simple hedonism, whose rules are to avoid hard work, look for fun, and get nice things, like money.

> The thing I like about myself is—*the way to handle boys*
>
> Usually she felt that sex—*helpes me on up the road farther*
>
> Women are lucky because—*they can get married and live off the men*
>
> Most men think that women—*are just something to use*
> *—are mearly around to get what they can off of them*
>
> A woman's body—*is made for the enjoyment of men*
>
> A wife should—*respect her husband and make him feel he is the King of his Castle and she can always have her way*
>
> When I am nervous, I—*stare at a person in the eyes and mock them*
>
> My mother and I—*get along when she has money*
>
> Men are lucky because—*I feel they get almost anything they want*
>
> Raising a family—*do not let children run the household*
> *—I want my family to obey me*
>
> A woman feels good when—*something she wants is done*
>
> A good mother—*should always please her children*
>
> If I can't get what I want—*I ask my father for it!*

Complaints against parents may occur at any level. Those at this level often seem to be describable as dependent complaining. A similar theme is that work is onerous or, at best, a means to an end, rather than an opportunity.

> If my mother—*would only baby sit more often*
>
> Sometimes she wished that—*her mother would understand*
> *—someone els would cook supper*
>
> When she thought of her mother, she—*complained that she was not loved*
>
> The worst thing about being a woman—*is hard work*
>
> Women are lucky because—*they don't have to work as hard as men*

Raising a family—*is a hard job for the mother*

Education—*I think Education is good for finding a job*

For a woman a career is—*money in her hand and a good job*

The Delta subject does not see herself as responsible for trouble or failure. Like the I-2 subject, she may see herself as a pawn of fate. You are lucky or unlucky; things just happen over which you have no control. This is not psychologically inconsistent with her concern over who is controlling whom, even when it may seem logically contradictory.

Women are lucky because—*some women are lucky*

Sometimes she wished that—*good things would happen*

Raising a family—*could be fun but sometimes it turns out differently*

My conscience bothers me if—*I happen to lie about something*

The worst thing about being a woman—*is when trouble appears to happen*

Usually she felt that sex—*was just something happen to a woman*

More common than blaming bad luck for trouble or failure is to blame other people, as does the I-2 person. One of the most distinctive Delta responses expresses the notion that one should be with the right people and avoid the wrong ones.

If my mother—*whould trust me Id be alright*
    —had told me so
    —would straighten out I wouldn't be here

What gets me into trouble is—*my sister she told*
    —running around with the wrong group

Being with other people—*makes you feel good if your with the right crowd*
    —means a lot to me if they are the right class of people

A good mother—*should not hesitate to speak up when she thinks her daughter might be in the wrong company*

Even where blame is not shifted to other people, it is external and somehow impersonal. The Delta subject seems to say that if her mouth or eyes or figure is to blame, then she is not.

What gets me into trouble is—*my figure*
> —*what my sister call trouble for me is that I talk with my eyes they say to men I don't really mean.* '(*Smile*)
> —*the car and going out with a boy of a different religion*

My main problem is—*keeping my mouth from getting me in trouble*

A woman's body—*is full of temptations*

The Delta person can be shamed, but she does not show real remorse nor does she assume real responsibility. What is wrong is to be caught. A person gets away with whatever he can, by deception or pretense if necessary. Rules are seen as loss of freedom.

When they avoided me—*they make me feel shame*

Whenever she was with her mother, she—*hid because she was ashamed of her*
> —*acted like a perfect little angle*

My conscience bothers me if—*I feel that someone is watching me*
> —*I let it*

Women are lucky because—*they can usually get by with more things than men*

A pregnant woman—*can always get away from heavy work*

What gets me into trouble is—*when my brothers or sisters tattle on me, and I don't have a way out*
> —*my step father, he speck for me to stay in the house all day & night*

If my mother—*went out of town for a while I could have a good time*

I am—*sick of this place and want to go home*

The Delta subject may take pride in her sexuality, flouting it for all to see. At the same time, the virtues she advocates show that control of sexual impulses is problematic for her.

The worst thing about being a woman—*is having a rotten lover or husband*

When I am with a man—*boy!*

I am—*a sex maniac*

A wife should—*never lie to her husband or doing anything behind his back that isn't nice*
      —not go out with other men

At times she worried about—*having a baby which had no father*

The Delta person may picture herself as invulnerable to hurt or weakness on the one hand, or she may think in terms of retaliation for injury on the other. In either case she shows her need for self-protection.

When they avoided me—*I laughed because my intentions were to avoid them*
      —I turned the tables

When my mother spanked me, I—*laughed*
      —hit her back

When she thought of her mother, she—*When she think of mother,*
      —it doesn't bother me I never knew her

Sometimes she wished that—*her grandchildren would be 10 times as mean as her children*

She displays hostile, callous humor, often directed against those giving the test. Similar deprecatory attitudes may be attributed to others. Such responses are particularly frequent on items that evoke sympathy, sentiment, or idealization from other respondents.

Raising a family—*is for Catholics*
      —is easy on ADC

Being with other people—*is fine (but not behind bars)*

When they avoided me—*they avoided my dog also*

When she thought of her mother, she—*thought of Blatz Beer*
      —wept bitter, bitter tears on her mink coat

A woman should always—*be sweet and nice Ha Ha*

I feel sorry—*I came today*

My main problem is—*a dislike for research questionnaires*
      —trying to answer these questions right now

My conscience bothers me if—*I waste precious time taking tests like this*

While omissions are scored I-3, some evasive responses that are distinctly hostile in tone are scored Delta.

A good mother—*went that way*

A wife should—*be married*

What gets me into trouble is—*none of your business*

DELTA/3: TRANSITION FROM SELF-PROTECTIVE TO CONFORMIST

The Delta/3 rating has been used primarily as a compromise for categories of response that are proportionally more frequent among subjects below I-3 but not uncommon among subjects at I-3 and I-3/4. In some cases the absolute number at I-3 or higher may exceed those below I-3, but that is because our samples contain fewer subjects below I-3 than at I-3 and I-3/4.

The most conspicuous theme refers to concrete aspects of traditional sex roles. More broadly, obedience and conformity to social norms are simple and absolute rules. Emotions are at least quasi-physiological rather than cognitively differentiated. Thus one finds physical causation in the responses where at higher levels psychological causation would be implied. Cleanliness and physical appearance in its concrete aspects are stressed. We omit examples, since whether these themes are classed I-3, Delta/3, or lower depends on the particular stem.

I-3: CONFORMIST

Any item is likely to have some nondiscriminating categories of response. Since our rule is to rate every response, we have to provide a rating for them. Where the category is completely nondiscriminating, we use the I-3 rating arbitrarily, but then we build our method of assigning TPRs to take that convention into account. Some categories of response fail to discriminate I-3 protocols from those at lower levels but make satisfactory discrimination between I-3 and those higher; those responses in general are listed at Delta/3. In describing typical characteristics of I-3 protocols, we shall rely on discriminating categories listed at the I-3 level, ignoring responses placed there by default. Some of the responses listed, however, will come from categories that do not discriminate I-3 from I-3/4 protocols; in those cases there are often similar categories at I-3/4 for other items.

The I-3 subject structures the world in a conceptually simple manner. Formulas for what does happen or what ought to happen tend to be stated in absolute terms, without contingencies or exceptions. When a particular category of persons or situations is mentioned, a sweeping generalization is often given, as if it applied to all members of the category rather than to just certain ones of them. Behavior is governed by rules and is often judged by absolute standards of right and wrong. The words "right" and "wrong" alone are far from exclusive for this level; they are used frequently by those at lower levels and by those at I-3/4.

My mother and I—*were never very close*

A woman's body—*is beautiful*
        —should always be covered

The thing I like about myself is—*that I never get too mad*
        —that I like fun with everyone

If my mother—*gives me advice, I take it because I know she is always right*

Education—*is very important for everyone*

Raising a family—*is a matter of importance to any women's life*

A pregnant woman—*cries easily*
        —is happy

Men are lucky because—*they are so free to do as they choose*

A good mother—*always understands her children*
        —teaches her child write from wrong, and give him or her spanking when needing

Whenever she was with her mother, she—*did as she was told*

My conscience bothers me if—*I break God's will's and commands*

Superlatives are often used; things are the best possible or the worst. Sentimental idealization is common. These characteristics hold also for the I-3/4 subject.

A good mother—*is the best yet*

A pregnant woman—*should look her best at all times*

My father—*is a great guy*

Most men think that women—*are the most needed things there are*

Being with other people—*is the best thing to do*

A woman's body—*is her most prized possession*

The I-3 person describes herself in socially acceptable terms. Her faults and her troubles are often trivial or conventional, and sometimes they are even virtues. Conventional social norms are accepted without question or personal evaluation. Clichés are frequent, often moralistic ones.

>What gets me into trouble is—*my big mouth*
>   —*I give my children to much*
>
>My mother and I—*are close*
>
>If I can't get what I want—*I try harder*
>
>When people are helpless—*I try to help them*
>
>When I am with a man—*I try to act like a lady*
>
>A wife should—*love, honor, and obey her husband*
>
>My father—*is tall, dark, and handsome*
>
>Education—*is important*
>
>Raising a family—*is a big responsibility*
>
>A woman's body—*should be her pride and joy*
>
>When I am with a man—*feel great*
>
>The worst thing about being a woman—*is trying to keep up with styles*
>   —*putting up with menstrual periods*
>
>My conscience bothers me if—*I lie*
>   —*tell a story*

Among the most important social norms for the I-3 subject are those that define the conventional sex roles. The social norm requires that one be satisfied with one's sex role. Therefore it is not contradictory when the same person says that men are lucky to be men, women lucky to be women, or when she says that women are lucky to have babies, men lucky that they cannot do so. Many responses of this type do not sharply differentiate the I-3 subject from those at Delta/3 and at I-3/4. Where they differ, responses classed Delta/3 tend to refer to more specific chores, while those classed I-3/4 tend to be a bit more interpersonal in emphasis or to refer to implicit standards.

>Men are lucky because—*they can be fathers*
>
>Women are lucky because—*they are women*
>   —*their place is in the home*
>
>A wife should—*act like a wife*

When I am with a man—*I try to act feminine*

A woman should always—*get married and have children*

Most men think that women—*should not be head of the family. I agree*

The worst thing about being a woman—*there is'nt any worst thing*

The I-3 and I-3/4 women value a pleasing, friendly personality and like to be part of a group. They depend on popularity and expressions of social approval. Belonging makes them feel secure. They often disapprove of hostility and aggression, which the Delta subject may flaunt, even when they admit to anger or temper. They may ignore hostile provocations.

If my mother—*is kind and generous*

A woman should always—*be friendly and nice*

When I am with a man—*I am polite*

The thing I like about myself is—*no one is a stranger a smile for all*

What gets me into trouble is—*my temper*

When they avoided me—*I felt unwanted*
—I smiled and kept on my way

Being with other people—*makes you feel like you belong*

When a child won't join in group activities—*he needs friendship*

A woman feels good when—*she is complimented*
—she is in a group of other people her age
—she is surrounded by her family

Concern for physical appearance is one of the most distinctive marks of the I-3 level as compared to I-4 or higher. Attractiveness to men is sometimes mentioned and probably often implied, but it is not the only factor involved. There is also preoccupation with concrete and external aspects of life. Many of the responses of this type do not discriminate I-3 from I-3/4 subjects. Concern for appearance obviously does not disappear at higher levels, but it is expressed differently.

A woman should always—*keep her figure*

A pregnant woman—*should try to make herself look as well-groomed as possible*

At times she worried about—*the way she walked*

Sometimes she wished that—*she was two inches shorter*
            —she was pretty

My main problem is—*my weight*
            —that my face is broken out

When I am with a man—*I put my best face forward*

The worst thing about being a woman—*is having to pin up your*
            hair every night

Women are lucky because—*they get to wear pretty cloths and*
            makeup

A woman feels good when—*she is dressed up*

Interpersonal interaction is described in terms of behaviors rather than in terms of differentiated feelings, motives, or traits, as it is at I-4. Talking is frequently mentioned, being the behavioral version of social interaction in general.

Whenever she was with her mother, she—*talked alot*
            —was usually sewing

If my mother—*goes shopping I like to go with her*

When she thought of her mother, she—*smiled*

My mother and I—*have fun by teasing each other, and by cook-*
            ing together

A good mother—*talks with her children*

What gets me into trouble is—*answering back*

When they talked about sex, I—*join right in*
            —sit there and just listen
            —left the room

When I am nervous, I—*chatter*

Inner life is mentioned only in terms of generalities and banalities, such as happy, sad, fun, close, embarrassed, and, of course, love and understanding.

Whenever she was with her mother, she—*felt pleasant*

The thing I like about myself is—*that I am happy*

When I am with a man—*I am very bashful*

Being with other people—*is fun*

When people are helpless—*I feel sorry for them*

When a child won't join in group activities—*he may be shy*

A good mother—*is one that loves and understands her children*

When they avoided me—*it worried me*

When they talked about sex, I—*don't like it*

At I-3 sex and love are never mentioned as two aspects of a single relation. The rare responses at this level mentioning both sex and love treat them as contrasting ideas. Love seems to be synonymous with caring for, which in turn is taken in its concrete meaning of taking care of. Hence love seems to be an aspect of dependence and security needs, though this conclusion is inferential.

Usually she felt that sex—*was less important than love*

A woman should always—*be true to her husband in love and sex*

A wife should—*take care of her home and family*

Men are lucky because—*they have a family to care for*

A pregnant woman—*needs love and support*

A woman feels good when—*she is loved*

When I am with a man—*I feel very secure*

Feelings are sometimes denied, but more characteristic is vague, evasive, or noncommittal response. Inner conflict is not acknowledged, though the succession of contradictory responses on a protocol is evidence that it exists at least in some I-3 subjects. Occasionally it will be manifest, though not acknowledged, in a single response.

When I am nervous, I—*I am not nervous*

If I can't get what I want—*I do without*

My mother and I—*my mother is dead*

When they avoided me—*nobody ever did*
　　　　　　　　　　　　—no comment

The thing I like about myself is—*myself*

Women are lucky because—*I don't know*

Education—*one semister colledge*

I feel sorry—*for some people*

At times she worried about—*a lot of things*
                              —nothing

When they avoided me—*I just get up and leave the room, I hate*
                      to be avoided

Men are lucky because—*they will never know, the joyous pangs*
                       of childbirth

There is an emphasis on concrete things, on outcomes rather than proc-
esses. The good life is the easy one, with work all done and with lots of
money. Another aspect of the I-3 woman's concrete view is her tendency
to class people in terms of superficial, often demographic, characteristics.

A woman feels good when—*she succeeds in raising a happy family*
                         —she has the housework done and the
                          children in bed

Raising a family—*is a wonderful job if you get it done*

At times she worried about—*getting poor grades*

Sometimes she wished that—*she had a million dollars*

For a woman a career is—*one way to keep happy and to have a*
                         few things she wants

My main problem is—*I don't like to cook*

Women are lucky because—*they can relax during the day*

When people are helpless—*they are a burden*

Most men think that women—*have it easy*

I am—*a student*

If my mother—*were living she'd be a grandmother*

My father—*works for the St. Joseph Lead Co.*

I feel sorry—*for orphans*

My mother and I—*wear the same size dress*

I-3/4: TRANSITION FROM CONFORMIST
TO CONSCIENTIOUS

While the I-3 woman lives in a simple world, where the same
thing is right always and for everyone, the person at I-3/4 sees multiple
possibilities and alternatives in situations.

My mother and I—*agree on many things but misunderstand on others*

A good mother—*is hard to define*

Being with other people—*is fine if its not constant*

A woman's body—*comes in many shapes & sizes*

A pregnant woman—*is happy but uncomfortable*

Raising a family—*is a career in itself and has both joy and sorrowful moments*

For a woman a career is—*everything, for others it isn't*

I am—*impossible to describe by any one adjective or noun*
—a little stumped for an answer—too many possibilities

In place of the I-3 tendency to classify actions in mutually exclusive categories of right and wrong, the I-3/4 subject tends to think about appropriateness, what is right for the time and the place and the situation. There are contingencies, exceptions, and comparisons, though they are global and often banal. More complex and differentiated contingencies and comparisons appear at I-4.

Usually she felt that sex—*was taboo for small children to learn about*

When they talked about sex, I—*feel there is a time and place for everything*

A pregnant woman—*is very fortunate if she really wants the child*

Education—*is fun, if you get into the swing of it*

When I am with a man—*I feel great (if I like him)*
—I feel more grown up than what I am

For a woman a career is—*important—until she marries and has a family*

When she thought of her mother, she—*wondered if she could ever be such a person*

My mother and I—*get along better than average*

A woman should always—*listen and never talk unless she has something important to say*

My main problem is—*saying the wrong thing at the wrong time*

My conscience bothers me if—*I scold my daughter unnecessarily*

Self-consciousness is prototypic for the I-3/4 transition, along with a rudimentary self-awareness and self-criticism. More differentiated and specific self-criticism, as well as other reflexive traits, are characteristic for the I-4 level. Another aspect or manifestation of self-consciousness is discomfort in a social situation. There may also be a feeling of loneliness, being aware of being alone, or even a desire to be alone.

My conscience bothers me if—*I do wrong, and realizes it*

What gets me into trouble is—*my own mistakes*

When I am nervous, I—*make it hard on everyone around me*

I feel sorry—*when I lose my temper*

When they avoided me—*I felt as if I was different and not as good as them*

A pregnant woman—*sometimes feels funny in a crowd*

When they talked about sex, I—*felt a little on edge*

Whenever she was with her mother, she—*got embarrassed*

I feel sorry—*for people when embarrassed in a crowd*

When I am with a man—*I am quiet and shy*

Being with other people—*Scares me because I am so self-conscious —i like a lot. Sometimes it gets lonly at home*

The worst thing about being a woman—*is when you have no friends*

I feel sorry—*for very old people who have lost the feeling of belonging*

When a child won't join in group activities—*he may prefer to be alone*

If my mother—*moved out of town I would be lonesome*

The I-3/4 subject has a stronger awareness of feelings than does the I-3 person. While she is still interested in appearance, this interest is often or usually expressed in terms of feelings.

When I am with a man—*I am conscious of being a woman —I feel prettier*

Most men think that women—*are too sensitive*

My main problem is—*not knowing how I really feel about love —is my moods of despondency*

A good mother—*not only loves her children but shows it*

I feel sorry—*for those who have never loved or been loved*

When she thought of her mother, she—*got a warm inner glow*

A pregnant woman—*is usually concerned about her appearance*

A woman feels good when—*she looks good and knows it*

If my mother—*would forget about her grey hair she'd be fine*

The worst thing about being a woman—*is the worry about figure, face, etc.*

The I-3/4 subject is more aware of individual differences in attitudes, interests, and abilities than is the I-3 person, but she mentions them in more global and banal terms than does the I-4 subject.

What gets me into trouble is—*my sarcastic attitude towards everything*

At times she worried about—*being smart enough*
        —being nervous

Most men think that women—*are incapable of doing the same jobs as them*

If my mother—*was more patient I could discuss matters with her better*

The thing I like about myself is—*my intelligence*

When a child won't join in group activities—*his interests may be elsewhere*

A good mother—*is interested in all that her children do*

The traits or prototraits seen at I-3/4 partake of moods ("patient"), norms ("feminine"), or virtues ("considerate"). The notion of femininity has ambiguous and even contradictory connotations. Probably unsophisticated women always mean something different from what psychologists, psychiatrists, and others in the helping professions mean when they talk of the "feminine role." For this reason we try to avoid the term except when quoting our respondents. Both because of the intrinsic ambiguity and because experience shows it would lead to errors, we never score on a word alone but always take the whole thought into consideration. The virtues emphasized are homely ones, reminiscent of the Boy Scout oath, and they merge with elementary and vague social concerns. A common concern is being helpful.

When I am with a man—*I feel very feminine and happy*

Most men think that women—*should be more feminine*
—are not as stable as themselves

A good mother—*is patient*
—should be considerate and love children

Whenever she was with her mother, she—*was always considerate*
and helpful

I am—*a very sincere person*

When people are helpless—*the community should extend a willing*
hand

I feel sorry—*for suffering humanity*

The thing I like about myself is—*my honesty*
—I like to help people

Sometimes she wished that—*war was an unknown word*
—she could do more for others

What gets me into trouble is—*trying to help others*

The I-3/4 woman has a deepened interest in interpersonal relations. Moreover, interactions are described in terms of feelings or traits rather than in purely behavioral terms, as is often the case at I-3. The feelings are not necessarily more loving; aggressive and hostile feelings may also be openly acknowledged.

When they talked about sex, I—*talked right along without feeling*
funny at all

The thing I like about myself is—*that I love to meet new people*
and I make friends easily

A woman feels good when—*she's with someone who loves her*

When my mother spanked me, I—*cried, my feelings hurt more*
than anything else

What gets me into trouble is—*not liking to hurt other peoples*
feelings

My father—*was a yes man to my mother*
—is a tyrant

The trouble that bothers the Delta subject, with its connotation of being caught, becomes replaced by problems for the I-3/4 person, with connotations of seeking solutions. Behavior is seen as having a reason or motive, but this is stated in general. Specific reasons and motives are given for specific behaviors at I-4. At I-3/4 understanding is mentioned, with or without interpersonal connotations.

A pregnant woman—*problem is just beginning*

A woman's body—*is usually a problem to her*

Being with other people—*helps one to forget himself and his problems*

When they avoided me—*I said there is a reason for all behavior*

When people are helpless—*I wonder why*

When my mother spanked me, I—*knew it was for a valid reason*

When a child won't join in group activities—*a parent should find out why*

My mother and I—*understand each other*

My father—*really understands the problems of teens*

A wife should—*try to understand and sympathize*

Elementary conceptions of purpose, goals, models, and expectations are present at I-3/4. Such conceptions are more sharply defined at higher levels; a clear conception that a person's behavior exhibits a pattern is rated I-4. Those below I-3/4 lack the degree of time perspective implied by purposes and goals. Models and expectations seem to involve a degree of conceptual complexity and abstraction that is lacking below I-3/4.

Education—*is the one ultimate goal everyone should have*

My main problem is—*what I will do when I graduate*

A woman should always—*set a good example*

What gets me into trouble is—*high expectations*

A woman feels good when—*she has a purpose*

A pregnant woman—*has something wonderful to look forward to*

I am—*a girl of* [age deleted] *hoping someday to fall in love and be happily married*

The I-3/4 woman may display an interest in opportunities, contrasting with the I-3 stress on the easy life and plenty of money, but not so definite as the I-4 interest in achievement.

Men are lucky because—*they have more opportunities in life*

The worst thing about being a woman—*is not being able to stand on our own two-feet*

For a woman a career is—*her way of rising up in the world*

Banal or ordinary responses about health, illness, death, religion, and God are more common at this than at other levels.

A pregnant woman—*is a person who God has blessed*
—*should take very good care of her health in order that she will have a healthy baby*

I feel sorry—*for bereaved families*

At times she worried about—*her husband's health*

My main problem is—*illness in the family*

The worst thing about being a woman—*is so many things go wrong with you*

A woman's body—*is a wonderful gift from God*

I am—*a child of God*

Sometimes she wished that—*she had more money or was a better Christian*

My conscience bothers me if—*I don't go to church*

I-4: CONSCIENTIOUS

True conceptual complexity is shown by the I-4 person, contrasting with conceptual simplicity at I-3 and multiplicity at I-3/4. The I-4 subject not only displays complex thinking but also perceives complexity.

My mother and I—*have some things in common, but generally do not think alike*

Education—*is an ongoing, stressful but rewarding experience*

A woman's body—*is a very complex structure*

A good mother—*conceals the fact*

When she thought of her mother, she—*was confused*

Usually she felt that sex—*was nice but mysterious*

For a woman a career is—*not essential but very stimulating and fun*

My father—*is a sweet but unmature man*

A response by an I-4 person will often combine alternatives that are polar opposites, each separately rated at I-3 or I-3/4. These polarities are not so global, so stereotyped, nor usually so evaluative as the good-bad, clean-dirty, right-wrong polarities of lower levels. Above the I-4 level even these differentiated polarities decrease.

> A woman should always—*be a lady in the parlor and a whore in the bedroom*
>
> A woman's body—*should be to please a man, in love, not disgust him, in lust*
>
> Most men think that women—*are too mannish, yet try to be too sexy*
>
> A good mother—*should give her children good discipline and lots of love*
>
> When I am with a man—*along, I try to enjoy myself and yet still act like a lady*
>
> Usually she felt that sex—*should be beautiful and not dragged through the gutter*
> *—was an obligation rather than pleasure*
>
> Raising a family—*may be hectic, but never dull*
> *—is an enjoyable responsibility*
>
> I am—*eager to be friendly, but shy with new friends*

Absolute statements and rules are often replaced by ones in comparative and contingent form; these comparisons and contingencies are not so global and banal as the ones seen at I-3/4.

> Women are lucky because—*they can tolerate many emotional crises that men cannot bear so well*
>
> Men are lucky because—*there are many avenues open for them to pursue occupations which are not open to women*
>
> My mother and I—*share some unfortunate traits*
>
> When my mother spanked me, I—*accepted it, but when she scolded me, I cried*
>
> When I am with a man—*I feel normal, according to who the man is and what he means to me*
>
> Raising a family—*can be a wonderful experience if all work together*

My mother and I—*get along good if my brother isn't around*

When people are helpless—*I sympathize, unless they are unwilling to try to help themselves*

A woman's body—*a wonderful thing if she uses it for righteous things*

Seeing the many possibilities in situations and the alternative courses of action, the I-4 subject sees life as presenting many choices. She is not a pawn of fate but holds the origin of her own destiny. She may have an excessive feeling of controlling or molding others, which contrasts with respect for others' autonomy at I-5.

Women are lucky because—*they have a large choice and many careers in this day and age*

If my mother—*would only decide on what she wants in life and pursue it*

My main problem is—*choosing the right college*

Sometimes she wished that—*she had not been so hasty with some of her decisions*

My conscience bothers me if—*I am not doing anything to help myself*

Men are lucky because—*they have great control over their own destinies*

A woman's body—*is what she makes it*

A pregnant woman—*is a wonderful woman and will have a person's whole life in her hand*

Women are lucky because—*they are in a position to influence change for the betterment of humanity*

The achievement motive is at its height at the I-4 level. Her motto is *ad astra per aspera.* In addition to objective accomplishment, she strives for self-improvement. Because of the concern for achievement, procrastination, wasting time, and disorganization are seen as problems.

Sometimes she wished that—*she could accomplish something worthwhile*

Women are lucky because—*they are considered great when they achieve something that only men were able to do*

I am—*disorganized*
    —*going to work to my capacity*

My main problem is—*not enough ambition*

Men are lucky because—*they can be more independent and strive for higher levels of achievement*

A woman should always—*strive to improve herself in every way*

The thing I like about myself is—*desire for improvement—intellectual and moral*

Education—*is very important in rounding out one's personality*

Being with other people—*enlightens me, give me new ideas thought and the like*

Raising a family—*takes a lot of careful planning and organizing*

I feel sorry—*when I don't get everything done on time*

What gets me into trouble is—*procrastination*

The I-4 subject has a strong sense of responsibility, she thinks of her duties, and at times she feels guilt over the consequences of her actions, as opposed to guilt over breaking rules per se at I-3/4 or I-3. Along with responsibilities goes a conception of privileges, of rights, and of justice or fairness. Indeed, responsibilities may be interpreted as privileges.

Raising a family—*is certainly no job for an irresponsible person*

A pregnant woman—*has a great obligation to fulfill toward someone beside herself*

I feel sorry—*when I don't fulfill all my duties*

When I am nervous, I—*take it out on my children and husband*

I am—*a woman who cares*

The worst thing about being a woman—*is that you are depended upon at all times*

If my mother—*were alive I would be more understanding of her now. I wish she were*

Sometimes she wished that—*she was a child again, with no decisions to make*

A woman should always—*try to live according to her conscience*

My conscience bothers me if—*I don't do what I believe is fair or right*

Women are lucky because—*they are women! and have all the privileges and responsibilities that go with being a woman*

Men are lucky because—*they have the responsibility for establishing a home and providing for their families*

When people are helpless—*they are entitled to help*

When my mother spanked me, I—*knew I deserved it*
                   —*felt the punishment was not justified*

The I-4 woman has her own self-evaluated standards, not only moral but also esthetic. Her conceptual complexity permits her to distinguish moral from esthetic standards. Her values make her sensitive to proportion and priorities.

At times she worried about—*little trivial things*

My conscience bothers me if—*I do not follow my "standards"*

My mother and I—*have different standards of right and wrong*

What gets me into trouble is—*my quick temper under minor circumstances*

A woman's body—*can be a beautiful object in an esthetic sense*

I feel sorry—*for people who do not make an attempt to find out what is really important in life*

Education—*is important or high in my heirarchy of values*

A wife should—*be first a wife, then a mother*

She has long-term goals and ideals, concepts that appear only in the most general form at I-3/4 and are virtually absent below that level. She distinguishes means from ends and is concerned with purpose in life.

The thing I like about myself is—*my philosophy of life*

Raising a family—*is an important part of one's contribution to society and fulfillment of himself*

A woman should always—*follow her goals in life*

My mother and I—*are in disagreement on family life, educational goals and a number of other things*

A woman's body—*derives its main purpose in bearing children*

Education—*is not an end in itself*

I am—*not sure what I want to do as an occupation, or to be as a person*

She has a richly differentiated inner life. Experiences are savored and appreciated, she finds joy and fulfillment in life, as do subjects at all higher levels.

Education—*is an enriching life experience*

Women are lucky because—*they can enjoy the wonders of holding a newborn baby*
—*of everything—I love being a woman*

Men are lucky because—*their jobs are so meaningful*

For a woman a career is—*what is most self-fulfilling*

Usually she felt that sex—*makes life richer*

My father—*enjoyed beauty*

I feel sorry—*for people that do not know the real joys of life*

Sometimes she wished that—*she could always be so happy*

She has a vivid sense of individual differences in the long-term dispositions that underlie behavior. Her descriptions of people are more realistic-sounding, because she perceives more complexities. When parents are idealized, there is a more emotional tone than in the idealization at the I-3 level.

I feel sorry—*for strict conformists*

My father—*was a dedicated family doctor*
—*is a wonderful person whom I love deeply*

The thing I like about myself is—*my flexibility*

When she thought of her mother, she—*saw a domineering, selfish, exact person*

Women are lucky because—*they have intuitive insight*

Men are lucky because—*they seem emotionally stronger than women*

Most men think that women—*I do not know what "most men think." However I believe they think women only "slightly" inferior to themselves*

Closely related are differences in interests and emotions, which may vary with the situation and the moment. Since she values what is interesting, the I-4 subject may be more likely to complain about routine and boring tasks than women at lower levels, who seem to complain more about the sheer effort.

> A wife should—*disregard her ill feelings to keep peace in the family*
>
> When my mother spanked me, I—*was surprised*
>
> The thing I like about myself is—*my interest in so many different things*
>
> If my mother—*were only as gay as she used to be*
>
> The worst thing about being a woman—*is routine housekeeping*
>
> For a woman a career is—*an escape from the tediousness of being a housewife*
>
> Women are lucky because—*we can follow our own interests and talents without the business obligations*

The I-4 person has a clear conception of the problem of impulse and control. She is aware of herself, reflects on herself, and describes herself and others in terms of reflexive traits. She is self-critical, but she also has self-respect.

> If my mother—*were a little less impulsive, it would probably be better for her*
>
> What gets me into trouble is—*I sometimes act impetuously*
> *—inappropriate self-discipline*
>
> When my mother spanked me, I—*got angry and wanted to hit her back (but didn't)*
>
> When I am nervous, I—*find it hard to control the tears*
> *—usually am aware of it*
>
> Whenever she was with her mother, she—*tried to keep from losing her temper*
>
> Women are lucky because—*they can control themslves more than men*
>
> The thing I like about myself is—*I try to solve my own problems before asking for help*

My main problem is—*that of finding myself and what I want*

When I am with a man—*I am more conscious of my appearance and actions*

My father—*an extremely hard-working and self-reliant person*

When they avoided me—*I took stock of myself to find possible reasons*

I am—*not a leader, but I feel I am a good worker*

A woman should always—*love herself in order to love her husband*

A good mother—*forgets not herself*

Interpersonal interaction is intensive; she displays a clear conception of mutuality, and, more variably, companionship, sympathy, identification, and so on. Where the I-3/4 person will talk about feelings, the I-4 has more differentiated ideas, such as trust, respect, needs, and emotional support.

Raising a family—*should be a mutually gratifying experience for both husband and wife*

If my mother—*were in my place, I'de be real mean to her*

My mother and I—*are quite distant in relation to feelings and expressing thoughts in personal subjects*
—*get along very well, we seem to think and feel the same way about things*

A wife should—*share problems as well as be considerate*
—*be cooperative*
—*be willing to support her husband emotionally*

When I am with a man—*I enjoy his company and hope he enjoys mine*

Usually she felt that sex—*was a sharing experience*

My conscience bothers me if—*I break the trust of someone who trusts me*

Sometimes she wished that—*she was capable of more love and understanding for her family*

I feel sorry—*that people distrust each other*

My main problem is—*my relationship with my older son*

When she thought of her mother, she—*thought of pleasant hours*
shared
—loves & respects her but
doesn't want to be exactly
like her

A woman feels good when—*she is appreciated and respected*

A good mother—*is alert to the needs of her children*

The ability to see matters from the other person's point of view is a connecting link between the deeper interpersonal relations of the I-4 subject and her more mature conscience.

If my mother—*disagrees with me, I look at her point of view*

Being with other people—*is one way of finding you're not the*
only one with problems

My father—*is very kind, understanding but we just don't seem to*
see eye to eye on some matters

A wife should—*never stop her husband from doing what he feels*
is right
—try to understand her husband's frustrations

When a child won't join in group activities—*his wishes should be*
deferred to

When people are helpless—*they need to be offered help in a posi-*
tive manner and one they are able to
accept

When they talked about sex, I—*was interested and respected what*
they said

When they avoided me—*I just let them go their way as I don't*
believe in pushing yourself where you're
not wanted

Where the I-3 person at times seems almost to reduce interpersonal relations to behavior, particularly talking, the I-4 person thinks in terms of communication and expression. The I-4 person is communicating or expressing ideas, feelings, and abilities. At higher levels, though the vocabulary is not much different, there is more connotation of deepening relations with others and of realization of self.

Being with other people—*is a challenge to put what you know*
and think against what they know and
think

My main problem is—*sometimes I find it hard to convey my feelings and I feel sometimes I'm over sympathetic*

Whenever she was with her mother, she—*kept her innermost feelings to herself*

Usually she felt that sex—*should be an expression of love*

A pregnant woman—*often has an inner glow*

Women are lucky because—*have opportunities to learn many ways of self-expression*

She sees intentions and motives as well as consequences of behavior. A clear notion of psychological causality is seen at the I-4 level, anticipated by a vague idea of reasons at I-3/4, and followed by more complex notions of psychological causality at higher levels.

If my mother—*wasn't such a cold fish, we'd all be better adjusted*

When people are helpless—*it is often because of circumstances they can not help*
—they may be too disturbed to be rational in the situation

When I am nervous, I—*either talk a lot or become depressed*

When a child won't join in group activities—*there is usually a family or mental problem*
—he will probably be a very unhappy adolescent

My conscience bothers me if—*I hurt someone on purpose*
—Offend some one, unintentionally

When my mother spanked me, I—*was angry unless I definitely knew the reason*

When they avoided me—*I felt they had some guilt complex*

The I-4 woman is aware of herself and others as learning, growing, developing, as having grown from childhood. She has a long time perspective. Such notions are surprisingly rare at lower levels.

When my mother spanked me, I—*was mad then, but glad for all the spankings I got, now*

When they talked about sex, I—*knew I was growing up and should*
hear about it

My mother and I—*are not really very close but we are improving*

A woman should always—*strive to satisfy her own interests and*
develop her own potentials

Women are lucky because—*they have more of an opportunity to*
see their children go through the var-
ious stages

Raising a family—*is the extension of one's self into the future*

My main problem is—*helping my son to develop*

When she thought of her mother, she—*yearned for her childhood*

The I-4 subject puts things in a broad social or temporal context. Concerns of lower I-levels for appearance, body, sex, money, social approval, and so on, are not absent but are integrated into a larger social or personal context. Appearance, for example, is expressive of feelings, as compared to the I-3/4 interest in feelings about appearance.

Most men think that women—*are important to society*

Being with other people—*gives one an opportunity to learn about*
many things

Education—*is of major importance for peace*
—is more than "book learning"

At times she worried about—*war*

Usually she felt that sex—*was as basic as eating and sleeping*

A woman's body—*is quite a miraculous thing, reproductively*
speaking
—is an intimate part of her personality

For a woman a career is—*a fortress for life against poverty*

Raising a family—*is the most enjoyable time of life*

The I-4 woman sees patterns in behavior. Abilities and traits are an aspect of patterning, but so also are expectations, roles, and social mores. Banal or vague references to roles are found at this level; at higher levels there is clearer, more explicit, and less stereotyped role conception.

A woman should always—*try to be an example for her children*
for their home life is their pattern for
their adult life

Women are lucky because—*they can fulfill many roles these days*
—less is expected of them than of men

A pregnant woman—*is fulfilling her God given purpose*

A wife should—*make her marriage her life's primary focus*
—always be what her husband thinks she is

Men are lucky because—*they have a less rigid code than women*

The worst thing about being a woman—*is not being expected to*
achieve as much as men
in the same field
—is overcoming the male
image of a woman
—is having to act like the
stereotype so often

What gets me into trouble is—*not complying with my standards—*
set by my parents and community
'(which is pretty seldom)

The I-4 person distinguishes appearances from underlying feelings and
contrasts the physical with the mental or spiritual. At lower levels the
latter distinction is not made spontaneously, while at higher levels their
integration and mutual interdependence may occasionally be mentioned.

Most men think that women—*are as equal as them but just don't*
want to admit it

When they avoided me—*I try to convey the impression that it*
doesn't bother me

The thing I like about myself—*my control of appearance and ex-*
pression

Women are lucky because—*they are not expected to hide their*
emotions

My main problem is—*thinking of non-revealing statements for this*
test

A pregnant woman—*is physically ugly but spiritually beautiful*

When my mother spanked me, I—*was deeply hurt, but not physi-*
cally

I am—*a thinking reasoning individual possessing a body & soul*

A good mother—*raises physically and mentally healthy children*

She is concerned with the problem of dependence-independence, but she has not clearly separated emotional dependence from other kinds, such as financial dependence. She does not see, as do those at I-4/5 and higher, the inevitability and desirability of emotional interdependence.

> Men are lucky because—*they can have an independent life outside the home*
> *—they do not have to be dependent as long as women*
>
> Women are lucky because—*their dependency needs are acceptably recognized*
> *—they have more freedom after marriage to pursue interests i. e. they are not tied down to jobs*
>
> My main problem is—*overprotective parents*
>
> The worst thing about being a woman—*learning when not to be so independent*
>
> Sometimes she wished that—*she had declared her independence long ago*

While the I-4 subject is aware of differences, she is also aware of our common humanity. She sees people as individuals, but a deeper appreciation for individuality as such comes at higher levels.

> A good mother—*cares about her child as an individual*
>
> Men are lucky because—*they were made in the image of God*
>
> I am—*student, human, ?—*
>
> My father—*I love because he treats me like I am, human*
>
> Most men think that women—*are human, just as they are*

I-4/5: TRANSITION FROM CONSCIENTIOUS TO AUTONOMOUS

Above the I-4 level, most responses are unique, but not all unique responses are rated above I-4. Though the exact wording is rarely replicated, categorical aspects can be pointed out. In general, responses illustrate other categories in addition to the one where they are listed. Except where explicitly stated, the characteristics of the I-4/5 level are also found in I-5 and I-6 responses.

The I-4/5 subject tends to have complex conceptions more often than subjects at lower levels. A frequent type of complexity, and an appreciable proportion of responses rated I-4/5 (and I-5), consists of combinations of popular or at least replicated responses rated singly at lower levels, with at least one aspect ratable at I-4 or higher. She has available to her in one breath, so to speak, the thoughts that subjects at lower levels commit themselves to as alternatives.

Raising a family—*requires love, good humor, and practicality*

Most men think that women—*should be feminine, honest, and interesting*

Being with other people—*is a good and stimulating (and reassuring) experience*

My mother and I—*are independent though devoted*

A woman's body—*is a beautiful and intricate structure, one of nature's masterpieces to be respected*

At times she worried about—*things that will never happen, and things she can do nothing about*

A woman should always—*respect herself as well as respecting men*

When they talked about sex, I—*respected their remarks and contributed my ideas but did not prolong the subject*

A woman feels good when—*she is complimented about her looks, intelligence & cooking*

If I can't get what I want—*I feel depressed, frustrated or disciplined—depending upon what I couldn't have & why*

For a woman a career is—*her greatest interest, whether it be her home or a profession*

Where the I-4 person often sees polar, incompatible opposites, the I-4/5 person is more likely to see paradox, a quasi-contradiction in nature rather than a forced choice.

Most men think that women—*are difficult to understand, but wonderful to be with*
—should be dependently independent

Women are lucky because—*they have an easier role in life than men although sometimes it is dull and boring*

A woman feels good when—*she knows she is being feminine and intelligent at the same time*

When I am with a man—*I want to be desired and respected*

My conscience bothers me if—*I willfully or unwillfully hurt anyone*

My mother and I—*were not alike in any way but I loved and admired her*
—have always been very close—possibly too much so for our own good

Interpersonal relations are cherished, their value probably partly supplanting the value for ability and achievement at I-4. Relations are seen as continuing or changing over time.

The thing I like about myself is—*I seem to have a way of "getting through" to other people*

A woman feels good when—*a man loves her & thinks that she makes him a more complete person*

I feel sorry—*for people who have hollow & mechanical relationships*

At times she worried about—*the lack of harmony at home*

What gets me into trouble is—*talking before considering its effect on other people*

Sometimes she wished that—*she could visit old friends*

A wife should—*never stop trying to "catch" her husband!*

My mother and I—*have become better friends now that I'm grown*

A woman should always—*strive for growth and increasing depth in her marriage*

There is greater complexity in conception of interpersonal interaction. Not only do persons affect others, but the relations between persons affect others and are, in turn, affected by circumstances, such as the traits of those involved. The I-4 subject talks of communicating and expressing ideas and feelings; these notions are deepened and made more complex at the I-4/5 level.

My mother and I—*have been brought closer together through hardships*

When they avoided me—*I suddenly realized I brought it on by being indifferent to them on previous occasions*

A wife should—*put her husband first because if the marriage is right children can glean much from this*

At times she worried about—*her husband's worrying about her being sick*

If my mother—*were less of the "old school," we might have a closer relationship*

My father—*is not easy to understand but yearns for love and companionship*

Being with other people—*is not always communicating with them. I often prefer to observe them*

When they talked about sex, I—*recalled my parents' reluctants to discuss such with me*
—*always joined in, because it's a universal language*

The thing I like about myself is—*that I think I can sympathize with other people and am able to feel what they feel (empathy?)*

A good mother—*is one who communicates deeply with her family, has trust when in doubt & loves*

What gets me into trouble is—*that often I think and talk too fast too far afield, and sometimes others don't see the significant things I'd like to talk about*

Psychological causality has become complex, contrasting with vague statements of "reasons" and "problems" at I-3/4 and I-4.

When my mother spanked me, I—*got repulsed, because it was more nervous anger than actual discipline*

Being with other people—*is often a defense against being alone with oneself*

When I am nervous, I—*tend to become self-centered and over look the needs and desires of others*

If my mother—*had a job I believe she would be more content at home*

When people are helpless—*there is always some cause, which altho we can't always understand, we must try to*

There is a distinction between process and outcome and greater interest in process and change. This is an elaboration of the sense for growth and development which occurs in its simplest form at the I-4 level.

Education—*continues throughout life*

A pregnant woman—*has new and wonderful experiences awaiting her*

The thing I like about myself is—*my ability to tolerate stress and the capacity to meet new challenges*

A good mother—*helps her children grow emotionally and socially by providing numerous experiences*

When they talked about sex, I—*was confused as my friends were two years older than I at the time. I was 10 and very immature*

At times she worried about—*me, now she worries about daddy*

Usually she felt that sex—*was something dirty until she married and found it was something very fulfilling*

Dependence and independence remain a problem, or perhaps a pair of problems, but they are seen primarily in terms of emotional dependence or as emotional problems.

If my mother—*were less dependent upon her children, it would be easier for them to break away*

For a woman a career is—*helpful to make her feel independent*

Men are lucky because—*they are not so dependent on others for their love*

Whenever she was with her mother, she—*became a little girl again*

When people are helpless—*I want to help them become more self-confident & independent*

The worst thing about being a woman—*the conflict of being independent and self sufficient and being expected to be dependent such as on dates, etc.*

A good mother—*cares enough for her children, to let them go when they are ready*

A wife should—*try to live her life and to help her husband live his and togather*

A related problem is that of individuality, only vaguely anticipated at I-4 or occasionally even at the I-3 level by use of the word "individual" or "individuality." The sense of individuality is even stronger at the I-5 level.

A wife should—*love her husband, have his interests at heart but not lose her own individuality*
—*be what she is and not what a neighbor or book says she should be*

A woman feels good when—*she is accepted and loved as she is*

The thing I like about myself is—*I don't wonder constantly how others see me. Most often I couldn't care less*

When a child won't join in group activities—*respect his wishes—I hate groups. Beat him to death?*

A woman should always—*maintain her own code of morals—a sense of individuality*
—*remember to respect a man's ego but also expect him to respect hers*

Many I-4/5 responses present vivid and personal versions of ideas that appear as clichés on I-4 protocols; examples are varied roles, self-fulfillment, and the joy of life.

Raising a family—*should be the most fulfilling role a woman can play*

My father—*is perfect for the job (of being a father)*

Women are lucky because—*they can know the joys of managing a home and/or a career*

For a woman a career is—*one way to fulfillment as a person*

Men are lucky because—*they can isolate sexual involvement from
other areas of life more easily than women*

A wife should—*be as much her husband's mistress as his home
manager—in fact more of his "date" than cook!*

I am—*a woman, a wife, a student, and an individual person*

The worst thing about being a woman—*is the confusion in society's
expectations of women to-
day*

A woman should always—*be womanly but not "typically feminine," i.e., scatterbrained, silly, medi-
ocre, etc.
—be as mature and well developed person as she is able to be*

The thing I like about myself is—*the thrills I get by such tomboy-
ish things as jumping on a tram-
poline*

Education—*is a must because the more I learn, the more I enjoy
life*

When I am with a man—*I come alive*

The I-4/5 subject distinguishes inner life from outer, the psychological
order from physical order, psychological response from physiological response. Unlike the I-4 subject, who sees a sharp dichotomy between mind
and body, she sees interaction and integration.

A pregnant woman—*should relax and try to be more outwardly
directed during pregnancy
—is only as healthy and lovely in appearance
as her attitudes towards her unborn child
are healthy and lovely*

A woman's body—*often determines her feminine qualities. Beauty
is important—more than I have ever given
cognizance to
—is one thing she should take care of not only
for health reasons but because it gives her
self-confidence*

The I-4/5 person will often be aware of conflicting or contrasting emotions. Conflict tends to be within the self, instead of between one's own
needs and society's requirements, as is sometimes the case with I-3/4 and

I-4 subjects. The full force of intrapsychic conflict is not felt until the I-5 level, however.

When my mother spanked me, I—*felt rebellious and also ashamed*

When she thought of her mother, she—*felt both pride and depression*
—tried to think of only her good features and not her faults

The worst thing about being a woman—*is the confusion in roles*

Men are lucky because—*they do not have any conflict around career or marriage*

My conscience bothers me if—*I do something I feel is wrong & not if someone else feels it's wrong*

I feel sorry—*for myself when I think of the mistakes I've made of a major nature which were unnecessary*

As one goes up the scale of ego development, although inner life becomes progressively richer and more differentiated, the conception of the universe becomes progressively less egocentric. Many responses of the I-4/5 person have self neither as subject nor as object. Complex contingencies with self not central are not found on protocols at I-3 or lower and are rare at the I-4 level.

If my mother—*had been more aggressive she might have "done big things"*

My father—*is a fatherly man. Everyone of my girl freind like him. And all enjoy his company*
—is a source of concern to me because of preoccupation with perfection and his desire to control the situation

Whenever she was with her mother, she—*allowed her to feel she was needed*
—would run around her skirts and create an unpleasant scene, she being my girlhood friend who was a bit mischievous

A good mother—*tries to understand her children's viewpoint even if she can't always agree*

When she thought of her mother, she—*was sorry for this girl like*
                                                her who had no mother

I feel sorry—*for the aged who are misfits in our society*

The I-4/5 subject distinguishes appearance from reality, thus continuing
and deepening the distinction made by the I-4 person between inner feelings and outward appearances. The I-4/5 subject is more specific about
her attempts to cope with reality and to be objective.

Education—*is a terrific experience but does not always represent
                what it seems to*

Men are lucky because—*they can appear to be very independent
                                of others*

My mother and I—*seem to be close sometimes but we often have
                        misunderstandings*

What gets me into trouble is—*my inability to face life realistically
                                —my tendency to put off or avoid
                                unpleasant experiences*

My main problem is—*worrying needlessly*

At times she worried about—*imaginary illnesses*

If I can't get what I want—*then perhaps I should reevaluate the
                                situation*

The thing I like about myself is—*the ability, though hard at times,
                                        to be objective about myself
                                        —my calm attitude to accept a sit-
                                        uation for what it is*

A wife should—*be understanding and view her husband's actions
                as objectively as possible*

The I-4/5 subject goes beyond perceiving individual differences to true
toleration of others and to the concept of tolerance.

If my mother—*were not so broad minded and understanding it
                would present problems in our home since she lives
                with us*

The thing I like about myself is—*although my own ideals are very
                                        high, I think that I can under-
                                        stand and relate to others who
                                        feel differently*

> My conscience bothers me if—*prejudge other people before I really know them*
>
> When they avoided me—*I make it possible for them to do so gracefully*
>
> I feel sorry—*for anyone who lacks understanding and tolerance —for people who are so intelligent they can't relate or accept others who are less intelligent*

There is a glimpse at this level of a relativism that is clearer at higher levels. It may take the form of a comment on rather than a completion of the stem.

> When they talked about sex, I—*It depends on the frame of reference. If its being taken as a joke i don't listen, I may leave*
>
> The worst thing about being a woman—*in what society*
>
> A woman should always—*nothing is that absolute and universal*

Unlike subjects at lower levels, the I-4/5 person and those at higher levels will often reveal a broad view of life as a whole.

> I am—*striving to experience as many things as I can & get a broad view of how the human race lives*
>
> A pregnant woman—*should be happy because she is blessed with the ability to creat a new life*
>
> Sometimes she wished that—*she could gain a greater depth in her response to life*
>
> Usually she felt that sex—*can be a positive, beautiful thing as years of marriage add up*
>
> At times she worried about—*God, man, and herself*

There is humor at the I-4/5 level, good-natured rather than hostile, though still somewhat artificial. It is not quite the same as the I-5 ability to see what is ridiculous in the nature of things. Humor is rare in the range I-3 to I-4, and when it occurs there, it tends to be conventional.

> A woman's body—*met to discuss the problems of todays children*
>
> Raising a family—*of bears is difficult; however, rearing humans is even more difficult*

I-5: AUTONOMOUS

A feature of I-5 protocols that cannot be illustrated in present format is the richness and variety of topics mentioned in a single protocol. No protocol should receive a TPR of I-5 unless there are responses from at least three of the following categories or themes. This rule is unlikely to conflict with automatic application of the ogive rules.

Where the I-4 subject will often see irreconcilable choices, the I-5 woman construes conflicting alternatives as aspects of many-faceted life situations, as how things really are. She has a high toleration for ambiguity.

A pregnant woman—*is a contradiction of unattractive bulk and vast femininity and womanliness*

Usually she felt that sex—*was delightful, intriguing, and very, very boring*

My mother and I—*love one another but do not understand each others ideas or happiness*
    —*had many mutual character traits, yet our total personalities were very different*

Raising a family—*is a full time job full of joys and sorrows and regrets for certain mistakes on my part*

My father—*is a brilliant & learned man but often dogmatic and selfish. I am proud of his position & intelligence*

I am—*a living, thinking, female, able and ready to compete or comfort*

Sometimes she wished that—*she had things she would not be happy with if she had them*

Most men think that women—*are worthwhile to be with, but depending on the type of man and type of woman thinkings differ*

Education—*is necessary for self-understanding and is experienced formally and informally*

The I-5 subject compares or collates three or more possibilities or aspects of a situation, such as appearances, actions, and feelings, again a departure from an either-or view one often sees at I-4. Such composite responses must have at least one facet from the I-4 or I-4/5 level to be rated I-5. In comparing these composite responses with similar categories at the I-4/5 and occasionally at the I-4 level, one notes at I-5 that the three

terms usually represent more sharply differentiated points of view than
at I-4/5.

> When they avoided me—*I wondered what the reason was. Whether*
> *it was something I had done, some un-*
> *related feelings they had, or if it were*
> *just by chance*

> A woman should always—*remember that she is first a woman, and*
> *look like it, act like it, and feel like it!*

> The thing I like about myself is—*that like most people, I like to*
> *do many different things, I*
> *find many things in life that*
> *are humorous as well as seri-*
> *ous, and I believe in God*

> Being with other people—*helps one to develop himself socially,*
> *mentally and emotionally*

> Most men think that women—*should be more gentle, idealistic*
> *and dependent than is possible*

> Women are lucky because—*we are often idealized, catered to, and*
> *have so many exciting roles to fill*

> When I am nervous, I—*seek physical activity, or solitude, or a*
> *novel*

> When people are helpless—*I pity them and admire those who try*
> *to change their situation. I have no re-*
> *spect for those who exploit their help-*
> *lessness*

> When they talked about sex, I—*accept well any scientific, medical*
> *or moral aspects, but can not be*
> *patient with the flippancy*

Where the I-4/5 person has begun to recognize inner conflict, the I-5
woman feels its full force. She strives to cope with it or to find some
means of transcending it or of reconciling herself to it.

> A woman should always—*strike a balance between her own wants*
> *and satisfactions and those of her family*

> The worst thing about being a woman—*is being torn between her*
> *duty as a creature of the*
> *modern world, and her*
> *duty to be an old-fash-*
> *ioned wife*

For a woman a career is—*something she would like to have but will give up to make a happy and solid home*

When they avoided me—*I felt ashamed and mad at the same time because they felt they were better than me and I didn't feel that they were*

Whenever she was with her mother, she—*was struggling for control*
                        —*felt torn between opposing emotions*

Sometimes she wished that—*she could give up her desires for a career and just be a woman*
                        —*she'd feel less guilty about things undone or unsaid regarding the mother-daughter relationship—the she being me*

She distinguishes social stereotypes from realistic views of people. She aspires to be realistic, objective, and unprejudiced.

Most men think that women—*are better than they really are; they do not see the faults which women find with other women*
                        —*are basically intelligent, and a needed part of their world, contrary to the popular "Madison Ave." concept of women as sex symbols*

The thing I like about myself is—*my abilities to face the actualities, sometimes pleasant, often not, about life and myself*

A pregnant woman—*is often idealized by everyone except herself*

I feel sorry—*for all who loose sight for the shortness of life on earth*
           —*for people who are blinded by prejudices*

The worst thing about being a woman—*is being lumped into a general category labeled "Women"*

Sometimes she wished that—*there were not so many tight, closed-in minds in the world*

What gets me into trouble is—*sometimes being satisfied with day-*
dreams instead of dealing with
things as they really are
—first impressions I have of people
and cannot change even when they
are untrue

A woman feels good when—*she is respected accepted and loved*
for what she is, not what other's
think she is

A good mother—*is not always perfect and it is better if she does*
not pretend to be

When she thought of her mother, she—*remembered her justice*
and calm

While the I-4/5 subject seems to be struggling with attaining her own
individuality in connection with the problem of emotional dependence,
the I-5 woman cherishes individuality and uniqueness in herself and
others.

A woman feels good when—*she has given of her unique self*

The worst thing about being a woman—*is the internal and exter-*
nal pressure to submerge
one's personality

A good mother—*tries to understand her children as individuals, is*
honest, and behaves naturally around them

A woman should always—*be herself whether she's intelligent or a*
"dumb broad"
—look for the best in her children—and
that way she can help them more

For a woman a career is—*dependent upon her need for it*

Branching off from the topic of individuality are several other characteristics of the I-5 subject. She is concerned with self-realization, which in
part supplants the achievement motive and merges with enjoyment of
life. Work may be onerous, not because it requires effort but because it
is stultifying. An important aspect of the enjoyment of life is relations
with other people. Like the I-4/5 woman, she cherishes relations with
people, but the I-5 woman expresses this in a more complex way or in
context of other ideas.

Education—*means a lot to me—I'll stagnate if I never do anything creative*

At times she worried about—*losing her dreams and ideals and falling prey to daily "ruts" and monotony*

Men are lucky because—*when they are "loved" all the way their goals become more meaningful*

A wife should—*try to help her husband achieve his self-fulfillment but at the same time should try to achieve her own "growth" too*

I feel sorry—*for those who do not appreciate the beauty of nature*

A woman should always—*value and treasure those qualities which make her a woman*

A woman's body—*is a delight to her in many ways*

Women are lucky because—*I feel that life offers them deeper emotional experiences than men*

My father—*is unending in his search for knowledge and his efforts to help others*

My main problem is—*deciding what my purpose in life is and what I can do to achieve this purpose*
—*is my inability to have a lasting relationship with men*

Being with other people—*is a joy since relationships with people give life meaning*

My mother and I—*should have been closer. Why we weren't I don't know, except I was always afraid of disappointing her and as an adult I never wanted to burden her with my problems*

When I am with a man—*I enjoy men very much, more so as I get older*

The I-5 woman expresses her respect for other people's need for autonomy in clear terms. The problem of identity, which also arises out of the matrix of individuality, appears only in general or cliché form; maximum appreciation of identity as a problem is present only at the I-6 level. However, the I-5 subject has a clear conception of roles and the associated problems for women.

When a child won't join in group activities—*he must continue to enjoy his interests and be permitted to activate any later interest for companionship*

A good mother—*is one that balances protective love with larger and larger amounts of freedom as the child matures*
—*should be loving, patient, should have fun with her children, but always remember she is the mother and not another child, the voice of authority*

When people are helpless—*it is best to aid them to help themselves than to prolong their helplessness and dependency on others*

A wife should—*be a good wife, and mother, but still have an identity of her own*
—*do whatever is required to be a good wife, within her own frame of reference for "good wife"*

A woman's body—*is only one facet of what and who she really is*

My main problem is—*what I am going to do or be and will I be of some use to someone*

When I am with a man—*I react in relation to whether I'm fulfilling a professional role, or am "being a woman"*

For a woman a career is—*difficult because of the conflicts of the role of woman—as a wife and a self-sufficient person*

Raising a family—*after marriage, is woman's basic traditional role. This tradition is being modified, but is still true for most women*

My mother and I—*don't get along in our personal lives—only in business*

The I-5 person sees more complex psychological causality than the I-4/5 person. She sees herself in an interpersonal context, and she sees the complexity and circularity of social interaction.

My mother and I—*share many of the same feelings so that we*
cannot work together easily

Raising a family—*requires sufficient maturity of each parent and*
a loving, stable relationship between them

If my mother—*were less a "career woman" and more* woman *my*
dad would be happier
—*were different, I would be different too. If she*
were more interested, I'd care more. If she'd care
more, I'd be more interested

When she thought of her mother, she—*appreciated many of the*
intangible things her
mother had given her
—*was overawed at her*
mother's insight and ca-
pabilities — things she
never realized as a child

Usually she felt that sex—*was good and could act as a healing*
and soothing balm to life

When I am nervous, I—*tend to be irritable and disrupt other*
people and their activities

She is concerned with communicating feelings. Her emotions are differentiated and vividly conveyed. They range from joy to poignancy to deep
sorrow or regret. Sensual experiences come through vividly.

If my mother—*could only know how many things I would like to*
tell her and how difficult I find it to say all that is
in my heart

A pregnant woman—*is attractive if her husband conveys this feel-*
ing to her both in words and in deeds

A good mother—*relaxes, and lets her children know it*

When my mother spanked me, I—*used to think she was a giant—*
but then I realized she wasn't
that strong

Whenever she was with her mother, she—*could feel that love that*
made their family so
close

My mother and I—*can become petty and quarrelsome—yet each*
can bear their innermost hearts to the other
without fear—we know, till death, each is for
the other

What gets me into trouble is—*heartbreak—lonliness, or a need for someone to love me alone*

The worst thing about being a woman—*is not being able to be proud of a child born out of wedlock*

Sex is seen in a context of mutuality, as an aspect of a relation to another person. Unlike most subjects at I-3 and I-4, but more like those at the lowest levels, she may mention sex directly or indirectly in responses to stems that do not mention it.

Usually she felt that sex—*is also an essential thing in marriage and should be enjoyed by both or you might as well not expect a very happy marriage*

Most men think that women—*are no good if their relations extend to more that 1 man. I think it depend on the treatment given her by the 1st man*

A woman feels good when—*she has soothed another into peace with himself*

When I am with a man—*I feel excitingly feminine*

A woman should always—*be well groomed, a willing sexual partner to her mate, and constantly boardening her mind*

The I-5 subject displays spontaneity, genuineness, and intensity. She will often have a light touch, fantasy, and a sensitivity to life's paradoxes. This is sometimes shown in a nonhostile existential humor.

If my mother—*were my daughter, I wonder how I would treat her*

Women are lucky because—*they can flout all sorts of little rules (Like being afraid of famous men) that men can't. . . .*

When my mother spanked me, I—*felt ashamed, but I never hesitated to go do the very same thing behind her back*

A wife should—*be a companion, a friend, a mother, a psychiatrist, a washing machine, a dish-washer, an alarm clock, & a vacum cleaner among other things*

When they talked about sex, I—*usually took a righteous stand of some sort*

I am—*at times a question mark, at times just a period, but many times an exciting exclamation mark*

Concern for broad social perspectives or issues may be expressed. Men and women are part of a common humanity. Such ideas are expressed in more original, or subtler, or more elaborated form than at the I-4 level.

Education—*is, or can be, a means to a more comprehensive understanding of life and people and self*

A wife should—*have interests outside the home as well in order to maintain contact with the world of ideas and current events*

Men are lucky because—*they are free to pursue approximately the same goals they have been pursuing for hundreds of years*

When they talked about sex, I—*could clarify my philosophy on the subject*

When I am with a man—*I try to view him as I would another person rather than constantly being aware of the sex difference*

The thing I like about myself is—*that I like all humanity, I'm glad to be one with them*

I am—*woman living and creating life*

What gets me into trouble is—*my honesty in matters involving injustice and pettiness*

My conscience bothers me if—*in some small way, I do not live up to my ideals, or if I have given the wrong impression*

A woman should always—*try to do something about cruelty, dire poverty and the unhappiness of others*

I-6: INTEGRATED

Characteristics of I-5 responses that are prominent at I-6, usually in combination, are existential humor and a feeling for paradox, respect for others' autonomy, search for self-fulfillment, value for justice and idealism, opposition to prejudice, coping with inner conflict, reconciliation of role conflicts, appreciation of sex in the context of mutuality, and reconciliation to one's destiny. Some form of conceptual complexity is always present, whether in terms of conflict, contradiction, alternative constructions of situations, or subtler complexities such as the notion of intolerance of prejudice or the notion of potential for development. Responses at this level are often vivid, touching, and even poetic. Most responses at I-6 unite the specific and the general, and they unite concern for inner life, usually presented as differentiated inner perceptions, and for outer life, often presented in terms of relations with others. Perhaps the only general rule that can be given is that these responses combine several thoughts that would separately be rated I-5.

When people are helpless—*they need others help to grow and become more self sufficient, if there is potential for development. Lacking potential they need protection*

I feel sorry—*for the disadvantaged and particularly the negro to the point that I am outraged and intolerant of prejudiced people*

At times she worried about—*money, health, the state of the world, and whether her son needed new shoes right now*
—a war which destroyed the world before she fulfilled her dreams

For a woman a career is—*a matter of choice with respect to her assessment of her self in terms of the world in which she lives*

A woman feels good when—*her sex life goes well, and when, in all respects she and her husband are "sympatico"*

When I am with a man—*I often enjoy the chance to better understand how male and female can complement each other*

A woman should always—*as should a man, treat other individuals with respect and work toward the betterment of the whole of people not just of herself*

Most men think that women—*are necessary evils when considered collectively, and are wonderful when considered individually (that is to say—wife, mother, sister, lover.)*

Women are lucky because—*they can feel a new life born within them; they are usually loved and cared for within the haven of a man's gentle strength*

My father—*has greatly enriched and influenced my life by his immense common sense logic and faith in the person*

The worst thing about being a woman—*cannot be generalized, as one woman makes an asset of the same situation decried by another*

The one new category at I-6 is that of search for identity. Clichés about "who am I" or being oneself do not qualify but only responses that on other grounds would be classed at least as I-5. The problem of identity appears in terms of reconciliation of roles, striving for one's own autonomy, individuality, and self-fulfillment, and recognizing other people's right to theirs.

Raising a family—*can break your heart and be wonderful too. One sometimes learns almost too late to accept and love and not try to change*

A wife should—*try to make some sense for herself out of the strange dual role the modern world has placed her in . . . so that she is free to make her husband happy*

My main problem is—*I am afraid, I lack courage to be what I want to be because it is different from what my parents feel I should be*

The worst thing about being a woman—*is accepting your position as a woman and an individual, but once found ceases to be the worst and becomes the best*

My mother and I—*get along, but I need to get away to develop myself. I praise her because she is a woman, and a person. I am a person, but not yet a woman*

When she thought of her mother, she—*hoped to be like her in some ways, but different in others, because she was herself, not her mother*

For a woman a career is—*a means of fulfillment, helping make her an intellectual, interesting person, so that she may be a better wife-companion*

A good mother—*lets go, loves without demanding conformity to her own ideals and standards—and helps to guide if possible*
—*is kind, consistent, tender, sensitive and* always *aware a child is master of its own soul*

CHAPTER 5

Instructions to Raters

T his manual is intended to be self-teaching. In recent years we have systematically inducted new raters into our work using written materials only, in order to force ourselves to incorporate the essentials in our written instructions and to test how far we have succeeded in doing so. At the end of a prescribed course of training, which can be completed in one or two months, new raters produce ratings equivalent to those of experienced raters who have worked together for many months or years, as Chapter Three has shown. At the end of the self-training course, individual differences appear to outweigh experience as determinants of rating ability. All of our raters have been reasonably intelligent and intellectually sophisticated; we have not tested the limits of the personal qualities necessary to become an adequate rater. We do not believe the manual can be used effectively without following a training program about like the one outlined here.

Since many users of this manual will be clinicians, we stress two points. First, every response is to be rated without regard to other responses on the protocol. We call this out of context rating and think of it as the psychometric as opposed to the clinical attitude. To get results comparable to ours, the psychometric attitude must govern rating of each response. It is entirely compatible, however, with taking a clinical view of the total protocol subsequently in deciding on the total protocol rating (see Chapter Six).

Second, the self-training program has been worked out carefully and is meant to lead to successively deeper levels of understanding of ego development and its manifestations in sentence completions. This understanding is the indispensable tacit component. All of the exercises in Appendix C should be completed and checked with our scoring before beginning those in Appendix D. All of the protocols in Appendix D should be rated and the ratings checked against ours before rating any other clinical or research materials. Otherwise the ratings will almost certainly contain excessive errors; moreover, the rater might ingrain in himself incorrect interpretations of the method. These precautions are doubly important where the method is extended to groups of people or to sentence stems other than the kinds we have used, since the tacit component is more important in such cases.

SELF-TRAINING PROGRAM

The first step in learning to rate for ego level is to master the concept of ego development as it is presented in Chapters One and Four. A rapid scanning of some of the item manuals (Part II) may also help to master the concept. No matter how detailed and explicit a manual such as this may become, familiarity with the concept will always remain as a tacit component of the rating process. A computer program will never equal the performance of an intelligent and sensitive rater, for the same reason no computer program can produce adequate translations from one language to another—in both cases the ultimate criterion is meaning rather than word usage.

The second step is to learn to rate each of the thirty-six items. This step should be followed even where the rater intends later to work with a form that substitutes other stems for certain ones in the present manual. What we have learned about ego development is dispersed throughout the thirty-six item manuals. Our experience indicates that with mastery of the present thirty-six-item form there is substantial transfer to new items. In particular, raters trained on the present form for women and girls appear to do about as well with a similar but not identical form for men and boys; however, in our work only raters with considerable experience beyond the basic training exercises have attempted to rate male protocols.

Raters find it necessary to immerse themselves in an item thoroughly to master it. Therefore it is difficult to work on more than one or two items per day at this stage, even though most raters do not require half a day per item, at least after the first few.

Detailed knowledge of the present chapter is required prior to or in conjunction with beginning to rate items. For each stem the manual should be read, noting introductory comments and category titles and scanning the examples in each category. The introductory comments discuss the kinds of completions found for that particular stem for each I-level in terms of theory and the stimulus-pull of the stem. Category titles help identify the most commonly occurring content areas obtained for that stem at each level. Responses listed as examples are meant to show the range of content included within the category; they are not an exhaustive list, and they do not include most of the obvious examples.

After familiarizing oneself with the manual for a particular stem, the responses to that stem given in Appendix C should be rated. All responses should be rated before checking the ratings against ours, since the examples are intended to lead to a thorough knowledge of the item manual. The rules of procedure for rating a single response are given in the next section. After checking his ratings against ours, the rater should try to understand our reasoning where our rating differs from his own. He then proceeds to the next item.

When the SC test is used as a clinical instrument, one would ordinarily rate all thirty-six responses of a single protocol at one time. We refer to this as rating in context. Rating out of context refers to rating all responses to a single stem given by a number of subjects without knowledge of any subject's response to other stems. The purpose of rating out of context in the present case is to master the scoring manual. In other cases it can serve various research purposes. We have used out-of-context rating systematically in evaluating and revising the scoring manual. The attitude of disregarding context is essential to obtain distributions of ratings comparable to those used in Chapter Six as a basis for total protocol rules. Every investigator should program his research so as to foster this psychometric attitude toward item rating.

The third step in the self-training program is to learn to rate total protocols. The procedure for going from the distribution of thirty-six item ratings to a TPR will be described in Chapter Six. Practice protocols are provided in Appendix D. The rater should record his rating of each response of a protocol and then determine the TPR. Our ratings are provided for him to check his against. In rating the protocols in Appendix D, the user will save time by again rating all responses to one item, then all responses to the next item, and so on. By this time the rater should be rating about half the responses by reading category titles only. Of the remaining responses, about half are decided easily by reading the examples listed in three or four germane categories. About one quarter of the responses will require more thought. High-level protocols, since they contain more original responses, take longer to rate. After all thirty-six items are rated, the total protocol is read seriatim before deciding on a total protocol rating, as detailed in Chapter Six. Only after completing his rating of the total protocol should he check his item ratings against ours. Alternatively, and perhaps preferably, the rater may follow the above procedure for the first ten protocols and check them, then rate and check the second set of ten protocols.

The most common error of beginning raters is to be swayed too much by the topic or content of the response. Actually, virtually any topic can be discussed at any level, but subjects at different levels will discuss it in a different manner. To cope with this problem, most category titles are followed by cross-references to the categories at other levels that are most closely related in topic and hence may be the hardest discriminations. We do not cross-reference categories at the same level. The purpose of the manual is to discriminate different levels, and we have no evidence that useful information is encoded in discriminations between categories within a level. However, during the self-training program, the rater should record the category as well as the level in order that he may compare his reasoning with ours, in lieu of a more personal teaching situation.

Popular categories of response are denoted by stars. A single star denotes a category given by about 3 to 10 per cent of a diverse sample, usually our sealed sample; two stars denote a category given by about 10 per cent or more.

PROCEDURE FOR RATING SINGLE RESPONSES

Our ground rules are: Rate every response. Rate the response as a whole. Rate on the level of meanings, in particular, what the subject meant to say. We do not make deep-level inferences about what the subject really means but rather try to take the meaning of the completion at its face value. Since we are concerned with meaning rather than word choice or word count, some inference may be necessary in many cases, but deep-level inference is excluded. Snap judgments should not be made, but lengthy rumination about a single response does not improve the rating.

In matching a response to the scoring manual for an item, there are essentially four possibilities. The response may fit one category (Rule

1), it may combine parts corresponding to two or more categories (Rules 2 and 3), it may be meaningful but fit no particular category (Rule 4), or it may be omitted or too fragmentary to be meaningful (Rule 5). The rules should be applied in sequence.

Completions may be simple or compound. Most responses will be simple, presenting just one idea, and should be rated following Rule 1 or, failing that, Rule 4. Formulation of rules for rating compound responses has occupied us off and on for many years, and we are still trying to put them into clear, simple form. The version presented here is slightly different from the one given to raters in the past, but we believe it will lead to the same I-levels as the version used during studies reported in Chapter Three. Despite the difficulty in stating the rules clearly and simply, we apparently communicate well enough to our raters, since a small study showed that unclassified responses correlated just as well with TPRs as did those responses put in categories.

A compound response mentions more than one idea, though it need not be a compound sentence. The dictionary defines compound as meaning to put together, as elements or parts, to form a whole. The elements that the subject may put together in a completion may be re-iterations of the same ideas, "sad and unhappy," clichés, "love, honor, and obey," contrasting ideas, "both boring and worthwhile," or different aspects of a situation, "look, act, and feel." Many categories and many examples within categories present compound responses of these different types, so most responses can be rated following Rule 1. Rules 2 and 3 cover rating of compound responses not found in the manual.

Rule 1: *Match the content of the completion with one of the listed category titles.*

Before deciding that a category is appropriate inspect the examples given, remembering that many obvious examples have been deleted. If there are cross-references after the category title, check the titles and examples of the categories indicated. The completions you score in a category may be in a different verbal style, use different vocabulary, and so on, as compared to the examples given. Your task is to decide whether the response at issue shares whatever the common content of the category is. One should not, however, force a response into a category where its fit is dubious, but rather proceed to the methods of categorization under Rules 2, 3, and 4.

Examples:

Simple response. "A woman should always—*watch her weight.*" This completion fits the category, "—be attractive, well groomed" (I-3, category 1).

Compound responses:

A. Pseudo-compounds, clichés. "A woman feels good when—*she is dressed neat and clean.*" By the dictionary "neat" and "clean" are different ideas, but such a phrase has become a single banality for our subjects. (Another is "love and understanding.") Such responses are usually rated I-3. In this case the response would fit I-3, category 1, "Concern with appearance of self, house."

B. Pseudo-compounds, repetitions. "My main problem is—*I am sometimes too shy and self-conscious.*" "Shy" and "self-conscious" are actually semirepetitious, containing two versions of a single thought. Such responses often combine responses from a single category and should be rated at the level and in the category from which the parts are examples. In this case, the completion fits the category, "—being shy, self-conscious" (I-3/4, category 5).

C. True compounds. True compounds are here defined as those responses containing two or more contrasting ideas or alternative aspects of a situation. "When they talked about sex, I—*felt uneasy, but joined in, and then tried to change the subject.*" This completion describes both feelings and actions. The category, "Compound response, at least three ideas, feelings and actions" (I-4/5, category 5) would be the appropriate category for rating this response. "When they talked about sex, I—*usually would rather listen than participate in the discussion.*" This completion contrasts the two behaviors "listen" and "participate." One category provides for this contrast, "—listened but said nothing, little" (I-4, category 6), so the response would be rated there. Other examples of true compounds are "Raising a family—*may be hectic, but never dull*" (I-4, category 4); "Being with other people—*can be stimulating & boring*" (I-4, category 5). Both these responses contain contrasting ideas that are neither repetitions nor clichés. When rating such a compound response, check to see if there is a category provided for such a combination of ideas. If there is not, follow the procedures under Rules 2 or 3.

Rule 2: *Where the combination of two or more elements in a compound response generates a more complex level of conception, rate the response one-half step higher than the highest element.*

Conceptual complexity has proved to be an important clue to I-level and is by no means a direct function of intelligence. Contrasting two ideas or two aspects of a situation has turned out to be a surprisingly frequent way of showing conceptual complexity. Two contrasting I-3 ideas may generate an I-3/4 response, although this is not frequent. More frequently, two contrasting I-3/4 ideas generate an I-4 response, two or three contrasting I-4 ideas generate an I-4/5 response, and three con-trasting ideas, at least one at the I-4/5 level, generate an I-5 response. Additional considerations are required to justify an I-6 rating, as ex-plained in Chapter Four. This rule has no application below the I-3 level.

> Rule 3: *Where the combination of ideas in a compound response does not generate a higher level of conceptual complexity, rate the response in the less frequent category, or rate in the higher category.*

These two considerations usually agree. If the higher category is over I-3, the higher rating is always used. Where one category is at I-3 and the other is at a lower level, the category at I-3 will often be popular or at least a more frequently occurring one, and one would give the lower rating. In case of doubt rate up. Where both elements come from the same level, for research and training purposes the response is assigned to the less frequent category, but the rating is of course not affected by this convention. (These rules differ slightly from those used in construct-ing the manual, and we do not guarantee that they have been followed in all cases in this volume.)

Examples:

"I feel sorry—*for people who are lonely and helpless.*" No cate-gory contains such a combination, nor are there similar examples under any category heading. There is a category for "are helpless" at I-3 and one for "are lonely" at I-3/4. The response is rated I-3/4, category 6.

"The thing I like about myself is—*I am good and I am not fat.*" "I am good" would be rated Delta, category 2. "I am not fat" would be rated Delta/3, category 1. There is an example in the Delta category, "*I am good at times and I am short.*" Hence the response is rated in that category. Since the appearance category at Delta/3 is popular, this de-cision accords with the first part of Rule 3, rating in the less frequent category.

"A woman should always—*try to keep herself neat, 'on the ball,' and thoughtful of others.*" "Neat" would be rated I-3, "on the ball" would be rated I-3/4, and "thoughtful of others" would be rated I-3/4. As a category exists at I-4, "Three different traits, at least one at I-3/4," this response is rated there according to Rule 1. If there were no such category for this stem, the response would be rated I-4, unclassified, ac-cording to Rule 2.

"What gets me into trouble is—*people and my mouth.*" "People" is rated I-2, category 1. "My mouth" is rated I-3, category 1. As the latter is a popular category, the response is rated I-2, category 1.

"A woman should always—*be pleasant and attractive.*" Separate categories are provided at I-3 for "be pleasant" and "be attractive." As the latter is a very popular category, the response is rated I-3, category 2.

"When a child won't join in group activities—*they are either shy or prefer not to.*" This response combines thoughts that would be classed at I-3, category 6 and I-3, category 7. Since the latter is a popular category, the response is rated I-3, category 6.

"A good mother—*sets limits, controls and directs.*" This is a pseudo-compound response. Each element would belong in I-3, category 13; therefore, the whole response is so classified.

"If my mother—*is kind and generous.*" This is a pseudo-compound response. It also ignores the grammar of the stem, but that fact is disregarded in rating. It appears at I-3, category 13.

> Rule 4: *In the case of a meaningful response, where there is no appropriate category and Rules 2 and 3 do not apply, use the general theory to arrive at a rating.*

We have intentionally deleted unusual responses that had no special theoretical interest, in part because without replication we had no way of verifying whether we had placed the response correctly. There will always be a certain percentage of such responses, no matter how complete the manual. When he obtains one, the rater assigns it whatever I-level he believes is correct, unclassified. There are several steps used in sequence in arriving at the I-level. One uses the materials in order of increasing remoteness from the stem at hand; more remote materials are used only when more immediate ones do not provide basis for rating. First one looks to see if similar ideas are found in categories or in unclassified examples for some level, perhaps substituting "father" or "parent" for "mother," for example. If that step does not yield a rating, one next rereads all the introductory remarks for the item manual, to see if the response comes within any of the general expectations presented there for the several levels. If the rater still is unable to decide where to place the response, he should rely on Chapter Four, which shows how ego level is manifest in SCs in general. Only when no guidance can be found in Chapter Four should he depend on the basic concept, Chapter One, and try to guess how a given response is related to ego level apart from experience with other SC protocols. The rater should be aware that the more latitude the method gives him for generating his own hypothesis, the greater the danger that personal biases may enter. Some important precautions are discussed presently.

Examples:

"A woman's body—*is a noble creation.*" Though this response fits no category for the stem, at I-3/4 are "—is sacred, holy; is God's gift; is a creation of God" (category 5) and "—is wonderful, marvelous" (category 7). The response, though fitting neither category, can be rated I-3/4, unclassified, because of its similarity in content to the two categories mentioned.

"Being with other people—*is not nice.*" There is no category for this response at any I-level for the stem. At I-2 is "—is nice, OK (unelaborated)" (category 1). Because this response is simply the negative statement of the idea classed I-2, it would be rated I-2, unclassified.

"When they avoided me—*I didn't worry.*" At I-3 is "—I feel sad, funny, bad; I worry" (category 3). Unlike the example given above, this response would not be rated I-3, unclassified, even though the positive statement of the idea is in a category at I-3. Following Rule 1 the response can be rated in Delta/3, category 1, "—it didn't bother me; I don't care." Be sure there is no appropriate category for a response before rating it unclassified.

"When they talked about sex, I—*looked away.*" Here again there is no appropriate category for the response. Given as an unclassified example at I-3 is *"turned my ear away."* As the response in question also describes a similar action, it would be rated I-3, unclassified.

"I am—*often very lonely.*" Though there is no category for this response, the rater should notice that "happy" is classed I-3, and "usually happy" is classed I-3/4. The introduction to the I-3/4 categories for this stem states that at this level there is "reference to long-term rather than to immediate feelings." Because the response refers to long-term rather than to immediate feelings, it would be rated I-3/4, unclassified.

"At times she worried about—*her impulsive behavior.*" Not only is there no category for this response, there is no guide for rating it contained in the introductory remarks for that item. However, in reviewing Chapter Four, the rater should note that responses to other stems indicate that at I-4 impulses are acknowledged and distinguished from the corresponding acts. Thus, the response would be rated I-4, unclassified.

Rule 5: *Where the response is omitted or too fragmentary to be meaningful, it is rated I-3.*

Although many grammatically incomplete sentences are ratable, occasionally no response is given or a completion cannot be scored because the subject has been vague, has free-associated to the stem, or has given too fragmentary a thought. In such cases, the rule is to score the completion I-3. Indicate the completions you have scored under this rule by writing "Rule 5" by the number on the scoring sheet.

Examples:

"My father—*was a governor emlope."* This response can be interpreted as a badly misspelled version of "was a government employee," and can be rated following Rule 1 in I-3, category, 11, "Occupations."

"When they talked about sex, I—*mean girl."* Though the response is grammatically incomplete, the several interpretations of the subject's possible meaning, that those talking about sex are mean (bad), that she herself becomes mean (bad, mad) in this situation, that to the subject sex means girls (female sex), all lead to an I-2, unclassified, rating.

"When they avoided me—*I think them."* The subject has not said enough to allow the rater to interpret her meaning. She may mean, "I thank them," in which case the response can be rated following Rule 1 in Delta, category 2, "—I laugh, am glad." But it is also likely that the subject did not complete her thought, "I think they . . ." In this case there is no clue as to the appropriate rating. Because of the uncertainty about the subject's meaning, this response must be rated I-3, Rule 5.

Some other responses rated I-3, Rule 5, are:

"When people are helpless—*sometimes"*

"Raising a family—*church"*

"Most men think that women—*are very fb"*

"Women are lucky because—*they"*

RECORDING THE RATINGS

Most users of this manual probably will not be interested in obtaining category ratings for each response; I-level ratings will suffice for most purposes. A new rater should score responses for both I-level and category at first even if his purpose requires only I-level ratings. By doing so the rater will force himself to keep the total classification scheme in mind and will be less likely to overlook some fine distinctions in meaning encoded in the manual. Actually, the sheer bulk of the thirty-six-item scoring manual prohibits even an experienced rater from scoring more than a few categories of responses without reference to the manual.

The following instructions for recording I-level and category ratings were given to the new raters used in the evaluation of the prepublication manual. The same format is used in the scoring keys in Appendices C and D.

Completions are to be scored for I-level and content category number unless otherwise indicated. These exceptions occur under Rules 4 and 5 of the instructions. Any notes that may be pertinent should be placed on the reverse side of the scoring sheet with the number of the completion to which they refer.

Examples:

The following four responses have been given to the stem, Education—.

1. is essential
2. is not
3. is necessary to maintain our democracy
4. is developed through contact with others

These responses are scored:

1. I-3, 1
2. Rule 5
3. I-4, 1
4. I-4, UC

The notations mean:

1. Completion is scored in content category 1 at the I-3 level.
2. This is the notation for an omitted or fragmented response.
3. Completion has been scored in content category 1 at the I-4 level.
4. This response is covered in Rule 4 of the instructions. The scoring signifies that there is no category appropriate to the completion, and the rater has hypothesized that the completion is best placed at the I-4 level. A note to explain the reasons may be added on the reverse side of the scoring sheet.

SOURCES OF BIAS

There are certain biases that may enter ratings that cannot be entirely guarded against nor even clearly tested for, yet must be discussed. These fall in three broad classes: traits of the subject that lead to response characteristics more obvious than the manifestations of I-level; characteristics of the subject or of the response that are as inferential as I-level; and characteristics of the raters.

Certain demographic and other traits of the subject are manifest in response characteristics more obvious than the manifestations of I-level, such as word choice, errors of spelling and grammar, and length of response. One could make a scoring manual on these characteristics alone, and it would be correlated with I-level. Our behavioristic brethren no doubt would be much happier with such a manual than with the one presented here. Such characteristics reflect intelligence and socioeconomic status more than they do I-level. In a somewhat different way, literary skill and professional training also enter in.

Number of words is correlated with I-level for a straightforward reason—that is, it takes on the average more words to express more complex thoughts and relations. This is not a spurious correlation. The correlation becomes spurious if we rate a response higher because it has more words, regardless of content. This is unlikely to take place if one uses the manual seriously. At least one scoring manual for judging adjustment from SCs has actually made mandatory penalizing responses that are unusually long. This will have the effect, on the average, of calling persons at high I-levels poorly adjusted. We rate neither up nor down according to number of words. While that rule holds without reservation for rating one item, conceivably one might occasionally shade a TPR rating down in the case of an extremely wordy subject. The reasoning would be that her extreme wordiness, where it is apparently a function of something other than I-level, consistently favored higher ratings for the separate items.

Errors of spelling and grammar are more likely to occur on low protocols than on high ones, again with a great deal of overlap. Such errors reflect directly intelligence and education, and, less directly, socioeconomic status. The correlation with I-level is, one must suppose, incidental. While there is certainly some correlation between I-level and intelligence, education, and socioeconomic status, this need not be interpreted as an artifact of measurement. There is no reason to suppose that retarded children or adults can achieve the highest ego levels; hence it is not a failing of the test that they do not achieve top scores. There are certainly very intelligent subjects that score low in I-level, and there are certainly individuals from the lowest social strata who score at I-4 or even occasionally at the I-5 level. We have at times found ourselves reasoning as follows: "Since this woman obviously comes from a low social class, to achieve this amount of insight represents a greater achievement than for someone in a more favorable environment. Therefore, let us give her the benefit of the doubt and raise the rating." At other times there has been the temptation to reason as follows: "This aspect of the response is more indicative of low social status than of low I-level. However, as they are correlated, chances are we will be right if we rate it low in I-level." Obviously, these two lines of reasoning cancel each other out. The only solution is to avoid as far as possible assigning any weight to intelligence, social status, errors in spelling and grammar, or use of plain or fancy words.

Certain words that we use to describe high protocols, "role conceptualization," "interpersonal relations," "sense of identity," "self-fulfillment," have become part of the cant of the helping professions. Some of our samples were drawn from such groups, including student social workers, graduate students in nursing, and psychology students. This lingo has of course also got through to the readers of women's magazines to some extent. What we look for in scoring, however, is not use of the words but evidences of the thought behind the words. The words by themselves usually stand out as clichés and often occur and usually are scored at the I-3/4 level. In general, individuals in the helping professions have not scored higher than other normal samples.

While the responses receiving highest scores have little professional lingo, they often are touching and poetic, humorous or sad, or both at once. None of our subjects to our knowledge has any special literary training or talent, surely no sample as a whole does. Again, one finds responses of some literary merit at all levels, some responses at high levels without any special literary quality. Such correlation between high I-level and literary merit as occurs again need not be spurious. A rich inner life is an aspect of high ego level by definition, and that such a rich inner life would also serve as an ingredient (though neither necessary nor sufficient) of literary talent is no new discovery. The literary quality per se is not the basis for scoring.

Similar considerations hold for age. The manual is not intended for ages below adolescence; our experience is that it is satisfactory down to about twelve years, though we have used it down to age nine. Some stems are inappropriate for younger children. A preliminary study showed no increase in I-level between ages twenty and fifty. A study cited in Chapter Three showed consistent and appreciable increases in ego level during adolescence. In any case, age-contingent scoring is specifically excluded. This rule corresponds to an implicit rule for intelligence tests. One expects mental age to rise during adolescence, but that does not mean more lenient scoring standards are adopted for younger ages. Indeed, if the decision to score a response right or wrong depended on the respondent's age, one would have no clear way to demonstrate age changes. Hence we decided never to score a response according to whether it came from someone of a certain age, or, on similar considerations, of a particular marital or parental status. The manual must accordingly be used in that fashion.

Two aspects of the response, somewhat more inferential than the foregoing sources of bias, are arbitrarily excluded from consideration in rating—the question of the truth of the response and the problem of pathology. We do not maintain that whether a person discriminates reality correctly is totally irrelevant to I-level, nor that pathology is uncorrelated with it. In general, the manual has been constructed by systematically ignoring the questions of truth and of pathology, and it must be used the same way.

The exigencies of research are such that we could not possibly know the factual status of the great majority of items where it might be an issue, for instance, "My main problem is—*I'm too fat.*" Since we usually do not know the reasonableness of such statements, and since we have never checked how reasonableness may be used as a cue for I-level, we exclude it as a consideration even where the rater may feel he can make a good guess. By way of justification, there are always a variety of ways of expressing any fact. "I'm too fat" could have been expressed in terms of lack of self-discipline, for example, and there are always an indefinitely large number of facts to express. The girl after all picked her weight to worry about rather than her school grades, boys, relations with parents, and so on. Even if a high I-level subject makes a few such remarks, there are all the other items for her to display other aspects of her thinking. The occurrence of a few I-3 responses does not affect the TPR. In discouraging consideration of the factual status of a remark we are, furthermore, discouraging many risky inferences that would introduce more error than truth into the ratings. The rule must not be pushed to absurdity, however. When the subject states "I am—*a secret spy for the Russians,*" she is joking and expects us to know it. Such information can be used in rating.

In general, quite serious pathology may escape notice in a SC protocol. Hospitalized schizophrenics may produce protocols indistinguishable from those of normals. Although we have many protocols from patients in mental hospitals, they have not been used to construct the manual. When pathology is evident in a response, we try so far as possible not to be influenced by it in our rating. Since it is more or less in the nature of pathological responses to be unique, this caveat is given less assistance by the detailed scoring manual than the other warnings. Since high-level responses also tend to be unique, and since the stem that triggers the subject's sick thoughts may lead to a lengthy, involved answer, a sick response can be confused with a high response. On the other hand, some raters may react to evident pathology by a desire to downgrade the response. Alternatively, pathology can lead to eruption of impulsive responses that belie the subject's characteristic ego level, and thus lead to low ratings. The extent to which ego regression takes place and is made evident in an instrument such as the SC test is one we have not attempted to study, nor could it be studied prior to construction of some effective measuring technique. In general, we would have to admit that pathology in a subject is a possible serious source of error. With an experienced, well-trained, and insightful rater it would probably not lead to overestimation of I-level. With an inexperienced or non-insightful rater, it could lead to overestimation of I-level. In either case it could lead to underestimation; however, if we assume that ego regression takes place under pressure of pathology, then it is not clear whether the SC test reflects or ought to reflect the highest ego potential or the current level of functioning. The test can be assumed to be valid only where the two more or less coincide or differ to the extent found in normal respondents.

A related limitation on use of the test is in connection with psychotherapy of any kind. The level of verbal exchange tapped by the SC test is too close to that of the therapeutic exchange not to be affected by it. The effect can be a spurious elevation or depression of the I-level as manifested on the SC test. Direct quotation of wise sayings and admonitions of the therapist will ordinarily lead to too high a rating. On the other hand, therapy encourages and works by bringing to the level of open verbalization the very hostile, sexual, self-interested motives whose suppression is a mark of some stages of ego growth. While therapy operates to abrogate the inhibitions in speech, it does not ordinarily lead to a corresponding regression in behavior. Hence a patient having successfully undergone therapy might actually seem to be lower in ego level, even though he operated at a higher level in ordinary life. These effects are not guesses but are, in part at least, observations from some preliminary studies. The long-sought instrument to evaluate the effects of psychotherapy is, for the foregoing and other reasons, not to be found in the present scoring manual.

A final group of biases refers to the characteristics of the rater rather than of the subject. One's own problems, and by no means necessarily neurotic ones, tend to be overestimated. If money is a major problem, then one wants to read high I-level into complaints about money problems. If religion is a major interest, one wants to see high I-level in religious professions; an antireligious rater may be similarly loath to rate religious answers as high as they deserve. An overweight rater will be touched by persons whose problem is being fat, one struggling with choice between marriage and career upgrades that conflict, and so on. Neurotic problems may be more insidious, since one does not always admit to having them. One cannot work with the scoring system for long without coming to feel that high is good. Since our accumulated experience by now encompasses most of life's common problems, reliance on the scoring manual is a substantial protection against this kind of error. In the early stages of the work a corresponding protection was obtained by working in groups, compromising differences with relentless mutual criticism. In later stages empirical feedback performed this function. Any reader who feels inclined to substitute his own judgment for that of the manual opens the way to this probably most serious of all biases. The manual must surely contain mistakes, but they are most likely in the rare categories, not those concerned with life's universal problems. Correction of mistakes must be founded on experience comparable in extent to that used for construction and evaluation of the present version.

A final bias is the end-of-the-rainbow effect. Not only is high seen as good, but one longs to believe that the achievement of high I-level will be crowned with peace and contentment. Responses expressing those feelings, along with self-satisfaction, do indeed occur occasionally at high I-levels. When we have attempted to build such a description into a scoring manual, however, the raters invariably and probably justifiably applied it so as to include far too many responses from I-3 and I-4 protocols. While peace and contentment may come with high I-level, they are not its distinctive marks. The absence of self-criticism at the I-3 level is probably even more conducive to verbal expressions of contentment. One could even argue that the mark of the highest level is not the solution of one's problems but openness to more problems and often to more poignant ones.

A question similar to that of rater bias is to what extent the I-level of the rater limits his ability as a rater. If we had a choice, we would limit use of the manual to persons at level I-4 or higher having some graduate training in psychology and above average intelligence. Can a person at the I-4 level learn to rate accurately at higher levels? Use of the SC method is based on the selective perception of facts in accord with one's own level. There is, however, a difference between what one selectively perceives and produces spontaneously in a free response situation and what one can deal with adequately when the material is presented. Thus one can in principle learn to score at a somewhat higher level than one's own. Our experience with many raters, few if any of us having claim to higher than an I-4 level of personal development, is that we do learn to rate consistently and validly beyond our own levels. Just as an impression, persons below the I-4 level have trouble discriminating responses in the range I-4/5 to I-6, in part because most such responses are unique and fit categories at best rather loosely.

CHAPTER 6

Deriving Total
Protocol Ratings

Given thirty-six item ratings for a protocol, the task remains of translating the distribution of ratings into a single rating for the protocol. This is the problem of the scoring paradigm, and it has no unique solution. Unfortunately most of the psychometric thinking and practice in this field is passed along by word of mouth in the "invisible college." There are no appropriate published references to most of the practices or to the reasoning behind them. The following account is meant to illustrate possible scoring paradigms rather than to present a balanced picture of other people's usages.

The first scoring paradigm translates into psychometric terms the notion that the trait at issue is primarily a capacity, one which the subject at any given moment may or may not exercise to its maximum extent. Kenneth Isaacs (1956), who holds this view, considers most characteristic of the person the highest level he displays, particularly in fantasies. Isaacs uses the TAT primarily. Each story is assigned to just one level, the highest level manifest in it, and a person is characterized by his highest score or by the second highest (which is not different in principle but a concession to the problem of reliability). David Hunt, using a SC test, similarly scores with regard to the highest level attained. In practice, to cope with the reliability problem, Hunt uses the average of the two highest or the three highest scores, again a modification in detail only.

A second paradigm takes as the protocol rating the mode of the distribution of item ratings. This model implies that the level most characteristic for a subject is the level where he most frequently operates. In the past Kohlberg (1964) has used this model. He uses incomplete stories that present a moral dilemma, following the person's completion of the story with a Piaget-type inquiry. Formerly he scored every thought, with a thought often being a single sentence; currently his method is being modified in the direction of scoring aspects of problems. In either case, a person is characterized by a distribution of ratings; to reduce that distribution to a single rating he formerly took the mode. Currently he is working on an alternative model, perhaps closer to our own notion of core functioning.

Another obvious and frequently used psychometric model involves taking the mean of the item ratings as the total protocol rating (TPR). Where the number of items is fixed, as in our case, with thirty-six stems and therefore thirty-six item ratings, the same results are obtained using the sum of item ratings. In this model each item rating is given equal weight as an estimate of the TPR, and the problem of reliability is met by averaging all ratings. This score has the merit of being almost perfectly correlated with the first factor score in an unrotated principal components factor analysis, at least with a sufficiently large number of items. There is an intuitive objection to this model, despite its merits. Suppose one were trying to decide whether a given protocol belonged at the conscientious or autonomous level. Normally one would expect an appreciable number of responses to come from lower levels on such a protocol. Whether those responses were at the impulsive, the opportunistic, or the conformist level is not germane intuitively. The sum-of-item-ratings paradigm would award a higher rating to the subject with conformist answers than to one with a mixture of conformist and lower level answers. A clinician, however, would tend to see the variety of themes and access to many developmental layers as itself often an indication of high ego level. Hence the presence of a few very low responses on a protocol with distinctive high responses may actually enhance the impression of high ego level. (Compare the psychoanalytic concept of "regression in the service of the ego.")

The notion of ego level as being the level of core functioning, which underlies some of our methodological choices, does not readily translate into these or any other scoring paradigm. We began by using the total configuration of the distribution of item ratings in assigning TPRs, guided by some intuitive rules for what kinds of distributions indicated what ego levels. This method has the advantage over the previous paradigms that it retains more information, and it is more like a clinician's diagnostic thinking, since it uses a configuration of responses, but it has the disadvantage of being subjective and hard to codify. As we came to think about it rigorously, we recognized another disadvantage. If there are K discriminable levels, this method involves roughly K^2 parameters. In an attempt to retain the advantages of this method yet reduce it to a simple set of rules, with no more parameters than there are discriminations to be made (one parameter less than the number of levels), we arrived at what we call the ogive rules, presented in this chapter.

All of the above scoring paradigms treat the separate items as interchangeable. From a rigorous, purely psychometric point of view a preferable model would assign a separate regression weight to each item, or to each scored level of each item, or, at the extreme, to each category of each item. In any of those cases the number of parameters that a scorer would have to cope with would involve either recourse to a computer or to a large table of parameters. It is doubtful if this method would substantially improve on the simple sum of item scores, which is essentially the score on the first principal component.

In the past, it seems to have been the case that every test constructor adopted one scoring paradigm which appealed to him for some reason without serious thought about other possible ones. In selecting a scoring paradigm, the following considerations have been adduced: It should be compatible with the formal aspects of the trait being measured. It should be objectively applied and convenient for use by a clinician in his office. It should show better correlation with criterion measures than alternative paradigms. Our ogive rules seem to meet these criteria, but they are not so compellingly derived from the givens of the situation as to preclude the possibility of a better scoring paradigm being proposed. Our intention is therefore to open rather than to close discussion of this issue.

OGIVE RULES

Tables 21 and 22 contain two sets of ogive rules to be applied to the cumulative frequency distribution of item ratings for any given pro-

Table 21

AUTOMATIC RULES FOR ASSIGNING TOTAL PROTOCOL RATINGS
TO THE OGIVE OF ITEM RATINGS

TPR is:	If there are:
I-6[a]	No more than 34 ratings at I-5
I-5	No more than 31 ratings at I-4/5
I-4/5	No more than 30 ratings at I-4
I-4	No more than 24 ratings at I-3/4
I-3/4	No more than 21 ratings at I-3
I-2	At least 5 ratings at I-2
Delta	At least 6 ratings at Delta
Delta/3	At least 6 ratings at Delta/3

NOTE.—Apply these rules in the order given, from I-6 to Delta/3.

[a] To receive an I-6 rating, the I-5 criterion must also be met.

Table 22

BORDERLINE RULES FOR ASSIGNING TOTAL PROTOCOL RATINGS
TO THE OGIVE OF ITEM RATINGS

TPR is:	If there are:	Borderline if there are:
I-6[a]	No more than 34 ratings at I-5	35 ratings at I-5
I-5	No more than 31 ratings at I-4/5	32 ratings at I-4/5
I-4/5	No more than 28 ratings at I-4	29 or 30 ratings at I-4
I-4	No more than 22 ratings at I-3/4	23, 24, or 25 ratings at I-3/4
I-3/4	No more than 20 ratings at I-3	21, 22, or 23 ratings at I-3
I-2	At least 6 ratings at I-2	4 or 5 ratings at I-2
Delta	At least 7 ratings at Delta	4, 5, or 6 ratings at Delta
Delta/3	At least 7 ratings at Delta/3	5 or 6 ratings at Delta/3

NOTE.—Apply these rules in the order given, from I-6 to Delta/3.

[a] To receive an I-6 rating, the I-5 criterion must also be met.

tocol. The first set, the automatic rules, requires no judgment from a rater other than that required to rate the individual responses. Given an ogive of thirty-six item ratings, these rules yield only one possible TPR. Note that protocols having more than twenty-one ratings at I-3 and fewer than six ratings at Delta/3 are scored I-3. The automatic ogive rules are the scoring method of choice for new raters inexperienced with the manual and the theory of ego development.

The second set of rules, the borderline rules, will not invariably yield a single TPR for all protocols. Some protocols will be classed borderline, between two I-levels, thus allowing the rater to use his judgment, based on his experience in judging level of ego development from sentence completions, in arriving at a final TPR. (Note, again, that the rating I-3 is given to protocols lower than I-3/4 and higher than Delta/3.) These were the rules used by all raters in the studies of the prepublication manual reported in Chapter Three (with additional leeway for overruling the rules, particularly for the sealed sample).

EXAMPLE

Assume the thirty-six item ratings for a protocol formed the following distribution.

Item Rating	I-2	Δ	Δ/3	I-3	I-3/4	I-4	I-4/5	I-5	I-6
Frequency	1	1	0	11	10	12	1	0	0

We obtain the following ogive.

Item Rating	I-2	Δ	Δ/3	I-3	I-3/4	I-4	I-4/5	I-5	I-6
Cumulative Frequency	1	2	2	13	23	35	36	36	36

Applying the absolute rules, the ogive in the example would be classified I-4. It is not I-6 because there are more than thirty-four ratings at I-5. It is not I-5 because there are more than thirty-one ratings at I-4/5. It is not I-4/5 because there are more than thirty ratings at I-4. But it has less than twenty-four ratings at I-3/4, so it would be classed I-4.

Application of the borderline rules to this ogive yields a borderline rating. Because there are twenty-three ratings at I-3/4 it falls between I-3/4 and I-4. Such a protocol would be reexamined by the rater for other cues (discussed below) that will help determine whether to rate it up (I-4) or down (I-3/4).

RATING A TOTAL PROTOCOL

In rating a protocol, the following steps should be taken in order. Newly trained raters follow steps 1, 3, and 4 only. When rating the practice protocols of Appendix D, however, the rater should follow all steps.

1. Rate each completion according to its own section of the manual and without regard to context. Record each rating. This should be considered a test scoring task and should be as objective as possible.

2. Read the whole protocol through, trying to form an impression of what kind of a person could have written it. Jot down this impressionistic I-level for the person.

3. Make a frequency distribution of your item ratings and then a cumulative frequency distribution (ogive).

4. Determine what TPR would be assigned using the ogive rules of Table 21 or, for experienced raters, Table 22.

Where the ogive TPR coincides with the impressionistic I-level, record this value as the TPR and go on to the next case. Where there is a discrepancy between the impressionistic and the ogive TPR, it is necessary to take a more analytic attitude. There is then a further series of steps, all of which should be taken before making a decision as to TPR.

5. Check all the preceding steps.

6. Look at the item rating distribution (as opposed to the ogive). In considering ratings above I-3, to some extent ratings should be more heavily weighted the higher they are. For example, if there is a marginal or even submarginal number of ratings at I-4 or above, if several of those are at I-4/5 and I-5, the protocol should probably be called I-4. Similar considerations hold for other ratings above I-3.

7. Evaluate nonpsychometric signs, that is, indications that do not affect the distribution. The following are important nonpsychometric signs that the rater should keep in mind.

(a) Repetition of particular words or phrases in three or more separate stems tends to be a low indicator, usually I-3 or below.

(b) Repetition of an idea or thought, such as responsibility or love, even if in varying language, may possibly indicate a more or less neurotic preoccupation. Several mentions of responsibility serve as a less good indicator of I-4 level than, say, mention of responsibility plus differentiated inner feelings plus complex responses. High levels are more strongly established when there are varied high-level indicators. Chapter Four can serve as a guide, since it gives themes that cut across items. Thus, richness and originality of the total protocol is a high-level indicator, although for original responses we do not have any hard and fast rules for differentiating signs of neurosis, signs of unusual intelligence and intellectual productivity, and signs of high I-level. An experienced and sensitive rater can, however, make such distinctions with reasonably good reliability with respect to total protocols. It is, of course, meaningless to ask whether a unique response is really a mark of neurosis, of intelligence, or of I-level; one can only meaningfully ask whether raters make correct inferences about the total protocol, that is, about the subject.

(c) While in general repetition is a low indicator, there may be I-3 and I-4 subjects who have a neurotic (or perhaps realistic) preoccupation with a particular low-level theme like interpersonal exploitation or drinking. Therefore I-2 and Delta ratings are also more secure if there are varied low-level indicators.

(d) Closeness to theory is also taken into account in evaluating the evidential worth of a particular response.

(e) Some special considerations apply to rating total protocols that are not entirely conveyed by the rules for rating items. Herewith we try to make some of these considerations explicit.

I-6 Ratings. Most samples will contain no I-6 subjects. For some purposes it may suffice to group I-6 cases with the I-5 cases. The following considerations are helpful where it is desired to retain distinctions at the highest levels. Where approximately half the item ratings are over I-4, the subject is a strong candidate for an I-6 TPR. In addition, we look for responses that integrate inner and outer life, self and other, present and future, immediate and long-term concerns, personal and social, trivial and important, and particularly responses that integrate several of the foregoing. To be rated I-6 a protocol must also satisfy requirements for an I-5 TPR.

I-5 Ratings. A TPR of I-5 is never given unless there are at least three different types of I-5 responses, or three different I-5 themes. Typical themes are coping with inner conflict, role conceptualization beyond the banal "wife and mother" level, complex psychological causation, psychological development, self-fulfillment, and conceptual complexity, for example, comparison of three different aspects of a situation, or three methods of coping, or three possible causes. Conceptual complexity can also be shown in the complexity of interpersonal interaction seen, such as the relation between two people affecting a third person, perhaps their child.

I-2 Ratings. Apart from responses rated I-2, one typically finds several of the following features on I-2 protocols: brief answers throughout, often with some omissions; flat affect, almost to the point of being inappropriate; alternatively or in combination with flat affect, evidence of unsocialized impulsivity (drinking, sex, getting mad), with some answers actually sounding impulsive; repetitive answers; little concern with interpersonal relations except as people serve as sources of supplies; dichotomization of the world into nice, clean, good-to-me versus nasty, dirty, mean-to-me. We try to distinguish an I-2 type of illogical response ("Men are lucky because—they are happy") from language barrier, whether due to foreign birth or semi-illiteracy. "If I can't get what I want—I would get a 3 bath room house," apparently misreading "can't" as "can." Language barrier is not a clue to I-level.

Delta Ratings. Where the I-2 may be unable to compose an original, germane response to each item, some Delta subjects just refuse to do so. They may omit some responses but are more likely to give hostile evasions. Some such responses are scored I-3, since they also occur at other levels, but where they set the tone of the whole protocol, they weigh strongly for a Delta rating. Where the tone of the protocol is dominated by themes such as exploitation, domination, and obedience, the protocol is probably Delta even though the individual responses are mostly I-3, and even though I-3 themes such as love are also present. Appearance, formerly considered an I-3 theme, occurs at lower levels often enough that for some items it is given a Delta/3 rating. I-2 responses are not uncommon on Delta protocols, nor is a sprinkling of I-3/4 and I-4 responses. However, a single clearly formulated reference to long-term values and ideals strongly contraindicates a rating of I-3 and, still more, a rating below I-3. In distinguishing I-2 from Delta protocols, we consider the general haplessness (more likely in I-2) and beginning sensitivity to social requirements (more likely in Delta). Thus, although the Delta person may be as selfish and self-centered as the I-2, she will disguise her hostility in the form of hostile humor in deference to social norms.

Some categories of response characterize protocols below I-3 but do not distinguish I-2 from Delta protocols; usually they are assigned to the Delta level as a compromise. Partly for this reason, a large number of Delta responses may weigh more in favor of an I-2 rating than a Delta rating. The ogive rules are constructed so that the I-2 rating should be ruled out before the Delta rating is considered.

The ratings I-2/Delta and Delta/3 can be used as compromise ratings for TPRs, although there are few such item ratings and no generalized descriptions of them. They are thought of as transitions and hence have characteristics of both levels.

APPENDICES

APPENDIX A

Instructions for Administering the Sentence Completion Test

The following are the instructions we now use. They represent what we consider to be the optimum amount of information to be given subjects. In the past we have used slight variations of this form. These instructions should be read to the subjects when they have received the form. We assume that minor variations in phrasing do not matter.

Now I would like you to fill out this sentence completion form. You see that these are incomplete sentences. Please finish each one. Notice that there are two pages; please make sure you have completed each one.

Responses to be used by experimenter if subjects request further help in completing the form:

Please finish the sentence in any way you wish. [or]
There are no right or wrong answers.
[In answer to the question, "Who is 'she'?"]:
It can mean anyone. [or]
Just think of it as anyone you wish.

APPENDIX B

Current Forms of the Washington University Sentence Completion Test for Measuring Ego Development

Included here are all our current sentence completion forms for men as well as for women. Except where noted, all are printed on two pages with a space for the subject's name at the top of the second page, in order to guard against separation of the pages. We always use only one side of the page. This makes the responses more legible and provides extra space for subjects who need it.

The following is a brief description of the forms presented.

Form 9-62 for Women. The manual in this book was constructed for the thirty-six items in this form. A few items that make a direct or covert reference to sex were being removed by investigators using the test in high school and grade school settings. These items do not cause difficulty for subjects, and their omission is purely a political matter. However, rather than have ad hoc versions proliferate, we have now constructed our own version for these purposes, the following form.

Form AB 10-68 for Girls. Five items were replaced to retain a total of thirty-six items, so that the psychometric properties remain essentially the same. This form is printed on three pages instead of two, to give more space for writing.

Form 11-68 for Women. This is the revised version of Form 9-62, with replacement of four of the least interesting items. To score this version one will use intuition and general knowledge for the few items not included in the manual. However, an experienced rater will have no difficulty. This form is presently the best test for women and girls where it is possible to use it.

Form 9-62 for Men. This is the original thirty-six-item men's form.

Form 10-68 for Men. Eight items from Form 9-62, including those items referring to sex, were deleted and eight others added.

Form 10-68 for Boys. This form is identical to Form 10-68 for men, but it is printed on three pages instead of two.

Form 11-68 for Men. This is the best test for men and boys where relations with principals or other authorities permit use of a few items that may have a direct or indirect reference to sex. The items are selected on the basis of extensive experience with Forms 9-62 for men and women.

A scoring manual for men and boys is planned to cover all items in Forms 10-68 and 11-68. Thus the scoring manual will cover forty-one items, though to get results comparable to ours *only thirty-six items should be used,* preferably either Form 10-68 or Form 11-68. Although the scoring manual is not yet available, many items can be scored using the manual for women. An intuitive person can score other items after training himself with the manual for women. What we have learned about ego development is dispersed throughout the present manual. Therefore a person intending to score other forms than Form 9-62 for women should follow all the exercises outlined in Chapter Five.

SENTENCE COMPLETION FOR WOMEN (Form 9-62)

Name .... Age ....

Marital Status .... Education ....

Instructions: Complete the following sentences.

1. Raising a family
2. Most men think that women
3. When they avoided me
4. If my mother
5. Being with other people
6. The thing I like about myself is
7. My mother and I
8. What gets me into trouble is
9. Education
10. When people are helpless
11. Women are lucky because
12. My father
13. A pregnant woman
14. When my mother spanked me, I
15. A wife should
16. I feel sorry
17. When I am nervous, I
18. A woman's body
19. When a child won't join in group activities

20. Men are lucky because
21. When they talked about sex, I
22. At times she worried about
23. I am
24. A woman feels good when
25. My main problem is
26. Whenever she was with her mother, she
27. The worst thing about being a woman
28. A good mother
29. Sometimes she wished that
30. When I am with a man
31. When she thought of her mother, she
32. If I can't get what I want
33. Usually she felt that sex
34. For a woman a career is
35. My conscience bothers me if
36. A woman should always

SENTENCE COMPLETION FOR GIRLS (*Form AB 10-68*)

Name .... School ....

Age .... Date .... Teacher ....

Instructions: Complete the following sentences in any way that you wish.

1. Raising a family
2. Most men think that women
3. When they avoided me
4. If my mother
5. Being with other people
6. The thing I like about myself is
7. A girl has a right to
8. When I get mad
9. My mother and I
10. What gets me into trouble is
11. Education
12. When people are helpless
13. Women are lucky because
14. When I am criticized
15. My father
16. Rules are
17. If I had more money
18. When my mother spanked me, I
19. A wife should

20. I feel sorry
21. When I am nervous, I
22. When a child will not join in group activities
23. Men are lucky because
24. At times she worried about
25. I am
26. A woman feels good when
27. My main problem is
28. Whenever she was with her mother, she
29. Sometimes she wished that
30. A good mother
31. The worst thing about being a woman
32. When she thought of her mother, she
33. If I can't get what I want
34. For a woman a career is
35. My conscience bothers me if
36. A woman should always

SENTENCE COMPLETION FOR WOMEN (Form 11-68)

Name .... Age ....

Marital Status .... Education ....

Instructions: Complete the following sentences.

1. Raising a family

2. A girl has a right to

3. When they avoided me

4. If my mother

5. Being with other people

6. The thing I like about myself is

7. My mother and I

8. What gets me into trouble is

9. Education

10. When people are helpless

11. Women are lucky because

12. My father

13. A pregnant woman

14. When my mother spanked me, I

15. A wife should

16. I feel sorry

17. Rules are

18. When I get mad

19. When a child will not join in group activities

20. Men are lucky because

21. When they talked about sex, I

22. At times she worried about

23. I am

24. A woman feels good when

25. My main problem is

26. My husband and I will

27. The worst thing about being a woman

28. A good mother

29. Sometimes she wished that

30. When I am with a man

31. When she thought of her mother, she

32. If I can't get what I want

33. Usually she felt that sex

34. For a woman a career is

35. My conscience bothers me if

36. A woman should always

SENTENCE COMPLETION FOR MEN (Form 9-62)

Name .... Age ....

Marital Status .... Education ....

Instructions: Complete the following sentences.

1. Raising a family
2. Most women think that men
3. When they avoided me
4. If my mother
5. Being with other people
6. The thing I like about myself is
7. A man's job
8. If I can't get what I want
9. I am embarrassed when
10. Education
11. When people are helpless
12. Women are lucky because
13. What gets me into trouble is
14. A good father
15. If I were king
16. A wife should
17. I feel sorry
18. When a child won't join in group activities
19. When I am nervous, I
20. He felt proud that he
21. Men are lucky because
22. When they talked about sex, I
23. At times he worried about
24. I am
25. A man feels good when
26. My main problem is
27. When his wife asked him to help with the housework
28. When I am criticized
29. Sometimes he wished that
30. When I am with a woman
31. When he thought of his mother, he
32. The worst thing about being a man
33. Usually he felt that sex
34. I just can't stand people who
35. My conscience bothers me if
36. Crime and delinquency could be halted if

SENTENCE COMPLETION FOR MEN (Form 10-68)

Name .... Age ....

Marital Status .... Education ....

Instructions: Complete the following sentences.

1. Raising a family
2. When a child will not join in group activities
3. When they avoided me
4. A man's job
5. Being with other people
6. The thing I like about myself is
7. If my mother
8. If I can't get what I want
9. When I was younger
10. Education
11. When people are helpless
12. Women are lucky because
13. What gets me into trouble is
14. A good father
15. If I were king
16. A wife should
17. I feel sorry
18. A man should always
19. Rules are
20. He felt proud that he
21. Men are lucky because
22. My father and I
23. A man feels good when
24. When I get mad
25. At times he worried about
26. When his wife asked him to help with the housework
27. My main problem is
28. When I am criticized
29. Sometimes he wished that
30. A husband has a right to
31. When he thought of his mother, he
32. The worst thing about being a man
33. If I had more money
34. I just can't stand people who
35. My conscience bothers me if
36. Crime and delinquency could be halted if

SENTENCE COMPLETION FOR MEN (*Form 11-68*)

Name .... Age ....

Marital Status .... Education ....

Instructions: Complete the following sentences.

1. Raising a family
2. When a child will not join in group activities
3. When they avoided me
4. A man's job
5. Being with other people
6. The thing I like about myself is
7. If my mother
8. Crime and delinquency could be halted if
9. When I am with a woman
10. Education
11. When people are helpless
12. Women are lucky because
13. What gets me into trouble is
14. A good father
15. A man feels good when
16. A wife should
17. I feel sorry
18. A man should always

19. Rules are
20. When they talked about sex, I
21. Men are lucky because
22. My father and I
23. When his wife asked him to help with the housework
24. Usually he felt that sex
25. At times he worried about
26. If I can't get what I want
27. My main problem is
28. When I am criticized
29. Sometimes he wished that
30. A husband has a right to
31. When he thought of his mother, he
32. The worst thing about being a man
33. If I had more money
34. I just can't stand people who
35. My conscience bothers me if
36. He felt proud that he

Examples and Scoring Keys for Practice Item Ratings

EXAMPLES

EXAMPLES FOR RATING ITEM 1: RAISING A FAMILY—

1. should be a great blessing for a couple
2. has its own reward
3. would have some stresses and strains but would also be a joy sometime
4. is difficult for just one parent

5. can be a wonderful and enriching experience
6. is a tough job
7. is hard work, but when done well, satisfying
8. is alright if you have the money to give them what they need
9. is a real big job and responsibility which should be enjoyed, and involving both parents
10. is a wonderful and rewarding experience
11. , some fun!
12. is a tremendous responsibility but can be very rewarding
13. is a full time job for mother with the help of father
14. I would like to
15. is the most important job of all
16. is a sincere privilege and a challenging opportunity
17. is a wonderful experience
18. is pleasure and work
19. is a big job and takes cooperation from both parents
20. is a challenging occupation

EXAMPLES FOR RATING ITEM 2: MOST MEN THINK THAT WOMEN—

1. are below their level
2. should act and be feminine
3. are good companions
4. have only physical qualities and no more
5. are wonderful and pretty
6. are good
7. spend too much money
8. are important but some men don't
9. are easy prey
10. are weaklings
11. are very interesting to be with but not as intelligent as they
12. should not
13. belong at home and not at work
14. are a push over
15. are wonderful but bad drivers
16. ?
17. are not as bright as men, nor as bright as they really are
18. should be their servants
19. are pretty nice people
20. are fickle

EXAMPLES FOR RATING ITEM 3: WHEN THEY AVOIDED ME—

1. it is probably for some reason
2. I was glad
3. they had not meant to do so
4. I wonder why—is it something about me, them, something that was done or said
5. it really didn't matter much
6. I asked them why
7. I cried and ran to mommy
8. I felt let down
9. it is because I have been thoughtless and remote
10. I was curious as to why
11. I became very hurt inside and wondered what was wrong
12. I talked to someone else
13. I did the same
14. I tried to cover up my feelings by pretending not to notice
15. I just go on and don't let it bother me
16. I dwelt in self pity
17. I wondered why and decided to find the reason
18. I kept out of their way
19. they don't care to be in my company
20. I smiled and walked on

EXAMPLES FOR RATING ITEM 4: IF MY MOTHER—

1. was living I would be happier
2. were here she'd be the happiest grandmother in the world
3. had more understanding about children our family would have been happier
4. were well again I would be very happy
5. comes here and tries to get me I'll promise her I'll never run away again
6. calls, I obey
7. was in good health we would go to Arizona
8. would stop being so hot tempered I feel she would be a charming person
9. had a better education she would have been a more capable mother
10. would stay as good as she is
11. would relax she would feel better
12. didn't fix my hair, I would be up a creek

13. hadn't been so understanding I don't think I would have been as well adjusted as I am today
14. could drive, it would make her very happy
15. were ill, I would help her
16. would quit smoking, I would be glad
17. would broaden her interests I think she could revitalize herself
18. was not with me, I would be very lost
19. were only here
20. was any different I wouldn't be happy about it

EXAMPLES FOR RATING ITEM 5: BEING WITH OTHER PEOPLE—

1. would be alright if you get with good people
2. gives me a feeling of being wanted
3. is sometimes a nuisance
4. is fun and rewarding
5. helps me get acquainted with more people
6. can be both stimulating and entertaining
7. makes me feel good, forget my problems
8. is very nice
9. is a joy
10. is fun and I never fail to feel how wonderful most people are
11. can be a pleasure if you understand them
12. I like
13. is enjoyable but everyone likes to be alone once in a while
14. is one of the most enjoyable aspects of living
15. you learn a lot
16. makes life interesting
17. is alright if I know them
18. helps me to see other peoples points of view and be more understanding
19. is vital at times but not always
20. makes me uncomfortable

EXAMPLES FOR RATING ITEM 6: THE THING I LIKE ABOUT MYSELF IS—

1. hard to figure out
2. that I stick at things
3. my personality. second best: my hair
4. my beautiful hair—also a pleasing personality
5. I have my health and strength

6. really nothing
7. adaptability
8. that most people can get along with me
9. my truthfulness
10. that I am a nice girl
11. self-reliance and ability to adjust to changing circumstances
12. kindness and thoughtfulness to others
13. my naturally curly hair
14. my intelligence
15. being me
16. I consider myself good at most sports and enjoy them
17. that I like to make new friends
18. that I don't have too much trouble getting along with people
19. someday, I'll be able to be a wife and mother
20. my delight with my family and home

EXAMPLES FOR RATING ITEM 7: MY MOTHER AND I—

1. are very close, we enjoy doing things together
2. sometimes quarrel, but on the whole we get along well
3. have never been as close as I wish we could have been
4. don't get along
5. go shopping and work together
6. have a good relationship and enjoy each others company
7. are not as close as my father and I
8. are very different personalities but usually agree
9. do not always get along
10. are close friends and love each other dearly
11. are getting closer to each other
12. are very close companions
13. seem more like sisters
14. are very close friends
15. get along very well, we seem to think and feel the same things
16. do not agree in many respects
17. enjoy discussing things together
18. talk about many things
19. are really too close, having spent our lives in close proximity
20. have the same color eyes

EXAMPLES FOR RATING ITEM 8: WHAT GETS ME INTO TROUBLE IS—

1. talking before considering its effect on other people
2. love

3. my friends
4. my children
5. my mouth and my temper
6. my little sister and me going steady, my parents disapprove
7. speaking what I think
8. eating too much
9. usually my big mouth. As I said I love talking to others and usually I talk too much
10. fighting with my sister
11. I have the tendency to overly criticize others
12. my habit of talking first and thinking later
13. my lack of patience
14. staying out too late
15. doing the wrong thing
16. my inability to face life realistically
17. my attitude sometimes
18. being with the wrong kind of girls
19. I can't control my temper
20. not thinking far enough ahead

EXAMPLES FOR RATING ITEM 9: EDUCATION—

1. is a good thing to have
2. is very interesting and important
3. is a continual thing
4. is important in leading a satisfying life
5. is a good thing
6. is not used by the population to its full advantage
7. continues through a lifetime
8. is an investment which cannot be lost
9. is the best thing if you can afford it
10. means a lot as far as advancement today
11. I think is important now days to get a job
12. is necessary to improve the moral standards of the U.S. and to improve the functioning of democracy
13. which everyone should have and I need
14. is necessary in our society
15. is of prime importance. Wish I'd realized it when I had an opportunity
16. is one of my chief values in life
17. is most important especially for boys
18. has always been important to me
19. would like more in ways
20. is important for both boys and girls

EXAMPLES FOR RATING ITEM 10: WHEN PEOPLE
ARE HELPLESS—

1. I feel I want to help them and do something for them
2. they need someone else to depend upon
3. it is usually their own fault
4. they should be helped by someone else
5. I feel pity and I try to help them as much as I can
6. they need assistance
7. I feel I should try to help them in some way
8. you should always
9. I love to help them
10. they should seek aid from an outside source
11. I try to be of the best service to them
12. they are pitiable
13. they feel dependent and are in need of support
14. I think someone should help them
15. they need all the love and attention they can get
16. others should come to their rescue
17. they deserve help
18. they are fearful
19. there is probably a good reason for it
20. I feel they should be offered help even if they don't ask for it

EXAMPLES FOR RATING ITEM 11: WOMEN ARE
LUCKY BECAUSE—

1. they don't always have to work
2. they are the better sex
3. they can be proud of the fact that after they have raised a family
   they have done their best
4. they wear neat things like heels and lipstick. Also they don't have to
   earn a living
5. well, they aren't
6. they don't have to wear long pants or shave daily
7. they seem to have a special warmth, can give freely
8. they don't work so hard
9. they usually don't have to make the living for the family
10. they are able to have and raise children
11. in some instances they have the advantage over men
12. of their just being a woman
13. they know the joy of raising children
14. they don't have to depend on men for everything now

15. they were chosen to be feminine
16. they can have a wide variety in life if desired
17. they can relax during the day
18. they are so sensitive to things
19. they are shown many courtesies
20. they can experience what it is to have a baby

EXAMPLES FOR RATING ITEM 12: MY FATHER—

1. is perhaps the best person I know
2. finds it very difficult to show himself freely with other people
3. doesn't live with us
4. and I get along just fine
5. is very good to me
6. died before I was born
7. is married to my mother
8. and I never have understood each other
9. is the most wonderful person in the world
10. I never knew
11. loves my mother
12. and I love each other
13. was a large, handsome man
14. my *stept* father—is a very wonderful person. & also my father
15. is so mean
16. is a wonderful person whom I love dearly
17. is a very gentle man
18. is a man whom I admire and respect
19. is conservative, strong and gentle
20. is a kind and understanding person

EXAMPLES FOR RATING ITEM 13: A PREGNANT WOMAN—

1. is most fortunate
2. has the joy of bringing a new life into the world
3. gets very sick sometimes
4. is a study of fulfillment, a continuing marvel at the creation of life
5. looks very awkward to me
6. walks funny
7. during its last stages is miserable
8. should feel proud and content
9. should be careful with herself from the first to the 9th month
10. is always out of shape and mostly sick a lot

11. should be a happy woman but it isn't always the case
12. repells me
13. go to the hospital
14. is usually happy even if she doesn't look very pretty
15. has a baby in her
16. is happy as a rule in spite of the physical discomfort
17. is likely to have emotional extremes
18. seems to take on a freshness and bloom
19. changes looks
20. sometimes looks darling

EXAMPLES FOR RATING ITEM 14: WHEN MY MOTHER SPANKED ME, I—

1. she never spanked me
2. was very angry and my feelings were hurt
3. knew I deserved every sting
4. cried and went into the other room
5. resented it at first
6. didn't always care anyway
7. went off somewhere by myself
8. slapped her
9. sometimes
10. would run to my father
11. hated her and thought she was unfair
12. cried and wished I were big enough to spank her
13. cried and would sulk for a while
14. used to have feelings of hatred toward her
15. was mad and cried
16. got hurt and angry
17. cried when I was a child
18. was mad for a while but soon forgot it
19. couldn't remember
20. gave way to rages as a child

EXAMPLES FOR RATING ITEM 15: A WIFE SHOULD—

1. always try to understand her husband
2. be a good mother and take care of her husband
3. try to be on the same intellectual level as her husband
4. be willing to be the lesser one
5. be a good wife to her husband
6. love her husband and provide a good home for him and their children

7. be a loving companion, a good housekeeper and mother
8. respect her husband's ideas
9. be able to prepare a good meal
10. compromise with her husband
11. take care of her husband
12. be trustful and true to her husband
13. work to please her husband
14. try to make her kids and her husband both happy
15. be very happy
16. always obey her husband
17. retain her own independence to a great extent
18. try to be well-rounded
19. fulfill her duties of marriage
20. not neglect her husband for her children

EXAMPLES FOR RATING ITEM 16: I FEEL SORRY—

1. for friendless people
2. for people who don't know what they want and are merely drifting and wasting
3. for the man reading this paper
4. that I seem to have wasted part of my life
5. for people who can't adjust to life
6. for the poor
7. for the blind, the crippled, and the sick
8. when I do things to others
9. for President Kennedy
10. for a person who is mistreated
11. for students who do not get the advantage of a college ed. if they have the ability
12. for very old people
13. for those people who have hardly anything to eat or who have to wear rags
14. when I cannot help the helpless
15. for people who aren't so lucky as I am
16. for too many people
17. for the unloved and lonely
18. for myself, at times
19. for people who are helpless and can't help themselves
20. for my sister

EXAMPLES FOR RATING ITEM 17: WHEN I AM NERVOUS, I—

1. lose my temper
2. get mad and upset
3. sometimes do things I won't normally do
4. I try my best to control myself
5. tend to overeat
6. get depressed afterward
7. sit down and relax
8. smoke quite a bit
9. am often crabby and want to be left alone for a while
10. start crying easily
11. am snappish
12. usually develop pains in my stomach
13. flush and hands tremble
14. cannot get settled to one thing
15. try to analyze why I am which sometimes makes it better
16. get excited
17. eat off my lipstick
18. try not to show it
19. work in my garden
20. bite my nails or eat fattening food

EXAMPLES FOR RATING ITEM 18: A WOMAN'S BODY—

1. is very useful
2. is frequently ugly
3. part of her total composition
4. is a thing to marvel at
5. should be well proportioned
6. should be kept clean and made as attractive as possible
7. can be lovely or otherwise
8. is precious and private only to her husband
9. is very delicate and should be a symbol of true art
10. is much stronger than a man's
11. is her pride
12. should always be well, clean at all times
13. is good
14. is very sensitive
15. something she should not be ashamed of
16. can be a real asset
17. is clean

18. is a temple of God
19. is not always most important
20. is made to have children

EXAMPLES FOR RATING ITEM 19: WHEN A CHILD WON'T JOIN IN GROUP ACTIVITIES—

1. one should try to discover why he will not
2. you should encourage him or her to join
3. it may be because he feels he isn't welcome
4. she's usually dull
5. he's not well
6. he should be left alone temporarily
7. he has emotional problems and needs professional help
8. there has got to be a good reason
9. he is a child that don't care to be around a lot of people
10. he should be encouraged but not forced to do so
11. it is often because he is self-conscious and he is afraid he won't be accepted
12. she is missing a lot of fun
13. he may not feel well
14. don't pressure him
15. it may indicate something is wrong
16. he is usually afraid or shy
17. it is the result of the child's shyness
18. it is because they may not have something he likes
19. I feel there must be something wrong with him and I try to help
20. he needs those activities available that he is interested in

EXAMPLES FOR RATING ITEM 20: MEN ARE LUCKY BECAUSE—

1. they ask a girl instead of having to be asked
2. they don't get pregnant
3. they can do more things with less criticism
4. they usually get their way in anything
5. they have an easy way to go
6. they can act as they wish without getting into trouble
7. they can make something of themselves
8. they do not have to keep house and have children
9. they don't seem to vary so much in their moods
10. they don't have to have children
11. they have strong will power and control a woman's world

12. they can do what they want
13. they do not have any conflict around career and marriage
14. they have much more social freedom
15. they don't have to worry about feeding the baby
16. they have an easier adjustment to daily details, easier organization
17. they are the Boss of the family
18. they can fall in love with women
19. their independent travel is more acceptable
20. they don't have the full responsibility of raising a family

EXAMPLES FOR RATING ITEM 21: WHEN THEY TALKED ABOUT SEX, I—

1. shyed over to the other side of the room
2. think that's all they have on their mind
3. wondered what the real reason was
4. listened eagerly
5. got mad when they talk about it
6. didn't contribute, I just listened
7. enjoy it very much
8. listened but did not join in
9. didn't have much to say
10. entered the talk if I had some opinion on the topic
11. didn't understand what they meant
12. joined in gayly
13. got scared at first
14. listened and added something once in a while
15. was interested in their viewpoint
16. don't mind listening
17. don't mind if the discussion is intelligent
18. listened as did every other student
19. blush and am embarrassed
20. was curious to know more

EXAMPLES FOR RATING ITEM 22: AT TIMES SHE WORRIED ABOUT—

1. how she would get home
2. all of us children
3. doing the wrong thing
4. her husband and children and how to pay the monthly bills
5. my not doing the things she thought I should be doing
6. little things

7. tests that were going to be taken
8. her physical condition
9. about the opposite sex
10. her personal relations with her closest friend
11. many things
12. getting pregnant before marriage
13. pleasing her husband
14. what the future held in store for her
15. how she looked when she went out
16. her homemaking capabilities
17. my depression
18. she always worries about me
19. my drive to do so much
20. doing the best possible job

EXAMPLES FOR RATING ITEM 23: I AM—

1. I think, a good wife and daughter
2. a young girl who is trying to find a purpose in life
3. lucky to have three little girls
4. what I am
5. very fortunate in many respects
6. a type of perfectionist
7. not as emotionally stable as I wish I were
8. always good
9. interested in folk music
10. anxious for the next year and a half to pass so Larry and I can get married
11. really at times quite stupid
12. glad to be a woman and mother
13. very unsure of myself
14. very much concerned about the welfare of others
15. fortunate to have found such fulfillment in my marriage
16. an average ordinary teenager
17. very fortunate to receive a good education
18. in love with life
19. a sophomore in college
20. sleepy this early in the morning

EXAMPLES FOR RATING ITEM 24: A WOMAN FEELS GOOD WHEN—

1. everything is coming along fine
2. she is complimented on her achievements or her looks

3. she feels her appearance is neat
4. she feels she is being treated as a woman should be treated
5. she is cherished and giving love to someone
6. she knows she looks good or when she receives a compliment
7. she prepared something and is complimented on it
8. a man tells her how pretty she is
9. when she knows she is wanted and there is a purpose in life for her
10. she has done something good
11. she is *free*
12. she is with the person she loves most
13. her efforts are appreciated
14. she is loved and respected
15. she knows she is appreciated
16. she has a family of her own
17. she's admired
18. she did her tasks well
19. she is with her "honey"
20. she knows her family is happy

EXAMPLES FOR RATING ITEM 25: MY MAIN PROBLEM IS—

1. how to make ends meet
2. a dislike for research questionaires
3. am I in love or not?
4. lack of time to accomplish everything
5. trying to pin down some concrete goals
6. that I fight too much with my steady
7. dieting
8. that I love to sleep late
9. keeping my patience
10. not being able to see boys and my stepfather
11. making close friends in a new city
12. planning menus
13. I try too hard to be accepted by those I like
14. being an ideal companion and mother
15. not enough time for all the activities I'd like to do
16. my visual handicap
17. my husband's drinking
18. helping my son develop
19. selfishness
20. solving my problems

EXAMPLES FOR RATING ITEM 26: WHENEVER SHE WAS WITH HER MOTHER, SHE—

1. felt like a baby
2. did anything she wanted when she wanted
3. laughed a lot
4. watched what she said and did
5. enjoyed herself
6. learned many things
7. laughed and talked
8. was pleasant and happy
9. was safe
10. seemed different than she did in school
11. was a very good girl
12. talked of their pleasant trip together
13. would never mind her
14. became a little girl again
15. used to fight
16. tended to be quieter
17. looked extremely happy
18. seemed to be having a wonderful time
19. enjoyed talking to her
20. was quite happy and felt loved and secure

EXAMPLES FOR RATING ITEM 27: THE WORST THING ABOUT BEING A WOMAN—

1. is having to watch out for her name
2. limited opportunity
3. is you can't travel as free as men
4. having kids
5. is dusting and doing dishes
6. is catching the right man
7. is not being able to play football. I love football
8. is that you can't do some things you might like to do
9. is to know you cannot have children
10. is being teased
11. is when you have no friends
12. is not being able to have the same chances as a man
13. is trying to act like one
14. having to wear a girdle
15. comes once a month
16. is that many of her tasks are repetitious and monotonous

17. is being faced with routine work
18. is not being able to go out by yourself
19. is getting along with other women
20. is being looked down on by men

EXAMPLES FOR RATING ITEM 28: A GOOD MOTHER—

1. loves her husband as much as her children
2. should be loving and above all understanding to her child
3. is one who is loved by her family no matter what
4. worry about her childrens
5. is very nice
6. cares for her baby
7. is a difficult term
8. I am, I think
9. always takes good care of her family
10. has family interest as well as outside interest
11. goes without things to give her children things
12. should trust her child
13. helps her children grow to be self-confident and independent
14. disciplines as well as loves her children
15. is interested always in her home and family's welfare
16. is what I got
17. is concerned about her role as wife and mother
18. is a desired goal
19. should always stay with her children
20. is the most important thing to children

EXAMPLES FOR RATING ITEM 29: SOMETIMES SHE WISHED THAT—

1. she could do better than she does
2. she would have a child
3. I would talk more
4. she was more attractive and intelligent
5. she could always be so happy
6. she wasn't in nursing
7. she could spend a year traveling to see all her old friends
8. she was already through high school and college
9. I'll be happy
10. she was dead during hours of labor
11. she could be more energetic
12. she were home and married

13. she had a rich man
14. she had a dryer
15. she could work instead of going to school
16. she had been born a man
17. she were in Paris
18. everything would go perfect
19. she could leave home
20. decisions were not so hard to make

EXAMPLES FOR RATING ITEM 30: WHEN I AM WITH A MAN—

1. I feel jittery
2. I enjoy his company and hope he enjoys mine
3. I am just as comfortable as with a woman
4. I try to be myself and not put on a show for him
5. I like to look nice and be interesting
6. I mostly try to control myself
7. I expect to go some place nice, not just the show
8. I enjoy male conversation
9. I feel like I am in heaven
10. love, I am very happy
11. I feel sexy
12. I have an enjoyable evening
13. I mind my manners
14. I feel prettier
15. for the first few times I am tense
16. it makes me feel more womanly
17. I think of being loved
18. I am a woman
19. I like to listen
20. I seldom know what to say

EXAMPLES FOR RATING ITEM 31: WHEN SHE THOUGHT OF HER MOTHER, SHE—

1. felt good inside
2. wondered what she was cooking
3. loves her
4. thought of "homey" things
5. sometimes wished things were as they used to be
6. remembered how gentle she was
7. usually got mad

8. always talked about her in glowing terms
9. longed to be with her
10. remembered when they had done everything together
11. thought of a precious love
12. usually had very tender feelings
13. laughed
14. burst into tears
15. had fond memories
16. she thought of all the love she was given
17. thought of a wonderful person
18. remembers when she was young
19. became aggressive
20. remembered what a great friend she was

EXAMPLES FOR RATING ITEM 32: IF I CAN'T GET WHAT I WANT—

1. I get it someway
2. I keep at it till I do
3. I try not to want it
4. I accept alternatives
5. I put up a fight
6. I cry and get mad
7. I keep trying in the right way
8. I work until I get it if I decide it is really important
9. I try to do something else but first I'll try all possibilities in regard to what I want first
10. I just get upset
11. I don't care that much
12. I try for something better
13. I forget about it or try to substitute in rare cases
14. I have a temper tantrum
15. I make the best of it
16. I try to get it all the more
17. I cry or convince myself I don't want it
18. I either give up or wait until things work out
19. I try and save money and get it for myself
20. I usually get mad but then I think it over and I'm okay again

EXAMPLES FOR RATING ITEM 33: USUALLY SHE FELT THAT SEX—

1. was a secret
2. was just another chore

3. is beautiful and a part of love
4. was gratifying
5. was a pleasant experience
6. was not important
7. wasn't nothing
8. was something bad
9. was a normal function and discussing it should not be taboo
10. was something dirty until she married and found out it was something very fulfilling
11. should not be talked about before marriage
12. OK at times
13. does her wrong
14. was over done on the screen
15. was a beautiful expression of deep love
16. was a normal part of the human experience
17. was horrible outside of marriage
18. was nasty
19. only nature
20. is important to some and unimportant to others

EXAMPLES FOR RATING ITEM 34: FOR A WOMAN A CAREER IS—

1. acceptable in our American society
2. a very good job
3. a substitute for real needs of love and being loved
4. very important, but a man's is more so since he's to be the bread winner
5. only one phase of married life
6. desirable if she is not married
7. something she did herself
8. a great thing to have
9. essential in time of need
10. good, but I feel that it should be combined with marriage; children
11. second choice
12. secondary to her husband and family
13. a very good thing
14. a hair stylist
15. a must
16. sometimes bad and sometimes good
17. a means of fulfillment
18. a way of finding self-identity
19. alright
20. as good as marriage

EXAMPLES FOR RATING ITEM 35: MY CONSCIENCE BOTHERS ME IF—

1. I waste time foolishly
2. I think I am trying to fool myself
3. I don't do work I know I'm supposed to do
4. I let it
5. I've done something wrong or if I've neglected to do something I should have done
6. I feel that I am not doing my best
7. I do wrong
8. I am untruthful or hurt others feelings
9. I do things or say things I shouldn't have said or did
10. I do something I know I shouldn't
11. I have been mean to someone
12. I have been selfish
13. my conscience doesn't bother me ever
14. I do not do what I believe in or if I neglect my son
15. I don't tell the truth
16. I do something that shouldn't be done
17. I mess around with a boy
18. I steal or do something bad
19. I don't study
20. I hurt another human being

EXAMPLES FOR RATING ITEM 36: A WOMAN SHOULD ALWAYS—

1. be pleasant and attractive
2. serve her family foremost
3. respect herself and others will follow suit
4. try to look her best
5. help her husband solve the family problems
6. keep herself clean
7. try to look nice
8. look after her family
9. value her womanhood
10. be gracious
11. care about her appearance
12. take care of herself and keep herself attractive
13. find self-fulfillment in some form
14. remain feminine
15. be thinking

16. command respect from a male
17. do what she feels is right
18. be neat and tidy
19. try to look, act, and feel as a woman
20. remember that she is one

SCORING KEYS

SCORING KEY FOR ITEM 1: RAISING A FAMILY—

1. I-4, 2
2. I-3/4, 1
3. I-4, 4
4. I-4, 8   This is also similar to the last example under I-3, 7. We interpret this response to convey mutuality rather than seeing husband as helper.
5. I-4, 3   Using Rule 3, "wonderful" would be I-3, 1, but "enriching" is I-4, 3.
6. Delta, 1
7. I-4, 6
8. I-3, 7
9. I-4/5, 5
10. I-3/4, 1   Using Rule 3, "wonderful" would be I-3, 1, but "rewarding" is I-3/4, 1.
11. Delta, 2
12. I-4, 5
13. I-3/4, 8   This might be seen as falling in I-4, 8, but it sounds more like the husband is seen as helper rather than as partner.
14. I-3, 9   This response does not sound like the personal, affective evaluation in category I-3/4, 11.
15. I-3/4, 7   However, this comes close to one example in I-4, 1.
16. I-4, 2   Using Rule 3, "challenging opportunity" would be I-3/4, 2, but "sincere privilege" is I-4, 2.
17. I-3, 1
18. I-3, 6
19. I-4, 8   Using Rule 3, "big job" would be I-3, 4, but "cooperation from both parents" is I-4, 8.
20. I-3/4, 2

SCORING KEY FOR ITEM 2: MOST MEN THINK THAT WOMEN—

1. I-3, 6
2. I-3/4, 6
3. I-3/4, 1
4. I-4/5, 5
5. I-3, 1   This is a composite of Delta/3, 2 and I-3, 1. Both are frequent. Rate up.
6. I-2, 1
7. I-3, 9
8. I-4, 10
9. Delta, 2
10. I-3, 7
11. I-4/5, 3

12. Rule 5
13. I-3, 11
14. Delta, 2
15. I-3/4, 3 This response resembles those in I-4, 2, but the two thoughts are just strung together. They do not contrast

directly enough to generate a higher level of complexity.

16. I-3, 16
17. I-5, 2
18. I-3/4, 7
19. I-3, 1
20. I-3/4, 2

SCORING KEY FOR ITEM 3: WHEN THEY AVOIDED ME—

1. I-3/4, 11
2. Delta, 2
3. I-4, 7
4. I-5, 1
5. Delta/3, 1
6. I-3/4, 9
7. I-2, 1
8. I-3/4, 2 The category I-3, 1 describes the same thing more externally.
9. I-4/5, 4
10. I-3/4, 9
11. I-4, 1

12. I-3/4, 5
13. I-3, 6
14. I-4, 2
15. I-4, 2 Use Rule 3.
16. I-4, UC This is similar to I-3/4, 2 but more introspective and self-critical.
17. I-4, 4
18. I-3/4, 6
19. I-3, 9
20. I-3, 7 This is close to one example in I-3/4, 3.

SCORING KEY FOR ITEM 4: IF MY MOTHER—

1. I-3, 1
2. I-4, 1
3. I-4, 13
4. I-3, 4
5. Delta, 6
6. I-3, 6
7. I-3, 18 This could also be classed I-3, 12.
8. I-4, 9
9. I-4, 4
10. I-3, 19
11. I-4, 2

12. I-3, 9
13. I-4/5, 1
14. I-3/4, 12
15. I-3, 5
16. I-3, 10
17. 1-4/5, UC This response is similar to those in I-4, 3, but "revitalize" has additional connotations of personal change.
18. I-3/4, 5
19. I-3, 2
20. I-3/4, 6

SCORING KEY FOR ITEM 5: BEING WITH
OTHER PEOPLE—

1. Delta, 1
2. I-3, 5
3. I-3, 8
4. I-4, 1   Use Rule 3.
5. Delta/3, 2
6. I-4/5, 4
7. I-3/4, 7   Use Rule 3.
8. I-2, 1
9. I-3, 1
10. I-5, 1   Use Rule 3.

11. I-3/4, 8
12. I-3, 2
13. I-4/5, 1
14. I-4, 3
15. I-3, 4
16. I-4, 1
17. I-3, 9
18. I-4, 7
19. I-3/4, 3
20. I-3/4, 4

SCORING KEY FOR ITEM 6: THE THING I LIKE
ABOUT MYSELF IS—

1. I-3/4, 11
2. I-4, 8
3. I-3, 1   Use Rule 3.
4. I-3, 1   Use Rule 3. This is a composite of I-3, 1 and Delta/3, 1, both popular. Rate up.
5. I-3, 13
6. I-2, 1
7. I-4, 4
8. Delta, 3
9. I-3/4, 6

10. Delta, 2
11. I-4, 5   This could also be I-4, 4.
12. I-3, 2
13. Delta/3, 1
14. I-3/4, 9
15. I-3, 16
16. I-4, 7
17. I-3/4, 2
18. I-3/4, 1
19. I-3, 10
20. I-3/4, 5

SCORING KEY FOR ITEM 7: MY MOTHER AND I—

1. I-3, 4   Use Rule 3. I-3, 4 is a less frequent category than I-3, 1.
2. I-3/4, 6
3. I-4, 4
4. Delta, 1
5. Delta/3, 1
6. I-4, 1   Use Rule 3.
7. I-3/4, 7
8. I-4/5, 1
9. I-3/4, 3

10. I-3/4, 1   Use Rule 3.
11. I-4, 3
12. I-3/4, 1
13. I-3/4, 7
14. I-3/4, 1
15. I-4, 11
16. I-4, 8
17. I-3, 4
18. I-3, 5
19. I-4/5, 4
20. I-3, 7

SCORING KEY FOR ITEM 8: WHAT GETS ME INTO TROUBLE IS—

1. I-4/5, 3
2. I-3, 13
3. I-2, 1
4. I-2, 1
5. I-3, 4   Use Rule 3. "My temper" would be in I-3, 4, the less frequent category.
6. I-3, 6
7. I-4, 2
8. I-3, 10
9. I-3/4, UC This is similar to the last example discussed in

the introduction to the I-3/4 level.
10. I-2, 2
11. I-5, 2
12. I-4, 5
13. I-4, 3
14. I-3, 8
15. Delta/3, 1
16. I-4/5, 1
17. I-3, 5
18. Delta, 1
19. I-4, 6
20. I-4, 4

SCORING KEY FOR ITEM 9: EDUCATION—

1. Delta, 1
2. I-3/4, 6
3. I-4/5, 1
4. I-4/5, 2
5. Delta, 1
6. I-4, 4
7. I-4/5, 1
8. I-3/4, 5
9. I-3, 8
10. I-3/4, 2
11. I-3, UC Similar to I-3, 5 and to Delta, 2. Rated up be-

cause of time perspective implied in "now days."
12. I-4, 1
13. I-3, 4   Use Rule 3.
14. I-3, 2
15. I-4, 14   Use Rule 3.
16. I-4, 13
17. I-3, 3
18. I-3, 1
19. Delta/3, 1
20. I-4, 10

SCORING KEY FOR ITEM 10: WHEN PEOPLE ARE HELPLESS—

1. I-3/4, 1
2. I-3, 4
3. I-3/4, 11
4. I-3, 2
5. I-3/4, 8   Use Rule 3.
6. I-3, 3
7. I-4, 2
8. Rule 5

9. I-3, 1
10. I-3/4, 4
11. I-3, 1
12. I-3/4, 8
13. I-4, 11 or I-4, 4
14. I-3, 2
15. I-3, 3
16. 1-3, 2

17. I-4, 3   19. I-4, 17
18. I-3/4, 5   20. I-3/4, 2

SCORING KEY FOR ITEM 11: WOMEN ARE LUCKY BECAUSE—

1. Delta/3, 1
2. I-3, 13
3. I-4, 4
4. I-3/4, 12   Use Rule 3.
5. I-3/4, 14
6. I-3, 6
7. I-4, 13   This response might be classed I-4/5, 4 if the two ideas are considered to be very different. They certainly are not contrasting ideas, however, and are more like a repetition.
8. Delta, 1
9. I-3/4, 12
10. I-3, 3   Using Rule 3, "they are able to raise children" would be in I-3, 3, the less frequent category.
11. I-3/4, 8
12. I-3, 1
13. I-4, 4
14. I-4, 10
15. I-3, 16
16. I-4, 9
17. I-3, 9
18. I-4, 13
19. I-3/4, 7
20. I-4, 1

SCORING KEY FOR ITEM 12: MY FATHER—

1. I-3/4, 1
2. I-4, 4
3. I-3, 18
4. I-3, 6
5. I-2, 1
6. I-3/4, 14
7. Delta, 2
8. I-4, 9
9. I-3/4, 1
10. I-3/4, 13
11. I-3/4, 4
12. I-3/4, UC   This response differs from those in I-3, 4 because of the two-way interaction.
13. I-3, 9
14. I-3, 1
15. I-2, 2
16. I-4, 1
17. I-3/4, 7
18. I-4, 8
19. I-4, 3
20. I-3/4, 7   Use Rule 3. "Kind" is in the less frequent category.

SCORING KEY FOR ITEM 13: A PREGNANT WOMAN—

1. I-3, 1
2. I-4/5, 1
3. I-2, 3
4. I-4/5, 1
5. Delta, 7
6. I-3, 10   This response fits Delta, 7 equally well and is called I-3 by default.

7. I-3, 6 This is similar to I-2, 4, but I-2 Ss do not think in terms of stages of pregnancy.
8. I-4, 4
9. I-3, 2
10. I-3, 10 Use Rule 3.
11. I-5, 3
12. I-3/4, 11
13. I-3, 9
14. I-4, 2
15. I-2, 1
16. I-3/4, 7
17. I-4, 5
18. I-4, 1
19. I-3, 10
20. I-3/4, 1

SCORING KEY FOR ITEM 14: WHEN MY MOTHER SPANKED ME, I—

1. I-3, 14
2. I-4/5, 3
3. I-4, 1
4. I-3/4, 12 Use Rule 3.
5. I-4, 3
6. I-3/4, 9
7. I-3/4, 12
8. Delta, 1
9. I-3, UC This could be interpreted as giving frequency, thus called I-3, UC, or as a fragmentary response, I-3, Rule 5.
10. I-3, 12
11. I-4, 2 Use Rule 3.
12. I-4, 5 Use Rule 3.
13. I-3/4, 2 Use Rule 3.
14. I-4, 7 This has a little more distance from the negative feelings than I-3/4, 7.
15. I-3/4, 6 Use Rule 3.
16. I-4/5, 3
17. I-3/4, 1
18. I-4, 8
19. I-4, 16
20. I-3/4, 3

SCORING KEY FOR ITEM 15: A WIFE SHOULD—

1. I-3/4, 5
2. I-3, 8 This could also be I-3, 7.
3. I-3/4, 8
4. I-4, 11
5. I-2, 1
6. I-3/4, 3 Use Rule 3.
7. I-3/4, 7 Using Rule 3, "good housekeeper and mother" would be I-3, 8, but "loving companion" is I-3/4, 7.
8. I-4, 3
9. I-3, 11
10. I-4, 2 But it could also be called I-4, 1.
11. I-3, 7
12. I-3/4, 11 Use Rule 3.
13. I-3/4, 1
14. I-3/4, 2
15. I-2, 3
16. I-3, 1
17. I-4/5, 1
18. I-4, 14
19. I-3, 6 The category I-4, 8 has more implication of a commitment to fulfill.
20. I-4, 9

SCORING KEY FOR ITEM 16: I FEEL SORRY—

1. I-3/4, 6
2. I-4, 1
3. Delta, 5
4. I-4, 14
5. I-4, 4
6. I-3, 2
7. I-3, 1
8. I-3/4, 17
9. Delta, 1
10. I-4, 11
11. I-4, 9
12. I-3, 3
13. I-3, 2
14. I-3/4, 4
15. I-3/4, 1
16. I-3, 6
17. I-3/4, 8   This could also be I-3/4, 6.
18. I-3, 12
19. I-3, 7
20. Delta, 1

SCORING KEY FOR ITEM 17: WHEN I AM NERVOUS, I—

1. Delta, 1
2. Delta/3, 1   Use Rule 3.
3. I-4, 3
4. I-4, 8
5. I-3/4, 8
6. I-4, 4
7. I-3, 7
8. I-3, 2
9. I-3/4, 16   Use Rule 3. I-3/4, 16 is a less frequent category than I-3/4, 14.
10. I-3/4, 12
11. I-3/4, 14
12. I-3/4, 1
13. I-3, 1
14. I-4, 1
15. I-4, 11
16. I-3, 10
17. I-3/4, 3   This could also be put at I-3, 3, but those are more stereotyped ideas of what to do when nervous.
18. I-3/4, 18
19. I-3/4, 11
20. I-3, 3   This could also be I-3, 2.

SCORING KEY FOR ITEM 18: A WOMAN'S BODY—

1. I-3/4, 8
2. I-3, 9
3. I-4, 14
4. I-3/4, 7
5. I-3/4, 1
6. I-3, 1   Use Rule 3. Delta/3, 1 and I-3, 1 are equally frequent categories. Rate up.
7. I-3/4, 2
8. I-3/4, 10
9. I-4, 4   Use Rule 3.
10. I-3/4, 15
11. I-3, 7
12. I-3, UC   This combines a response from the popular category Delta/3, 1 with "well," an unusual one. However, it lacks the connotations of personal effort in I-4, 2.

13. I-2, 3
14. I-3, 4
15. I-4, 13
16. I-3, 6

17. I-2, 3
18. I-3/4, 5
19. I-4, 15
20. I-4, 8

SCORING KEY FOR ITEM 19: WHEN A CHILD WON'T JOIN IN GROUP ACTIVITIES—

1. I-3/4, 1
2. I-3, 1
3. I-3/4, 7
4. I-3, 8
5. I-2, 1
6. I-3/4, 9
7. I-4, 4   Use Rule 3.
8. I-4, 1
9. I-3, 6
10. I-4, 6
11. I-3/4, 7   This combines the ideas of I-3/4, 6, 7, and 8, but they are very similar and the total does not seem more complex.
12. I-3, 10
13. Delta/3, 2

14. I-3, 2
15. Delta/3, 1
16. I-3/4, 6   Use Rule 3.
17. I-3, 7
18. I-3, 5   This is closer to I-3, 5 than to I-3/4, 12 because of the concrete reference to things.
19. I-3/4, UC   The first clause is similar to Delta/3, 1 but more personalized. The second clause is similar to I-3, 1, but "help" does not presuppose, as do the responses in I-3, 1, that the outcome must be joining up.
20. I-4/5, 3

SCORING KEY FOR ITEM 20: MEN ARE LUCKY BECAUSE—

1. I-3/4, 3
2. I-3, 17
3. I-4, 8
4. Delta, 3
5. I-3, 9
6. Delta, 2   It could be put in I-3, 14.
7. I-4, 12
8. Delta/3, 1   Use Rule 3. Delta/3, 1 is a less frequent category than I-3, 10.
9. I-4, 9
10. Delta/3, 1

11. I-4, UC   The second clause is similar to I-4, 2. The first clause is an I-4 idea.
12. I-3, 13
13. I-4/5, 5
14. I-4, 5
15. I-4, 7
16. I-5, 1
17. I-3/4, 1
18. Delta/3, 2
19. I-4, 5
20. I-4, 7

SCORING KEY FOR ITEM 21: WHEN THEY TALKED ABOUT SEX, I—

1. I-3, 3
2. I-3/4, 14
3. I-5, 1
4. I-3/4, 5
5. I-2, 1
6. I-4, 6
7. Delta/3, 3
8. I-4, 6
9. I-3/4, 13
10. I-4, 8
11. I-3/4, 8
12. I-3, 1
13. Delta/3, 4
14. I-4, 5
15. I-3/4, 7
16. I-3/4, 3
17. I-4, 7
18. I-4, 9
19. I-3/4, 2   Use Rule 3.
20. I-3/4, 6

SCORING KEY FOR ITEM 22: AT TIMES SHE WORRIED ABOUT—

1. I-3, 11
2. I-3, 1
3. I-3/4, 8
4. I-3, 8   Using Rule 3, I-3, 8 is the less frequent category.
5. I-4, 6
6. I-2, 1
7. I-3, 7
8. I-3, 5
9. Delta, 2
10. I-4/5, 4
11. I-3, 9
12. Delta, 1
13. I-3/4, 3
14. I-4, 2
15. I-3/4, 1
16. I-4, 9
17. I-3/4, 11
18. Delta/3, 1
19. I-4, 4
20. I-4, 5

SCORING KEY FOR ITEM 23: I AM—

1. I-3, 2
2. I-4, 9
3. I-3, 12
4. I-3, 19
5. I-3, 14
6. I-4, 16
7. I-4, 12
8. I-2, 1
9. I-4, 2
10. I-3/4, 4
11. Delta, 2
12. I-3, 15
13. I-3/4, 14
14. I-4, 3
15. I-4/5, 1
16. I-4, 7
17. I-4, 4
18. I-4, 1
19. I-3, 1
20. I-3, 4

SCORING KEY FOR ITEM 24: A WOMAN FEELS
GOOD WHEN—

1. Delta/3, 2
2. I-4/5, 1
3. I-3/4, 9
4. I-3/4, 6
5. I-4, 6
6. I-3/4, 9   Use Rule 3.
7. I-4, 1
8. I-3, 4
9. I-4, UC   Having a purpose in life is more like I-4, 3 than like I-3/4, 11.
10. I-3, 11
11. Delta/3, 1
12. I-3/4, 2
13. I-4, 1
14. I-3/4, 6   Use Rule 3.
15. I-3/4, 5
16. I-3, 8
17. I-3/4, 5
18. I-3, 11
19. Delta, 4   This could be called I-3/4, 2, but we interpret "honey" as a category, not a relation or expression of affection.
20. I-3, 10

SCORING KEY FOR ITEM 25: MY MAIN PROBLEM IS—

1. I-3, 3
2. Delta, 4
3. I-3/4, 2
4. I-4, 6
5. I-5, 1
6. I-3, 6   This response is not like I-2, 1, where fighting has the connotation of being punished for it.
7. I-3, 1
8. I-3, 15
9. I-4, 13
10. Delta, 2
11. I-3, 10
12. I-3, 5
13. I-5, 2
14. I-3, 4
15. I-4, 6
16. I-3/4, 3
17. I-4, 2
18. I-4, 1
19. I-3/4, 18
20. I-3/4, 16

SCORING KEY FOR ITEM 26: WHENEVER SHE WAS
WITH HER MOTHER, SHE—

1. I-3/4, 8
2. I-4, 13
3. I-3, 4
4. I-3, 10
5. I-3, 2
6. I-3/4, 15
7. I-3, 4   Use Rule 3.
8. I-3, 12   Use Rule 3.
9. I-3, 5
10. I-4, 8
11. Delta, 1
12. I-4, 9
13. Delta, 2
14. I-4/5, 3
15. Delta/3, 1
16. I-3/4, 10

17. I-3/4, 1   19. I-4, 1
18. I-4/5, 6   20. I-3/4, 2   Use Rule 3.

SCORING KEY FOR ITEM 27: THE WORST THING ABOUT BEING A WOMAN—

1.	I-3, 10	11.	I-3/4, 17
2.	I-4, 2	12.	I-4, 2
3.	I-4, 1	13.	I-3/4, 10
4.	I-2, 1	14.	I-3, 2
5.	I-3, 5	15.	I-3, 3
6.	I-3, 12	16.	I-4, 7
7.	I-3/4, 8	17.	I-4, 7
8.	I-3, 8	18.	I-3/4, 9
9.	I-3/4, 16	19.	I-3/4, 19
10.	I-3/4, 13	20.	I-3/4, 12

SCORING KEY FOR ITEM 28: A GOOD MOTHER—

1. I-4, 4
2. I-3, 2
3. I-4, 12
4. I-3, 6
5. I-2, 2
6. I-3/4, 5
7. I-3/4, 18
8. I-3, 18
9. I-3, 3
10. I-4, 5
11. I-3/4, 11   We put this in I-3/4, 11, though it is more concrete. It differs from I-2, 3 because it makes self-sacrifice explicit.
12. Delta, 1
13. I-4/5, 2
14. I-4, 1
15. I-4, 10
16. I-3, 18
17. I-4, 3
18. I-3/4, 17
19. Delta, 3
20. I-3, 9

SCORING KEY FOR ITEM 29: SOMETIMES SHE WISHED THAT—

1.	I-3/4, 9	9.	Delta, 1
2.	I-3/4, 3	10.	I-3/4, 11
3.	I-3, 10	11.	I-4, 7
4.	I-3/4, 9 Use Rule 3.	12.	I-3/4, 1 Use Rule 3.
5.	I-4, 3	13.	I-3, 1
6.	I-3/4, 8	14.	I-3, 1
7.	I-4/5, 3	15.	I-3/4, 8
8.	Delta/3, 4	16.	Delta/3, 2

17. I-3, 5
18. I-3/4, 4

19. Delta/3, 3
20. I-4, 1

SCORING KEY FOR ITEM 30: WHEN I AM WITH A MAN—

1. I-3/4, 3
2. I-4, 1
3. I-4/5, 3
4. I-4/5, 4
5. I-3/4, 16   Use Rule 3.
6. Delta, 3
7. I-3, 14
8. I-4, 3
9. I-3/4, 4
10. I-3/4, 12

11. I-2, 1
12. I-3/4, 1
13. I-3, 9
14. I-3/4, 8
15. I-4, 6
16. I-3/4, 7
17. I-3/4, 19
18. I-3, 11
19. I-3, 7
20. I-3/4, 14

SCORING KEY FOR ITEM 31: WHEN SHE THOUGHT OF HER MOTHER, SHE—

1. I-3, 2
2. I-3, 4
3. I-2, 2
4. I-4, 12
5. I-4, 11
6. I-3/4, 6
7. I-3, 10
8. I-3, 5
9. I-3/4, 14
10. I-4, 7   This is similar to I-3/4, 10, but there is more time perspective.
11. I-3/4, 4
12. I-4, 5

13. Delta, 2
14. Delta/3, 1
15. I-3/4, 1
16. I-3/4, 4   This response is also similar to I-4, 3. Many responses to this item are somewhat ambiguous in meaning because of the "she."
17. I-3/4, 5
18. I-3/4, 11
19. I-3/4, UC   While similar to I-3, 10, the idea seems a bit more differentiated.
20. I-4, 6

SCORING KEY FOR ITEM 32: IF I CAN'T GET WHAT I WANT—

1. Delta, 3
2. I-3/4, 2
3. I-4/5, 1
4. I-4, 7
5. Delta, 2

6. I-2, 2   Using Rule 3, I-2, 2 is less frequent than Delta, 1.
7. I-3/4, 2
8. I-4, 3
9. I-4, 4

10. Delta, 1
11. Delta/3, 1
12. I-3/4, 3
13. I-4, 5
14. Delta/3, 5
15. I-3/4, 6

16. I-3, 4
17. I-4, 5
18. I-4, 5
19. I-3, 6
20. I-3/4, 7

SCORING KEY FOR ITEM 33: USUALLY SHE FELT THAT SEX—

1. I-3/4, 1
2. I-4, 6
3. I-4, 7   Use Rule 3.
4. I-4, 4
5. I-4, 3
6. I-3, 3
7. Delta/3, 2
8. I-2, 1
9. I-3/4, 3   Use Rule 3.
10. I-4/5, 2

11. I-3/4, 1
12. I-3/4, 13
13. Delta, 2
14. I-3/4, 5
15. I-4/5, 1
16. I-4, 1
17. I-3, 2
18. Delta/3, 4
19. I-3, 1
20. I-4, 11

SCORING KEY FOR ITEM 34: FOR A WOMAN A CAREER IS—

1. I-3/4, 19
2. I-2, 1
3. I-4/5, 3
4. I-3/4, 16   Use Rule 3.
5. I-3/4, 15
6. I-3/4, 1
7. I-3/4, 17
8. I-3, 2
9. I-3/4, 3
10. I-4, 3

11. I-3, 5
12. I-4, 1
13. Delta/3, 1
14. Delta/3, 4
15. I-3, 4
16. I-3/4, 7
17. I-4, 12
18. I-4/5, 5
19. I-3, 1
20. I-3, 6

SCORING KEY FOR ITEM 35: MY CONSCIENCE BOTHERS ME IF—

1. I-3/4, 15
2. I-4, 12
3. I-3/4, 15
4. Delta, 3
5. I-3/4, 15   Use Rule 3.

6. I-4, 11
7. Delta/3, 1
8. I-3/4, 1   Use Rule 3.
9. I-3, 2   This could also be I-3, 4.

10. I-3/4, 3
11. I-3, 3
12. I-4, 2
13. Delta, 2
14. I-4/5, 3   Use Rule 3.
15. I-3, 1
16. I-3, 2

17. I-2, 1
18. Delta, 1   Using Rule 3, Delta, 1 is less popular than Delta/3, 1.
19. I-3, 7
20. I-3/4, 1

SCORING KEY FOR ITEM 36: A WOMAN SHOULD ALWAYS—

1. I-3, 2   Use Rule 3. "Pleasant" is in the less frequent category.
2. I-3/4, 13
3. I-4, 13
4. I-3/4, 2
5. I-4, 14
6. I-2, 1
7. Delta/3, 1
8. Delta/3, 2
9. I-5, 1
10. I-3/4, 4

11. I-4, 1
12. Delta, 4   Use Rule 3. Delta, 4 is a less frequent category.
13. I-4/5, 1
14. I-3/4, 1
15. Delta, 3
16. I-3/4, 8
17. I-3/4, 11
18. I-3, 1
19. I-5, 4
20. I-4, 2

APPENDIX **D**

Examples and Scoring Keys for Practice Total Protocol Ratings

EXAMPLES

PRACTICE PROTOCOL 1

1. Raising a family—is one of the most important things in life
2. Most men think that women—are persons who should be loved and care for by them
3. When they avoided me—it means I wasn't good enough for job or work they want done

4. If my mother—disaproved of something I did it would hurt me very much
5. Being with other people—is lots of fun if you know how to handle your behavior
6. The thing I like about myself is—I try to the best of my ability to do things right
7. My mother and I—went shopping last Saturday for new clothes
8. What gets me into trouble is—my big mouth and misunderstanding
9. Education—is the most important thing in life you should get as must as you can these days
10. When people are helpless—I want to help them the best I know how
11. Women are lucky because—they can bring life into the world and many other things which they are good for
12. My father—is a man who tries to help others
13. A pregnant woman—is very happy and content with life and has a glow about her which makes other people happy
14. When my mother spanked me, I—accept, because I know I did something wrong
15. A wife should—be as pleasant as possible when things go wrong
16. I feel sorry—for people are helpless and arent able to work things out for their selves
17. When I am nervous, I—can't do the things I want too
18. A woman's body—is a wonnderful part of nature and should be taken care of very time it is possible. It also is the most beautiful thing in the world.
19. When a child won't join in group activities—there is something wrong and it should be looked into by the parents
20. Men are lucky because—I think are equal to everyone. I don't see where they are lucky
21. When they talked about sex, I—join in to see if I can learn more about for it is a very important subject and you can the right things by talking about it
22. At times she worried about—the way she looks or acts in public
23. I am—very interest in cosmetology and want to learn all I can about it
24. A woman feels good when—a man tells her she is beautiful
25. My main problem is—not understanding difficult problems
26. Whenever she was with her mother, she—was just like an angle
27. The worst thing about being a woman—is always being hurt by someone you love
28. A good mother—is one that understands her childrens problems
29. Sometimes she wished that—she could be like someone else

30. When I am with a man—I want him to feel like a man and not a mouse
31. When she thought of her mother, she—was very unhappy
32. If I can't get what I want—I will do with out
33. Usually she felt that sex—was something terrible, but about understood it. She didn't think so and found the true meaning
34. For a woman a career is—something she can fall back on when in trouble
35. My conscience bothers me if—I do something or don't understand things
36. A woman should always—act like a women and do the best to her life something if she is married she should make her husband feel he is wanted

PRACTICE PROTOCOL 2

1. Raising a family—
2. Most men think that women—is trouble
3. When they avoided me—
4. If my mother—
5. Being with other people—is fun
6. The thing I like about myself is—getting boys
7. My mother and I—do not get along with each other
8. What gets me into trouble is—boys
9. Education—is what I hate
10. When people are helpless—I like to help them
11. Women are lucky because—
12. My father—is a very lucky man
13. A pregnant woman—will wait
14. When my mother spanked me, I—feel sorry for myself
15. A wife should—
16. I feel sorry—for my sisters
17. When I am nervous, I—tell lies
18. A woman's body—be long to her husband
19. When a child won't join in group activities—she paining a runaway
20. Men are lucky because—
21. When they talked about sex, I—like it
22. At times she worried about—
23. I am—a sex maniac
24. A woman feels good when—she is with her man
25. My main problem is—sex
26. Whenever she was with her mother, she—

27. The worst thing about being a woman—is boy will not leave you along
28. A good mother—should be at home was her children
29. Sometimes she wished that—she was a boy
30. When I am with a man—I feel good
31. When she thought of her mother, she—
32. If I can't get what I want—I fight for it
33. Usually she felt that sex—is good
34. For a woman a career is—sex
35. My conscience bothers me if—
36. A woman should always—be with her husband

PRACTICE PROTOCOL 3

1. Raising a family—is wounderful
2. Most men think that women—is silly
3. When they avoided me—I feill left out and a lone
4. If my mother—said to do something I do it
5. Being with other people—is a good thing, you done feel left out
6. The thing I like about myself is—my ways
7. My mother and I—are very close
8. What gets me into trouble is—my mouth
9. Education—is a good, and we drop ou going to need it
10. When people are helpless—I love to help them
11. Women are lucky because—they can raise a family
12. My father—is very good to me
13. A pregnant woman—is blessed, because some women want baby and is not blessed with them
14. When my mother spanked me, I—obey then
15. A wife should—be a good, faithful wife
16. I feel sorry—for one who can't help themself
17. When I am nervous, I—bit me nail
18. A woman's body—is her main problem, keeping it in shape
19. When a child won't join in group activities—it is something wrong with him
20. Men are lucky because—they can married and raise a family
21. When they talked about sex, I—don't like to be around
22. At times she worried about—my weight
23. I am—nice, and easy to get alone with
24. A woman feels good when—a man tell her she look nice
25. My main problem is—weight
26. Whenever she was with her mother, she—so small
27. The worst thing about being a woman—is being loud

28. A good mother—is the best kind
29. Sometimes she wished that—she could have children
30. When I am with a man—I enjoy it
31. When she thought of her mother, she—would cry
32. If I can't get what I want—get mad some time
33. Usually she felt that sex—is terrible
34. For a woman a career is—excited
35. My conscience bothers me if—I do wrong
36. A woman should always—be neat

PRACTICE PROTOCOL 4

1. Raising a family—requires considerable investment
2. Most men think that women—are an attractive necessity
3. When they avoided me—it aroused my curiosity
4. If my mother—had understood, how would I have been different
5. Being with other people—is fun
6. The thing I like about myself is—my stubborness
7. My mother and I—are incompatible
8. What gets me into trouble is—lack of tact and impulsiveness
9. Education—is an experience which results ultimately in change
10. When people are helpless—I want to help them
11. Women are lucky because—they are often endowed with the ability to be feminine and charming
12. My father—was an alcoholic
13. A pregnant woman—has some difficulty in getting about
14. When my mother spanked me, I—rebelled
15. A wife should—play many roles
16. I feel sorry—for those who have received so little affection & understanding
17. When I am nervous, I—want to escape
18. A woman's body—should be accepted by its owner
19. When a child won't join in group activities—perhaps he has emotional problems and needs professional help
20. Men are lucky because—they can be so independent
21. When they talked about sex, I—was interested
22. At times she worried about—all sorts of things
23. I am—proud to be a woman
24. A woman feels good when—she is flattered
25. My main problem is—depression
26. Whenever she was with her mother, she—was uncomfortable
27. The worst thing about being a woman—is the occasional necessity to be dependent

28. A good mother—has the ability to accept herself and the good & bad in her child
29. Sometimes she wished that—she were dead
30. When I am with a man—I am comfortable
31. When she thought of her mother, she—wrote her a letter
32. If I can't get what I want—then perhaps I should reevaluate the situation
33. Usually she felt that sex—was just a positive part of life
34. For a woman a career is—rewarding
35. My conscience bothers me if—I display an unnecessary lack of tact
36. A woman should always—abide to the rules at least to a reasonable extent

PRACTICE PROTOCOL 5

1. Raising a family—no. children
2. Most men think that women—crize
3. When they avoided me—feel funny
4. If my mother—if my Mother was a fat women I will be happy girl
5. Being with other people—make me look funny
6. The thing I like about myself is—I am a very nice Peson
7. My mother and I—go. Place together
8. What gets me into trouble is—is when I tell lie
9. Education—is go to Schools
10. When people are helpless—there are nurses
11. Women are lucky because—do good thing
12. My father—is a hard in Man
13. A pregnant woman—I dont no
14. When my mother spanked me, I—I get Sick
15. A wife should—be good to her hus.
16. I feel sorry—because I am tall
17. When I am nervous, I—Sick
18. A woman's body—is her Person thing
19. When a child won't join in group activities—I was
20. Men are lucky because—I becaus werk
21. When they talked about sex, I—I walk a away
22. At times she worried about—at time she with me
23. I am—a girl
24. A woman feels good when—a her man is with her
25. My main problem is—get up in the Morning
26. Whenever she was with her mother, she—was a Nice Person
27. The worst thing about being a woman—is you have'nt be women
28. A good mother—is a woman. let Raising

29. Sometimes she wished that—I could Keep her Baby
30. When I am with a man—I feel good
31. When she thought of her mother, she—is when she get sick
32. If I can't get what I want—I dont want it
33. Usually she felt that sex—none
34. For a woman a career is—is a good women
35. My conscience bothers me if—none
36. A woman should always—Keep her self clean

PRACTICE PROTOCOL 6

1. Raising a family—is joy and test of awakening acknowledge of one's self
2. Most men think that women—are people
3. When they avoided me—I assumed a poker face and later analyzed the incident
4. If my mother—were nearer we would enjoy moments of companionship
5. Being with other people—is wonderfully refreshing if there is communication
6. The thing I like about myself is—the occasionally refreshing varieties of mood and the moments I feel release and accomplishment through intense study of some interest
7. My mother and I—developed our appreciation and values of each other during my college days
8. What gets me into trouble is—procrastination
9. Education—is vitally growth enriching when one has his own awakening to/for it
10. When people are helpless—the greatest effort is to find a beginning avenue in which they climb out of this state
11. Women are lucky because—they have the opportunity to be creative physically and mentally and because warmth of expression is more acceptable in men than women
12. My father—has greatly enriched and influenced my life by his immense common sense logic and faith in the person
13. A pregnant woman—is nauseated!
14. When my mother spanked me, I—would feel "broken" I do not remember physical punishment from her
15. A wife should—sensitively develop her independent and common role in the family unit and outside
16. I feel sorry—for those who have rejected any hope of finding life purposeful and enlivening
17. When I am nervous, I—seek physical activity, or solitude, or a novel

18. A woman's body—assumes significance or background depending on her mood or the present situation
19. When a child won't join in group activities—he must continue to enjoy his interests and be permitted to activate any later interest for companionship
20. Men are lucky because—they have an easier adjustment to daily details, easier organization
21. When they talked about sex, I—participated
22. At times she worried about—becoming dull, apathetic
23. I am—woman living and creating life
24. A woman feels good when—she is giving and feeling its acceptance
25. My main problem is—procrastination
26. Whenever she was with her mother, she—was grateful for the mother's presence
27. The worst thing about being a woman—is being feminine and highly individual
28. A good mother—sees the *child* and as Whitman, trains him to grow away from her
29. Sometimes she wished that—an ocean and snow slopes were nearer
30. When I am with a man—I am delighted
31. When she thought of her mother, she—admired her ability to so well satisfy the father's needs
32. If I can't get what I want—I'm likely to be frustrated and spend a brief period of adjustment
33. Usually she felt that sex—was interesting and expressive
34. For a woman a career is—most desirable if she finds her interests there
35. My conscience bothers me if—allow myself to enhance a story by extra details
36. A woman should always—enjoy life

PRACTICE PROTOCOL 7

1. Raising a family—is a big responsibility
2. Most men think that women—are weaker and sometimes they are very bossy
3. When they avoided me—I could not find them
4. If my mother—is here with me, I will be very happy
5. Being with other people—is a nuisance to me
6. The thing I like about myself is—to be quiet
7. My mother and I—understand each other very well
8. What gets me into trouble is—misunderstanding
9. Education—is a must for everyone

10. When people are helpless—they are also hopeless
11. Women are lucky because—when they are young, they are taken care by parents, then by her husband and later on by her children when they are old
12. My father—is now so far away from me
13. A pregnant woman—needs a lot of rest and preparation for the coming event
14. When my mother spanked me, I—hated her
15. A wife should—obey her husband
16. I feel sorry—for the blind, the crippled and the sick
17. When I am nervous, I—want to stay alone
18. A woman's body—has about the same functions and structures as man's body
19. When a child won't join in group activities—there must be a reason for it
20. Men are lucky because—they are stronger
21. When they talked about sex, I—can join them without much difficulty
22. At times she worried about—nothing
23. I am—not happy now as when I was home in my country
24. A woman feels good when—she is flattered
25. My main problem is—a language barrier
26. Whenever she was with her mother, she—always argues
27. The worst thing about being a woman—is that she always talks too much
28. A good mother—is very hard to achieve
29. Sometimes she wished that—she were a grown-up so she could drive a car
30. When I am with a man—I feel uneasy
31. When she thought of her mother, she—many times resented her
32. If I can't get what I want—I'll try again
33. Usually she felt that sex—is a normal event of a life cycle
34. For a woman a career is—not necessary
35. My conscience bothers me if—I knew I have done something wrong
36. A woman should always—be patient

PRACTICE PROTOCOL 8

1. Raising a family—is very nice
2. Most men think that women—are very lovly
3. When they avoided me—it makes me mad
4. If my mother—go to Chicgo she is good to take me
5. Being with other people—makes me feel wonderful

6. The thing I like about myself is—I'm a very nice young lady
7. My mother and I—look very much alike
8. What gets me into trouble is—Boys there so bad
9. Education—[deleted—gave amount]
10. When people are helpless—I like to help them.
11. Women are lucky because—they don't have to work
12. My father—and my brother looks alike
13. A pregnant woman—is good to have a little baby
14. When my mother spanked me, I—just cry
15. A wife should—always stay at home and cook
16. I feel sorry—because I didn't go to Chicgo
17. When I am nervous, I—just can't hold anything
18. A woman's body—is very nice
19. When a child won't join in group activities—
20. Men are lucky because—there are nice looking women
21. When they talked about sex, I—just leave
22. At times she worried about—my father
23. I am—not going to go home now
24. A woman feels good when—there isn't anything wrong
25. My main problem is—that I don't fool around with boys
26. Whenever she was with her mother, she—didn't act right
27. The worst thing about being a woman—because you have children
28. A good mother—is very nice
29. Sometimes she wished that—you had somebody to love
30. When I am with a man—we just talk about thing
31. When she thought of her mother, she—didn't care
32. If I can't get what I want—I just don't get it
33. Usually she felt that sex—is nature
34. For a woman a career is—very nice for them
35. My conscience bothers me if—I dont have no one talk to
36. A woman should always—be neat and clean

PRACTICE PROTOCOL 9

1. Raising a family—is a complicated full time job
2. Most men think that women—are not quite so competent in careers outside the home
3. When they avoided me—I felt slighted
4. If my mother—would go out more she would be happier
5. Being with other people—is uncomfortable at times
6. The thing I like about myself is—I like other people
7. My mother and I—aren't very much alike

8. What gets me into trouble is—I expect people to be more than they are

9. Education—is a lifelong project

10. When people are helpless—they are usually afraid

11. Women are lucky because—they can express emotions more openly than men

12. My father—is perhaps the best person I know

13. A pregnant woman—should be very happy

14. When my mother spanked me, I—was afraid of her losing respect or love for me more than I was afraid of being spanked

15. A wife should—make her husband happy and then be happy because he is

16. I feel sorry—that people distrust each other

17. When I am nervous, I—get headaches

18. A woman's body—should be respected, as any human body should

19. When a child won't join in group activities—perhaps the child is afraid

20. Men are lucky because—they enjoy more freedom in what is considered proper for them to do

21. When they talked about sex, I—hoped they would keep the conversation on a level above the smutty

22. At times she worried about—her financial security

23. I am—not the person I would like to be

24. A woman feels good when—she is appreciated by men she respects

25. My main problem is—I don't have the courage to be the way I think I should be

26. Whenever she was with her mother, she—was very much afraid of being improper in her manners

27. The worst thing about being a woman—is that women are sometimes very cruel when they are afraid

28. A good mother—puts a childs welfare above the ideas of comfort

29. Sometimes she wished that—she was able to do just one thing really well

30. When I am with a man—I am interested in him as a person rather than entertainment for the evening

31. When she thought of her mother, she—felt sad that her mother had not had an easier life

32. If I can't get what I want—I usually substitute something else I want and try for that

33. Usually she felt that sex—is not a dirty thing but is misused by most people

34. For a woman a career is—not always possible but good because she

can make full use of her talents if she doesn't restrict herself to being a wife

35. My conscience bothers me if—I disappoint those whom I respect
36. A woman should always—deserve the respect she expects

PRACTICE PROTOCOL 10

1. Raising a family—requires a tremendous amount of responsibility
2. Most men think that women—are inferior
3. When they avoided me—i began to take a second look at myself
4. If my mother—only knew
5. Being with other people—is a stimulating experience
6. The thing I like about myself is—I'm not conceited
7. My mother and I—are related
8. What gets me into trouble is—my locquacity
9. Education—is necessary to make a place for oneself in the business world
10. When people are helpless—they become scared
11. Women are lucky because—they are female
12. My father—married my mother
13. A pregnant woman—is going to have a baby
14. When my mother spanked me, I—rebelled
15. A wife should—be understanding
16. I feel sorry—for my instructors
17. When I am nervous, I—start to giggle
18. A woman's body—is quite distinguishable from a man's
19. When a child won't join in group activities—he is shy and insecure
20. Men are lucky because—they wear the pants
21. When they talked about sex, I—listened
22. At times she worried about—offending others
23. I am—, you are, he is
24. A woman feels good when—someone complements her
25. My main problem is—overweight
26. Whenever she was with her mother, she—behaved
27. The worst thing about being a woman—is not a "durn" thing
28. A good mother—is 1 who is understanding and helpfull
29. Sometimes she wished that—she was young again
30. When I am with a man—"I can't say no"
31. When she thought of her mother, she—was happy
32. If I can't get what I want—I substitute or try again later
33. Usually she felt that sex—was wonderful
34. For a woman a career is—great, great, great, until she marries

35. My conscience bothers me if—I've done something I know I shouldn't do
36. A woman should always—be feminine

PRACTICE PROTOCOL 11

1. Raising a family—is a great deal of work & worry but there are compensating factors particularly when the children become adults
2. Most men think that women—have little or no practical or financial sense
3. When they avoided me—it probably was for a good reason and it's up to me to find the reason & correct the fault if it seemed pertinent
4. If my mother—were living, I could be much more appreciative
5. Being with other people—is stimulating
6. The thing I like about myself is—that I can always see the other "side"
7. My mother and I—seemed to have little in common
8. What gets me into trouble is—talking too much
9. Education—is important but not necessarily an end in itself
10. When people are helpless—they frequently need help toward self help
11. Women are lucky because—they can be mothers
12. My father—was a very understanding person
13. A pregnant woman—needs to be active
14. When my mother spanked me, I—resented it event when deserved
15. A wife should—be a help to her husband
16. I feel sorry—for those who can never be objective toward their problems
17. When I am nervous, I—usually escape by means of an absorbing book
18. A woman's body—should be kept healthy & reasonably attractive
19. When a child won't join in group activities—he may feel very unwanted & rejected
20. Men are lucky because—their horizons can be much less limited
21. When they talked about sex, I—participate in the discussion unless it has a "smutty" tinge when I leave as inconspicuously as possible
22. At times she worried about—finances & security
23. I am—glad to be a woman & mother
24. A woman feels good when—she is admired
25. My main problem is—not being able to project self confidence
26. Whenever she was with her mother, she—was deferential
27. The worst thing about being a woman—is when others feel it necessarily follows that she is unpractical & incompetent

28. A good mother—allows her children choices which gradually widen in scope commesurate with their age
29. Sometimes she wished that—people could accept you regardless of appearances
30. When I am with a man—I usual enjoy the broader outlook they usually bring to a situation
31. When she thought of her mother, she—realized how much help she had been to her
32. If I can't get what I want—I accept alternatives
33. Usually she felt that sex—proper & right in its place but over rated
34. For a woman a career is—not always necessary but can be very rewarding
35. My conscience bothers me if—I do that which is contrary to what I was taught as a child
36. A woman should always—keep an alert mind

PRACTICE PROTOCOL 12

1. Raising a family—you should have money
2. Most men think that women—are fools
3. When they avoided me—I would avoided them
4. If my mother—told me to come in at a certained time I would
5. Being with other people—Sometime will get you in trouble
6. The thing I like about myself is—I'm nobody's fool
7. My mother and I—were talking
8. What gets me into trouble is—Myself
9. Education—is where it's at
10. When people are helpless—because they can't help it
11. Women are lucky because—they have Sence
12. My father—is very nice to me
13. A pregnant woman—Should take it easy
14. When my mother spanked me, I—don't get spanked
15. A wife should—not trip on her husband
16. I feel sorry—for some people
17. When I am nervous, I—do anything but kill myself
18. A woman's body—is neat
19. When a child won't join in group activities—He's pitilfle
20. Men are lucky because—they have sence
21. When they talked about sex, I—get mad
22. At times she worried about—him pretty much
23. I am—who I am
24. A woman feels good when—she has the right man
25. My main problem is—getting up in the morning

26. Whenever she was with her mother, she—would act stuck-up
27. The worst thing about being a woman—is you go through so much trouble
28. A good mother—is a Mother to be like mine
29. Sometimes she wished that—I would get up
30. When I am with a man—I act very nice if I like him
31. When she thought of her mother, she—drop her head
32. If I can't get what I want—I don't want anything
33. Usually she felt that sex—disagree (Why) I don't I the question
34. For a woman a career is—
35. My conscience bothers me if—I tell a lie
36. A woman should always—try to be neat

PRACTICE PROTOCOL 13

1. Raising a family—is a big job
2. Most men think that women—need to get out and get a job
3. When they avoided me—I just walk away
4. If my mother—was well she would get a job
5. Being with other people—makes me feel good
6. The thing I like about myself is—that I have pretty brown eyes
7. My mother and I—don't look the same
8. What gets me into trouble is—not speaking at the right time
9. Education—is a very important thing to have
10. When people are helpless—they want you to do mostly everything for them
11. Women are lucky because—they don't have to do as much hard work like men folks
12. My father—and I look just alike
13. A pregnant woman—never should wear tight clothing
14. When my mother spanked me, I—cry and get mad
15. A wife should—nice to her husband
16. I feel sorry—for my mother
17. When I am nervous, I—drop things or make mistakes
18. A woman's body—should always be clean
19. When a child won't join in group activities—he should sat down and talk better
20. Men are lucky because—they can't have babies
21. When they talked about sex, I—listens very close
22. At times she worried about—her hair
23. I am—very cute

24. A woman feels good when—she gets a nice complainment
25. My main problem is—trying to be a mother and father
26. Whenever she was with her mother, she—would walk in front of her
27. The worst thing about being a woman—is having children
28. A good mother—would never leave her Kids
29. Sometimes she wished that—she was dead
30. When I am with a man—I feel comfort
31. When she thought of her mother, she—cried
32. If I can't get what I want—I will take it
33. Usually she felt that sex—is foolish
34. For a woman a career is—being a nurse
35. My conscience bothers me if—I do something wrong
36. A woman should always—carry her self in a lady like fashion

PRACTICE PROTOCOL 14

1. Raising a family—is the most exhaustive yet rewarding experience in which man can involve himself
2. Most men think that women—are poor drivers, gossips, and complainers
3. When they avoided me—I became very introspective and imaginative as to the reasons
4. If my mother—were in better health I would be happier
5. Being with other people—is exhilirating but usually leaves me exhausted. Generally I gain from this experience
6. The thing I like about myself is—my ability to adapt to almost any situation and my capacity for change and improvement
7. My mother and I—did not have a good relationship until I was divorced and living at home
8. What gets me into trouble is—the fact that I accept people too quickly, that is I tend to exchange confidences or believe all a person tells me when I first meet him
9. Education—is the key word to success in living and adapting to life situations
10. When people are helpless—physically I am full of pity and nausea, mental helplessness (retarded ect.) reduces me to tears and tends to give me a leaning toward belief in mercy killing, tho my morality will never accept it
11. Women are lucky because—they are never directly involved in War thru the Armed Services
12. My father—is a source of concern to me because of preoccupation with perfection and his desire to control the situation

13. A pregnant woman—is some one I would like to be in the indefinite future
14. When my mother spanked me, I—don't remember
15. A wife should—love her husband both his physical and spiritual person and do her best to make him comfortable. When he is emotionally secure he will in turn be making her happy
16. I feel sorry—for myself when I think of the mistakes I've made of a major nature which were unnecessary
17. When I am nervous, I—get headaches, an upset stomach, and talkative
18. A woman's body—was created to give and promote life to child and to provide comfort for man
19. When a child won't join in group activities—he shouldn't be forced; but one should seek out the reason and give help if necessary. It is not unhealthy to want to do things individually
20. Men are lucky because—they are not restricted from activities on the basis of sex. That is they can go where they want when they want
21. When they talked about sex, I—listen sometimes but generally I remove myself as I don't feel the subject is the "ice break" kind—I prefer to discuss with my doctor or clergyman.
22. At times she worried about—my ability to manage money. My mother thinks I am a spend thrift
23. I am—in love in an adult or "real" way and have never be happier or had such a sense of belonging or fulfillment
24. A woman feels good when—she knows she is attractive to a man and for me specifically when I feel I am contributing to someone els's happiness
25. My main problem is—letting others decide major problems for me— being unable to trust my own judgment
26. Whenever she was with her mother, she—was irritated. In my grandmothers last years she and my mother were often at odds. I knew they loved each other deeply and it hurt me to see them treat each other that way
27. The worst thing about being a woman—is the probability of "female trouble" and the social restrictions imposed by society (i.e. not travelling alone etc.)
28. A good mother—is demonstrative and always willing to help her children become independent individuals
29. Sometimes she wished that—she had finished college. My mother, when she is blue, feels her lack of college degree makes her inferior
30. When I am with a man—I like to feel I have his attention and admiration

31. When she thought of her mother, she—cried at my grandmothers funeral my mother wished she had spent more time with her mother
32. If I can't get what I want—I try to substitute or else rationalize the desire away
33. Usually she felt that sex—should be a private relationship
34. For a woman a career is—as impt. as for a man. Career simply means finding a task the fulfilling of which is individualy rewarding
35. My conscience bothers me if—I do less than my best
36. A woman should always—be neat in her personal dress and convey general warmth toward humanity

PRACTICE PROTOCOL 15

1. Raising a family—would be nice
2. Most men think that women—are sexy thing in world
3. When they avoided me—I think that something is wrong with me
4. If my mother—spank me I don't what I would do to her
5. Being with other people—are fun sometimes
6. The thing I like about myself is—that I nice to other people
7. My mother and I—are very close
8. What gets me into trouble is—my mother charge's account
9. Education—I hate school
10. When people are helpless—I would like to help them
11. Women are lucky because—they are married and living a happy life
12. My father—is a ploiceman
13. A pregnant woman—eat alot
14. When my mother spanked me, I—would have the slighted idea because I don't get them
15. A wife should—not cheat on her husband
16. I feel sorry—for who can't help there self
17. When I am nervous, I—bite my finger nail off
18. A woman's body—is her pride and joy
19. When a child won't join in group activities—something must be wrong
20. Men are lucky because—they are married to pretty wife
21. When they talked about sex, I—rather not be around
22. At times she worried about—weither I am going to get to work on time are not
23. I am—[deleted—gave age] and have 2 boys [deleted—gave names]
24. A woman feels good when—she is alone with her man
25. My main problem is—I spend to much money
26. Whenever she was with her mother, she—always felt like a baby
27. The worst thing about being a woman—is she have to many childrens

28. A good mother—is a good wife
29. Sometimes she wished that—she had never had any children
30. When I am with a man—I feel okay
31. When she thought of her mother, she—thought of her whole family
32. If I can't get what I want—I rather not worried about it
33. Usually she felt that sex—was a game
34. For a woman a career is—a wonderful thing
35. My conscience bothers me if—I can't have my own way
36. A woman should always—be neat and clean

PRACTICE PROTOCOL 16

1. Raising a family—would be fun
2. Most men think that women—are attractive
3. When they avoided me—I sought out others
4. If my mother—were here, she'd like the school
5. Being with other people—is a rewarding experience
6. The thing I like about myself is—my easygoing manner
7. My mother and I—get along very well
8. What gets me into trouble is—occasionally saying more than I should on a subject
9. Education—is a most rewarding and enriching experience
10. When people are helpless—they are likely to be unhappy
11. Women are lucky because—they can be wives and mothers
12. My father—was a wonderful person
13. A pregnant woman—walked down the street
14. When my mother spanked me, I—cried
15. A wife should—interest herself in her home and husband, but enrich her own outside interests as well
16. I feel sorry—for sick people
17. When I am nervous, I—feel jittery
18. A woman's body—can be a beautiful thing
19. When a child won't join in group activities—there could be many reasons for this behavior
20. Men are lucky because—They are encouraged to achieve to their ultimate ability
21. When they talked about sex, I—listened
22. At times she worried about—herself
23. I am—happy for her
24. A woman feels good when—she is loved
25. My main problem is—getting the work done
26. Whenever she was with her mother, she—was a different person

27. The worst thing about being a woman—is that not much is expected of you other than marriage and raising a family
28. A good mother—loves and understands her children
29. Sometimes she wished that—she could travel, too
30. When I am with a man—who is an interesting person, I enjoy listening to him talk
31. When she thought of her mother, she—felt comforted
32. If I can't get what I want—, I seek other goals until this one can be more obtainable
33. Usually she felt that sex—discussions should be held in mature groups
34. For a woman a career is—a beneficial and enriching thing
35. My conscience bothers me if—I've hurt someone
36. A woman should always—be feminine in most ways

PRACTICE PROTOCOL 17

1. Raising a family—is an eventual occupation of a wife usually
2. Most men think that women—are easily figured out
3. When they avoided me—I in return killed them with kindness
4. If my mother—were old then I'd be older than I am
5. Being with other people—is nice but a twosome is nicer
6. The thing I like about myself is—my changable nature; you never know how I will react
7. My mother and I—enjoy each other's company for lunch every now and then
8. What gets me into trouble is—the opposite sex, one in particular
9. Education—is broading to the mind
10. When people are helpless—someone should help them
11. Women are lucky because—they are females and at least have a chance to be feminine
12. My father—the greatest man alive
13. A pregnant woman—is about to become a mother
14. When my mother spanked me, I—usually got a little red on the behind
15. A wife should—never forget when to be a mistress to her husband
16. I feel sorry—for old maids
17. When I am nervous, I—usually eat something
18. A woman's body—is one of her best resources
19. When a child won't join in group activities—perhaps he likes to have a few minutes to himself
20. Men are lucky because—they don't have to bother with hair rollers when they go to bed at night

21. When they talked about sex, I—listened and learned
22. At times she worried about—being popular
23. I am—glad I'm a female
24. A woman feels good when—she gets married
25. My main problem is—I'm such a clown all the time
26. Whenever she was with her mother, she—acted more like a lady
27. The worst thing about being a woman—is our monthly problem
28. A good mother—is first a wife and then a mother and her children are secondarily to the husband
29. Sometimes she wished that—she had no problems
30. When I am with a man—I enjoy being treated like a woman
31. When she thought of her mother, she—thought of her father and the two together
32. If I can't get what I want—I work harder and do a better snow job and I eventually do get it
33. Usually she felt that sex—was interesting but that there is a time and a place for everything
34. For a woman a career is—fine until she is married
35. My conscience bothers me if—I have to lie to someone who trusts me
36. A woman should always—remember that she is first, last and always a female!

PRACTICE PROTOCOL 18

1. Raising a family—isn't so bad when you haven't got too many children
2. Most men think that women—are fools
3. When they avoided me—I just went on my merry way
4. If my mother—wouldn't work so hard she probably wouldn't be so weak now
5. Being with other people—sometimes makes me nervous
6. The thing I like about myself is—I Love children
7. My mother and I—aren't very close
8. What gets me into trouble is—sometimes I talk to much
9. Education—is a very important thing
10. When people are helpless—you are sopposed to try and help them
11. Women are lucky because—they don't have to work as hard as some men
12. My father—is a hard working man
13. A pregnant woman—is sometimes evil
14. When my mother spanked me, I—cried
15. A wife should—Keep things clean

16. I feel sorry—for sick people
17. When I am nervous, I—bite my nails
18. A woman's body—is not to be felt on
19. When a child won't join in group activities—don't make him
20. Men are lucky because—they don't have baby's
21. When they talked about sex, I—shut up
22. At times she worried about—me
23. I am—[deleted—gave age]
24. A woman feels good when—she's under a cool shower
25. My main problem is—responsibility
26. Whenever she was with her mother, she—kept quiet
27. The worst thing about being a woman—suffering so many pains
28. A good mother—shares her children troubles
29. Sometimes she wished that—she was in another town
30. When I am with a man—I get shy
31. When she thought of her mother, she—was very proud
32. If I can't get what I want—get mad
33. Usually she felt that sex—was shameful
34. For a woman a career is—something good
35. My conscience bothers me if—I do something wrong
36. A woman should always—try to keep her pride

PRACTICE PROTOCOL 19

1. Raising a family—means giving more than 50-50 and more than just love but caring, friendship, ect.
2. Most men think that women—are feminer and hope that they are ladies.
3. When they avoided me—it can possibly mean they are snubbing me or more likely that there is no attraction of opposite sex there.
4. If my mother—were any different, I should hope not.
5. Being with other people—gives me pleasure and enjoyment in sharing their company.
6. The thing I like about myself is—that I believe I'm alikable person and hope that others can get along with me.
7. My mother and I—are very close and yet I am still allowed my independence and voice.
8. What gets me into trouble is—my temper at the rare times that it flares.
9. Education—is one of my major goals and I hope to complete it.
10. When people are helpless—I feel a need to help and wish that I'm doing some good.
11. Women are lucky because—they are women.

12. My father—is an authorative person but a very "dear" one and I love him.

13. A pregnant woman—is woman that is beautiful for she is conceiving the future.

14. When my mother spanked me, I—felt mad and ashamed and at times unjustified but many times back when is when my temper got the best of me.

15. A wife should—be a wife and all the things it entails and hope to have a blessed union.

16. I feel sorry—for people who have had no love and people who do not know how to *care* for others and that special someone.

17. When I am nervous, I—have a habit of eating or dancing this is a time I should get busy doing something with my hands.

18. A woman's body—is sacred and beautiful and meant only for a special someone to fully entail.

19. When a child won't join in group activities—someone ought to try and talk with them and encourage them to because we, at sometime, have felt shy.

20. Men are lucky because—they are men.

21. When they talked about sex, I—can talk about it freely and openly if the person I'm talking with is taking a mature attitude.

22. At times she worried about—my temper and what I would become, but not as much now.

23. I am—me that has grown up and become a woman I hope in the right way.

24. A woman feels good when—she is loved and feels beautiful or feels she is doing good for others.

25. My main problem is—my shyness which can cause me to be awkward at times and be introverted.

26. Whenever she was with her mother, she—(my grandmother) would always say something of her childhood days I could tease her about.

27. The worst thing about being a woman—is the dissipointments and hurts received in the process of growing up.

28. A good mother—is one who nutures her children (if any) loves her husband to the utmost of her ability.

29. Sometimes she wished that—I would stop throwing temper tantrums

30. When I am with a man—I feel secure and wonderful if I enjoy his company and like him.

31. When she thought of her mother, she—always thought that she was behind in her letter writing or how she was doing.

32. If I can't get what I want—I have to learn to do without or find somemeans to obtain it by my own means.

33. Usually she felt that sex—was natural and beautiful and should be preserved till sacred marriage
34. For a woman a career is—making a place in the world, furthing her knowledge and understanding of people, and socializing.
35. My conscience bothers me if—I really do something wrong to another person or if I have to every so often borrow money from my folks.
36. A woman should always—be a woman and a lady.

PRACTICE PROTOCOL 20

1. Raising a family—is fun.
2. Most men think that women—are stupid.
3. When they avoided me—I avoided them.
4. If my mother—is wrong she is sorry
5. Being with other people—is fun.
6. The thing I like about myself is—I try to be fair.
7. My mother and I—are just like sister's.
8. What gets me into trouble is—too much food.
9. Education—is fine.
10. When people are helpless—they are sick.
11. Women are lucky because—they are fine.
12. My father—is dead.
13. A pregnant woman—is real fat.
14. When my mother spanked me, I—needed it.
15. A wife should—be gay.
16. I feel sorry—for you.
17. When I am nervous, I—am not feeling good.
18. A woman's body—is her pride.
19. When a child won't join in group activities—they don't feel well.
20. Men are lucky because—do as they please.
21. When they talked about sex, I—didn't say anything
22. At times she worried about—you.
23. I am—fine.
24. A woman feels good when—she is praised.
25. My main problem is—you.
26. Whenever she was with her mother, she—looked fine.
27. The worst thing about being a woman—is not being praised.
28. A good mother—is alway's alert
29. Sometimes she wished that—I wasn't as large as she.
30. When I am with a man—I try to be nice.
31. When she thought of her mother, she—thought of you.
32. If I can't get what I want—I just try something else.

33. Usually she felt that sex—was warm.
34. For a woman a career is—fine.
35. My conscience bothers me if—I do wrong.
36. A woman should always—be praised.

SCORING KEYS

ITEM RATINGS AND TPR FOR PRACTICE PROTOCOL 1

ITEM RATINGS

1. I-4, 1	13. I-4/5, 4	25. I-4, 7
2. I-4, 1	14. I-3/4, 11	26. Δ, 3
3. I-4/5, 5	15. I-4, UC	27. I-4, UC
4. I-4, 12	16. I-3, 7	28. I-4, 10
5. I-3/4, UC	17. I-4, UC	29. I-3/4, 10
6. I-3/4, UC	18. I-3/4, UC	30. I-4, 5
7. Δ/3, 1	19. I-3/4, 1	31. I-3/4, 15
8. I-3/4, UC	20. I-4, 17	32. I-3, 1
9. I-3/4, 1	21. I-4, 2	33. I-4/5, 2
10. I-3/4, 1	22. I-3/4, UC	34. I-3/4, 3
11. I-4, 3	23. I-4, 2	35. I-3, UC
12. I-3/4, 7	24. I-3, 4	36. I-5, 4

EXPLANATION OF RATINGS

5. Contingent response, not I-4 because it deals with behavior rather than feelings.
6. This resembles I-4, 8 except for the idea that there is one right thing to do.
8. Seems to reflect difficulties in communication.
9. This could also be I-3/4, 7.
17. This resembles I-4, 2.
18. Combination of I-3 and I-3/4 ideas.
22. This seems closer to I-3/4, 5 than to the similar I-4, 13. The difference here lies in being more concerned with herself than with how others think.
27. Not as high as I-4/5, 5 because of the absolute "always" and the cliché-like wording.
35. The first clause is rated Delta/3, 1. The meaning of the second clause is unclear. It could mean that the subject does not understand what conscience means, which is how we took it when rating out of context. This interpretation is contradicted by the rest of the protocol. It could mean guilt for lack of achievement, an interpretation con-

sistent with this subject's ego level being high compared to her
achievement level. Note that we do not change the item rating after
taking context into account.

DERIVING TPR

		Item Ratings						
2	Δ	Δ/3	3	3/4	4	4/5	5	6
Distribution	1	1	4	13	13	3	1	
Ogive	1	2	6	19	32	35	36	

One sees in this protocol vivid interpersonal feelings, guilt, trait
orientation, personal standards, and achievement.

TPR

I-4

ITEM RATINGS AND TPR FOR PRACTICE PROTOCOL 2

ITEM RATINGS

1. Rule 5	13. I-3, UC	25. Δ, 3
2. Δ, UC	14. Δ, 3	26. Rule 5
3. Rule 5	15. Rule 5	27. Δ, 3
4. Rule 5	16. Δ, 1	28. I-2, 1
5. I-3, 1	17. Δ, UC	29. Δ/3, 2
6. Δ, 4	18. 1-3/4, 10	30. I-3, 1
7. Δ, 1	19. Δ, 2	31. Rule 5
8. I-2, 1	20. Rule 5	32. Δ, 2
9. I-2, UC	21. Δ/3, 3	33. Δ/3, 1
10. I-3, 1	22. Rule 5	34. Δ, UC
11. Rule 5	23. Δ, 3	35. Rule 5
12. Δ, 3	24. Δ, 4	36. I-2, UC

EXPLANATION OF RATINGS

2. "Trouble" used in this manner is usually rated Delta.

9. Distaste for education can be I-2 or Delta. This response is more
   primitive and impulsive than Delta, 3.

17. Given as example at Delta, UC; the thought is similar to Delta, 3.

28. This response has an unfocused quality more similar to other I-2 re-
    sponses than to related ideas at Delta and I-3.

34. Blatant expression of sexuality, similar to unclassified example.

36. This response is ambiguous. It probably represents a Delta concern

for promiscuity expressed in a rather inappropriate, probably I-2 manner.

DERIVING TPR

Item Ratings

	2	Δ	Δ/3	3	3/4	4	4/5	5	6
Distribution	4	14	3	14	1				
Ogive	4	18	21	35	36				

According to the borderline TPR rules this protocol could be either I-2 or Delta. The themes of sex and aggression are strong, and there are other signs of impulsivity, but sex is not discussed in physiological terms as some I-2 subjects do. However, even for an I-2 protocol this one has unusually few responses at I-3 and I-3/4, especially when we consider that ten of the I-3 ratings result from omissions. We have not found interpretation of omissions to be reliable, but in the present case, where the rest of the protocol is impulsive and impoverished, the frequency of omissions is more compatible with an I-2 than with a Delta rating. The overall impression is unmistakably that of an I-2 person.

TPR

I-2

ITEM RATINGS AND TPR FOR PRACTICE PROTOCOL 3

ITEM RATINGS

1. I-3, 1	13. I-3/4, 9	25. I-3, 1
2. I-3, 4	14. I-3, 11	26. Rule 5
3. I-3/4, 2	15. I-3, 4	27. I-2, 4
4. I-3, 6	16. I-3, 7	28. I-3, 8
5. I-3, 5	17. I-3, 3	29. I-3/4, 3
6. I-3, UC	18. I-4, 10	30. I-3/4, 1
7. I-3, 1	19. Δ/3, 1	31. Δ/3, 1
8. I-3, 1	20. I-3, 18	32. Δ, 1
9. Δ/3, 1	21. I-3, 3	33. Δ/3, 5
10. I-3, 1	22. I-3, 4	34. Δ, 3
11. I-3, 3	23. I-3, 8	35. Δ/3, 1
12. I-2, 1	24. I-3, 4	36. I-3, 1

EXPLANATION OF RATINGS

6. This response may have some opportunistic connotation, but not clear enough to be scored Delta. Similar to I-3, 1 and I-3, 8.

9. By the rules, this ought to be called Delta, 1 because this category is less frequent than Delta/3, 1. However, this version, with its reference to dropouts, seems to belong at the higher level.

DERIVING TPR

	Item Ratings								
	2	Δ	Δ/3	3	3/4	4	4/5	5	6
Distribution	2	2	5	22	4	1			
Ogive	2	4	9	31	35	36			

By the ogive, this protocol would be rated Delta/3. Since at this time we have no clear conception of how a Delta/3 differs from a low I-3 protocol, we follow the ogive rule.

TPR

Delta/3

ITEM RATINGS AND TPR FOR PRACTICE PROTOCOL 4

ITEM RATINGS

1. I-4, 7
2. I-4, UC
3. I-3/4, 9
4. I-4, UC
5. I-3, 1
6. I-3/4, UC
7. I-4, 11
8. I-4, 4
9. I-4, 9
10. I-3/4, 1
11. I-4, UC
12. I-3, 15
13. I-3, 10
14. I-4, 6
15. I-4, 14
16. I-3/4, 8
17. I-4, 15
18. I-4/5, UC
19. I-4, 4
20. I-3, 12
21. I-3/4, 5
22. I-3, 9
23. I-3, 15
24. I-3, 2
25. I-3/4, 7
26. I-3/4, 11
27. I-4, 12
28. I-5, 3
29. Δ/3, 1
30. I-3/4, 2
31. I-3, 6
32. I-4/5, 2
33. I-4, 1
34. I-4, 12
35. I-4/5, 4
36. I-3/4, UC

EXPLANATION OF RATINGS

2. Though there is no contrast, this response is similar to I-4, 2.
4. Like I-4, 13 without blame.
6. Hard to know exactly how she means this. It is a trait less practical than those in I-3, 6 but less achievement-oriented than those in I-4,
8. The rating given is a compromise.
11. Conception of traits as capacities.
13. This could also be I-3, 6.
18. This is similar to I-5, 3 but less vivid.

33. This could also be I-4, 3.
36. "The rules" sounds more external than I-4, 7, but the qualification raises it above I-3; perhaps similar to I-3/4, 9 or I-3/4, 11.

DERIVING TPR

			Item Ratings						
	2	Δ	Δ/3	3	3/4	4	4/5	5	6
Distribution			1	8	9	14	3	1	
Ogive			1	9	18	32	35	36	

The general orientation is personal. There is concern with interests, achievement, and independence. The subject understands the concepts of roles and traits and makes abundant use of qualifications.

TPR

I-4

ITEM RATINGS AND TPR FOR PRACTICE PROTOCOL 5

ITEM RATINGS

1. I-3, 10	13. I-3, UC	25. I-3, 15
2. I-2, UC	14. I-2, UC	26. I-2, 2
3. I-3, 3	15. I-2, 1	27. Rule 5
4. I-3, UC	16. I-2, 1	28. Rule 5
5. Δ/3, UC	17. I-2, 2	29. I-3, 10
6. Δ, 2	18. I-3/4, 9	30. I-3, 1
7. Δ/3, 1	19. Rule 5	31. I-2, UC
8. I-3, 7	20. I-2, 3	32. I-2, 3
9. I-2, UC	21. Δ/3, 1	33. I-3, 14
10. Δ, 3	22. Rule 5	34. I-2, 3
11. I-2, UC	23. I-3, 1	35. Δ, 2
12. I-2, 2	24. Δ, 4	36. I-2, 1

EXPLANATION OF RATINGS

2. If she means "cries" it is a very impoverished association for this stem; if she means "crazy" it is I-2, 2.
5. The meaning is ambiguous; similar to Delta/3, 1.
9. Similar to I-2, 3.
11. The global "good" plus the sense that "Women are lucky when . . ."
14. The use of the present tense as in I-2, 1, and the physical "sick."
27. This could be interpreted to mean "you have to be woman," and scored Delta, 5.

31. Either the relation with her mother is seen exclusively in terms of dependency, or the negative emotion is expressed in physiological terms.

33. This could be scored I-2, UC, if "none" is interpreted as meaning "not good," or "don't like."

DERIVING TPR

Item Ratings

	2	Δ	Δ/3	3	3/4	4	4/5	5	6
Distribution	14	4	3	14	1				
Ogive	14	18	21	35	36				

A possibility is that rather than low I-level, this protocol reflects difficulties in understanding and using the language. However, many of the responses for which the meaning is clear are indicative of an I-2 TPR, not so much because of impulsivity but rather because of primitive thinking. This is suggested by the good-bad dichotomy, the physical expression of feelings, and the action-oriented rather than functional descriptions.

TPR

I-2

ITEM RATINGS AND TPR FOR PRACTICE PROTOCOL 6

ITEM RATINGS

1. I-5, UC	13. I-3, 9	25. I-4, 5
2. I-4, 8	14. I-4, 16	26. I-3/4, 3
3. I-4/5, 3	15. I-6, UC	27. I-5, 2
4. I-4, 2	16. I-5, 2	28. I-5, 1
5. I-4/5, 2	17. I-5, 3	29. I-4, 2
6. I-6, UC	18. I-6, UC	30. I-3/4, 4
7. I-4/5, 3	19. I-5, 2	31. I-5, UC
8. I-4, 1	20. I-5, 1	32. I-4/5, 3
9. I-5, 4	21. I-3/4, 12	33. I-4, UC
10. I-5, 1	22. I-5, 2	34. I-4, 13
11. I-5, 1	23. I-5, UC	35. I-4/5, UC
12. I-6, UC	24. I-4/5, UC	36. I-3/4, 15

EXPLANATION OF RATINGS

1. Explicit description of the effect of the family on one's growth. Similar to I-5, 1.

4. Similar to I-3/4, 2, but "moments of companionship" indicates a more differentiated view of the relationship.
6. The complexity, that is, the merging of "release and accomplishment," and the vividness of affect contribute to an I-6 rating.
12. Contributing to the high rating are time perspective, self-fulfillment, perception of her father as a unique and complex individual, and the ability to see the concrete from a very abstract perspective.
15. Combination of I-4/5 and I-5 ideas. The complexity of role development is succinctly expressed in this response.
18. The contrast of "significance or background" raises it above I-4/5, 2. The thought is similar to the other I-6 example.
23. For this stem it is unusual to find so abstract a conception, connecting the subject with the stream of life.
24. This response resembles I-4, 6 but is more abstract and original.
27. We interpret her intended meaning to be that the difficulty is in reconciling femininity and individuality.
28. The second clause by itself would be scored I-4/5, 3, but the first clause in conjunction with it leads us to the higher rating.
31. Distance from mother-daughter relation and appreciation of mother's contribution to mother-father relation.
33. Not as explicit, but similar to I-4, 2, 3, and 4.

DERIVING TPR

	2	Δ	Δ/3	3	3/4	4	4/5	5	6
Item Ratings									
Distribution				1	4	8	6	13	4
Ogive				1	5	13	19	32	36

The general level of the protocol is very high since two-thirds of the responses are above I-4. The search for identity is not apparent, but subject seems to be at peace with contrasting elements within herself.

TPR

I-6

ITEM RATINGS AND TPR FOR PRACTICE PROTOCOL 7

ITEM RATINGS

1. I-3, 3	5. I-3, 8	9. I-3, 4
2. I-3, 7	6. I-3, UC	10. I-3/4, 5
3. I-3, UC	7. I-3/4, 2	11. I-3/4, 6
4. I-3, 1	8. I-3/4, UC	12. I-3, 18

13. I-4, 9	21. I-3/4, 3	29. I-4, 11
14. I-3/4, 7	22. I-3, 12	30. I-3/4, 3
15. I-3, 1	23. I-3/4, UC	31. I-3, 10
16. I-3, 1	24. I-3, 2	32. I-3, 4
17. I-3/4, 16	25. I-3, UC	33. I-4, 1
18. I-3/4, 15	26. I-3/4, 14	34. I-3, 5
19. I-4, 1	27. I-3, 13	35. I-3/4, 3
20. I-3/4, 12	28. I-4, 17	36. I-3/4, 4

EXPLANATION OF RATINGS

3. This could be interpreted either as evasion or as hostile humor.
6. Similar to some responses in I-3, 8.
8. Seems to refer to difficulties in communication.
9. This could also be I-3, 3.
11. The predominant tone of this response seems to fit I-3/4, 6, although the long view of the life span would argue for a higher rating.
23. There are time perspective and comparison between situations, but the feelings are undifferentiated.
25. Cliché version of I-4, 15.
31. While we know the difference between anger and resentment, many subjects use the terms synonymously, and this response seems to be of that type.

DERIVING TPR

	2	Δ	Δ/3	3	3/4	4	4/5	5	6
Distribution				17	14	5			
Ogive				17	31	36			

TPR

I-3/4

ITEM RATINGS AND TPR FOR PRACTICE PROTOCOL 8

ITEM RATINGS

1. I-3, 1	7. I-3, 7	13. I-2, 1
2. Δ/3, 2	8. I-2, 1	14. I-2, 1
3. Δ, 1	9. I-3, 11	15. Δ/3, 2
4. I-3, 12	10. I-3, 1	16. I-2, 1
5. I-3, 2	11. Δ/3, 1	17. I-3/4, 4
6. Δ, 2	12. I-3, 9	18. I-2, 3

19.	Rule 5	25.	Δ, UC	31.	Δ, UC
20.	I-3, 2	26.	Δ, 2	32.	Δ/3, 2
21.	Δ/3, 1	27.	I-2, 1	33.	I-3, 1
22.	I-3, 1	28.	I-2, 2	34.	Δ/3, 1
23.	I-3, 5	29.	I-3/4, 2	35.	I-3, UC
24.	Δ/3, 2	30.	I-3, 7	36.	I-2, 1

EXPLANATION OF RATINGS

13. "Is good" is interpreted to mean "is going to."
16. Self-centered; confusion of "sad" and "sorry."
25. Like Delta, 2, but even more blatant.
26. This could be interpreted in the sense of I-3, 7.
31. This suggests the Delta reaction against ties to mother; it is also similar to Delta, 3.
35. Subject's meaning is unclear. She may not know what "conscience" means, in which case the response could be scored I-2; but she may also be expressing a concern with confession.

DERIVING TPR

Item Ratings

	2	Δ	Δ/3	3	3/4	4	4/5	5	6
Distribution	8	5	7	14	2				
Ogive	8	13	20	34	36				

There are only two responses above I-3, and neither provides a convincing picture of distinctive I-3/4 level thinking. Characteristics of the protocol are global dichotomies, sexual preoccupation, externalization of blame, concern with cleanliness, and getting things.

TPR

I-2

ITEM RATINGS AND TPR FOR PRACTICE PROTOCOL 9

ITEM RATINGS

1.	I-4, 9	4.	I-3/4, 12	7.	I-3/4, 8
2.	I-4, 5	5.	I-3/4, 4	8.	I-5, 2
3.	I-3, 1	6.	I-3, 3	9.	I-4/5, 1

10. I-3/4, 5	19. I-3/4, 6	28. I-4, 10
11. I-4, 14	20. I-4, 13	29. I-4, 10
12. I-3/4, 1	21. I-4, 7	30. I-5, UC
13. I-3, 1	22. I-4, 11	31. I-4/5, 1
14. I-5, UC	23. I-4, 12	32. I-4, 6
15. I-4, 2	24. I-4, UC	33. I-4, UC
16. I-4, 10	25. I-5, UC	34. I-4, 11
17. I-3/4, 1	26. I-4, UC	35. I-4, 10
18. I-4/5, UC	27. I-5, UC	36. I-4/5, UC

EXPLANATION OF RATINGS

14. Elaborated comparison of psychological versus physical consequences.
18. An elaboration of I-4, 11, similar to I-4/5, 3.
21. Similar in tone to I-4, 7.
24. The mutuality raises it above I-3/4, 5. It is somewhat similar to I-4, 6.
25. Similar in level to I-5, 1.
26. This could be rated I-4, 4.
27. The complex psychological causation and the linking of the diverse qualities "afraid" and "cruel" raise the rating above I-4/5.
30. This is similar to I-5, 2; perhaps it could be rated there.
32. I-4, 6 is preferred to I-3/4, 3 because there is an idea similar to that of goal.
33. This is a compound of I-4, 8 and I-4, 9.
34. Although several thoughts are strung together, they do not seem to generate any more complex idea than those in I-4, 11.
36. Despite its brevity, this is a complex and original idea.

DERIVING TPR

Item Ratings

	2	Δ	Δ/3	3	3/4	4	4/5	5	6
Distribution				3	7	17	4	5	
Ogive				3	10	27	31	36	

The theme of respect is somewhat repetitious, but each time it enters in a slightly different way. Other high-level themes are complex psychological causation, distinction between reality and idealistic expectation, recognition of conflicting alternatives, broad social perspective, and a beginning of the problem of identity.

I-5

ITEM RATINGS AND TPR FOR PRACTICE PROTOCOL 10

ITEM RATINGS

1. I-3, 3	13. I-2, 1	25. I-3, 1
2. I-3, 6	14. I-4, 6	26. I-3, 10
3. I-3/4, 10	15. I-3, 2	27. I-3, 1
4. I-3/4, 11	16. Δ, 1	28. I-3, 2
5. I-4, 1	17. I-3, 5	29. I-3, 3
6. Δ, 5	18. I-3, 10	30. Δ, 1
7. I-3, UC	19. I-4, 5	31. I-3, 2
8. I-3, 2	20. I-3/4, 6	32. I-4, 5
9. I-3/4, 2	21. I-3, 2	33. I-3, 4
10. I-3/4, 5	22. I-3/4, UC	34. I-3/4, 1
11. I-3, 1	23. I-3, UC	35. I-3/4, 3
12. Δ, 2	24. I-3, 4	36. I-3/4, 1

EXPLANATION OF RATINGS

7. Similar to unclassified responses at I-3.
20. The implication may be that they have authority (I-4, 1); however this is not specified. This is also similar to I-3/4, 1.
22. "Offending" seems to be the opposite of "pleasing"; so this could fit I-3/4, 3.
23. This is interpreted as nonhostile evasion.

DERIVING TPR

		Item Ratings						
	2	Δ	Δ/3	3	3/4	4	4/5	5	6
Distribution	1	4	0	18	9	4			
Ogive	1	5	5	23	32	36			

According to the ogive rules, this protocol is on the borderline between I-3 and I-3/4. Note that if we look at the low end, it is also on the border between Delta and I-3. I-3/4 is chosen as the TPR because most of the responses classed below and at I-3 seem to be just quick, flip answers, a way to complete the task quickly. The rest of the protocol indicates a self-awareness and self-consciousness and a concern with interpersonal traits typical of the I-3/4 level.

TPR

I-3/4

ITEM RATINGS AND TPR FOR PRACTICE PROTOCOL 11

ITEM RATINGS

1. I-5, 2	13. I-3, UC	25. I-4/5, UC
2. I-4, 5	14. I-4/5, UC	26. I-4, 6
3. I-5, UC	15. I-3, 3	27. I-5, 3
4. I-4, 12	16. I-5, 1	28. I-5, 1
5. I-4, 1	17. I-4, 15	29. I-4/5, UC
6. I-4, 1	18. I-4, 2	30. I-4/5, 2
7. I-3/4, 8	19. I-3/4, 7	31. I-4, 4
8. I-3, 2	20. I-4, 11	32. I-4, 7
9. I-4, 12	21. I-4/5, UC	33. I-4, 12
10. I-4, 6	22. I-3/4, UC	34. I-4, 12
11. I-3/4, 1	23. I-3, 15	35. I-4/5, UC
12. I-3/4, 8	24. I-3/4, 5	36. I-3/4, UC

EXPLANATION OF RATINGS

3. Similar to I-4/5, 2 but more elaborated.
13. Similar to I-3, 7 but stated positively.
14. Combination of two I-4 ideas, similar to example at I-4/5.
15. Whether the response is put at I-3, 3 or I-3/4, 7 is arbitrary, as arguments for either classification can be made. The argument that the response is less abstract than the I-3/4, 7 examples has been given more weight here.
21. Similar to I-4/5, 4.
22. This response seems to fall between I-3, 8 and I-4, 11.
25. This seems to be better than I-4, 9 but not as good as I-5, 2.
29. Implied contrast between feelings, traits, and so on, and their expression in appearance.
35. This response shows a long time perspective and some distance from conscience; hence it is scored higher than I-4.
36. "Alert mind" is closer to I-3/4, 9 than to Delta, 3.

DERIVING TPR

	2	Δ	Δ/3	3	3/4	4	4/5	5	6
Distribution				4	7	14	6	5	
Ogive				4	11	25	31	36	

Item Ratings

A wide variety of answers is given. High-level themes include continuity with the past, objectivity, autonomy, and objection to stereotypes.

TPR

I-5

ITEM RATINGS AND TPR FOR PRACTICE PROTOCOL 12

ITEM RATINGS

1. Δ, 4	13. Δ, 1	25. I-3, 15
2. I-2, 2	14. I-3, 14	26. Δ/3, 2
3. I-3, 6	15. Δ, 1	27. Δ, 2
4. I-3, 6	16. I-3, 6	28. I-3, 18
5. Δ, UC	17. I-3, 11	29. I-3, 10
6. Δ, UC	18. I-3, 1	30. Δ, UC
7. I-3, 5	19. I-3, UC	31. I-3, UC
8. I-3/4, 16	20. I-3, UC	32. I-2, 3
9. I-3, UC	21. I-2, 1	33. I-3, 14
10. I-2, 2	22. I-3, 2	34. Rule 5
11. I-3, 13	23. I-3, 19	35. I-3, 1
12. I-2, 1	24. I-3, 7	36. I-3, 1

EXPLANATION OF RATINGS

6. Suspicious, guarded response.
19. Similar in meaning to "I feel sorry for him," I-3, 11.
20. The same response is rated I-3 for Item 11.
30. This is not very different from Delta, 4. The contingency is self-centered.
31. The meaning is ambiguous. One could interpret it as an expression of emotion in physical terms and score it at I-2.
33. This could also be scored Rule 5.

DERIVING TPR

		Item Ratings						
	2	Δ	Δ/3	3	3/4	4	4/5	5	6
Distribution	5	7	1	22	1			
Ogive	5	12	13	35	36			

According to the ogive rules, the TPR is no higher than Delta and perhaps is I-2. Delta is chosen as the rating because of the preponderance of Delta themes such as exploitation, externalization of blame, and guardedness. The callous tone is probably more characteristic of Delta than of I-2 subjects.

TPR

Delta

ITEM RATINGS AND TPR FOR PRACTICE PROTOCOL 13

ITEM RATINGS

1. I-3, 4	13. I-3, 7	25. I-3/4, UC
2. I-3/4, UC	14. I-2, 1	26. I-3, 17
3. I-3, 7	15. I-2, 1	27. I-2, 1
4. I-3, UC	16. Δ, 1	28. Δ, 3
5. I-3, 2	17. I-3/4, 4	29. Δ/3, 1
6. Δ/3, 1	18. Δ/3, 1	30. I-3/4, 2
7. I-3, 7	19. Δ, 1	31. Δ/3, 1
8. I-3/4, 1	20. Δ/3, 1	32. Δ, 2
9. I-3, 1	21. I-3/4, 5	33. Δ/3, 2
10. Δ, 1	22. I-3, 4	34. Δ/3, 4
11. Δ, 1	23. I-3, 6	35. Δ/3, 1
12. I-3, 9	24. I-3, 2	36. I-3/4, 1

EXPLANATION OF RATINGS

2. This response is more unusual than most I-3 responses to this stem.
4. Similar to I-3, 18.
25. Both the striving and the combination of roles raise this response above I-3.
26. This could be interpreted in the sense of Delta, 4.

DERIVING TPR

	Item Ratings							
	2	Δ	Δ/3	3	3/4	4	4/5	5	6
Distribution	3	6	8	12	7			
Ogive	3	9	17	29	36			

By the ogive rules, the protocol would be rated Delta. However, with the exception of Item 32, the self-protective tone typical of Delta protocols is not found here. This consideration, plus the large number of responses scored Delta/3, influences the decision to rate up.

TPR

Delta/3

ITEM RATINGS AND TPR FOR PRACTICE PROTOCOL 14

ITEM RATINGS

1. I-4, 4	13. I-3/4, 12	25. I-4/5, UC
2. I-3/4, 2	14. I-4, 16	26. I-5, 2
3. I-4, 4	15. I-5, 4	27. I-4, 1
4. I-3, 4	16. I-4/5, 4	28. I-4/5, 2
5. I-5, UC	17. I-3/4, 1	29. I-4/5, UC
6. I-5, UC	18. I-4/5, UC	30. I-4/5, 7
7. I-4/5, 3	19. I-5, 1	31. I-4/5, UC
8. I-4/5, 3	20. I-4, 5	32. I-4/5, 1
9. I-4/5, UC	21. I-4/5, 5	33. I-3/4, 6
10. I-5, 3	22. I-4, 11	34. I-5, UC
11. I-3, 11	23. I-4/5, 1	35. I-4, 11
12. I-4/5, 1	24. I-4/5, 1	36. I-4, UC

EXPLANATION OF RATINGS

5. Combination of reactions as in I-4/5, 4, plus appreciation of personal growth.

6. This is similar to I-5, 2. Though only two ideas are mentioned, they represent a sophisticated and differentiated contrast (adaptation versus change).

9. This response is like I-4, 11, too instrumental to be called I-5. We called it I-4/5, UC as a compromise.

18. She gives two purposes, one biological, one psychological.

22. Two versions of one idea. The compound is not more complex than the elements.

25. Elaboration on I-4 ideas of being dependent and lacking confidence.

29. This response shows an ability to empathize with her mother; it is an unusual response for this stem.

31. Subject takes mother's point of view. If context is considered, it would probably be scored I-4, since it represents a recurrent theme on the protocol.

34. This is similar to I-4, 5 and I-4, 6, but the concern for what is individually rewarding raises it to I-5.

DERIVING TPR

				Item Ratings				
2	Δ	Δ/3	3	3/4	4	4/5	5	6
Distribution			2	4	8	15	7	
Ogive			2	6	14	29	36	

Although our raters differ on exactly how to rate the many unique responses on this protocol, we agree that it is an excellent example of an I-5 protocol. Among the high elements are the diversity of themes, contrasts (including those between inner and outer, general and specific, physical and psychological), a broad view of life, psychological causation, long time perspective, vivid and unique self-perceptions, respect for the individuality of others, and self-fulfillment. There is vivid evocation of other people as individuals and in terms of their relations with others. That the subject tends to dwell on her mother and the mother-grandmother relation indicates some preoccupation with them, but does not serve to lower the overall rating.

TPR

I-5

ITEM RATINGS AND TPR FOR PRACTICE PROTOCOL 15

ITEM RATINGS

1. I-3, 1	13. I-3, UC	25. I-3, 3
2. I-3/4, 10	14. I-3, 14	26. I-3/4, 8
3. I-3/4, 7	15. Δ, 1	27. I-2, 1
4. Δ, UC	16. I-3, 7	28. I-3, 10
5. I-3, 1	17. I-3, 3	29. I-2, 2
6. I-3, 2	18. I-3, 7	30. I-3, 1
7. I-3, 1	19. Δ/3, 1	31. I-3/4, 12
8. I-2, UC	20. I-2, UC	32. Δ/3, 1
9. I-2, UC	21. I-3, 3	33. Δ, 3
10. I-3/4, 1	22. I-3, UC	34. I-3, 1
11. I-2, 1	23. I-3, 1	35. Δ, 6
12. I-3, 11	24. Δ, 4	36. I-2, 1

EXPLANATION OF RATINGS

4. Revenge is implied. The I-2 reaction is rarely against the parents.
8. Mention of concrete, external thing.
9. Similar to Delta, 3, but more primitive and impulsive in tone.

13. This is a concrete action. It might be rated I-2, UC because of content and tone.
20. Similar to subject's response to item 11.
22. Being on time is more concrete than "Time limitations" (I-4, 7), and similar to responses in I-3, 7.

DERIVING TPR

	2	Δ	Δ/3	3	3/4	4	4/5	5	6
Distribution	7	5	2	17	5				
Ogive	7	12	14	31	36				

Item Ratings

There is some evidence of impulsivity in items 4, 8, 9, 13, 25, and 35. The general impression is one of dependence, waiting to be given to, and confusion of wish with reality, what psychoanalysts call primary process thinking.

TPR

I-2

ITEM RATINGS AND TPR FOR PRACTICE PROTOCOL 16

ITEM RATINGS

1. I-3, 1	13. I-3, UC	25. I-3/4, 13
2. Δ/3, 2	14. I-3, 1	26. I-4, 7
3. I-3/4, 5	15. I-5, 1	27. I-4, UC
4. I-4, 1	16. I-3, 1	28. I-3, 1
5. I-4, 1	17. I-3/4, 2	29. I-3/4, 5
6. I-3, 5	18. I-3/4, 2	30. I-4, 9
7. I-3, 2	19. I-4, 1	31. I-3/4, 2
8. I-3/4, 1	20. I-4, 12	32. I-4, 6
9. I-4, 8	21. I-3, 2	33. I-3/4, UC
10. I-3, 6	22. I-3, 3	34. I-4, 12
11. I-3/4, 1	23. I-3, 12	35. I-3/4, 1
12. I-3, 1	24. I-3, 5	36. I-3/4, 1

EXPLANATION OF RATINGS

6. This could also be I-3, 1.
13. Concrete action, which we suspect is an evasion of whatever this stem arouses in the subject.
27. Similar to I-4, 3.
33. Similar to I-3/4, 3 and I-3/4, 5.

Item Ratings

	2	Δ	Δ/3	3	3/4	4	4/5	5	6
Distribution				1	13	11	10	0	1
Ogive				1	14	25	35	35	36

According to the ogive rules, this protocol is at least I-3/4 and perhaps I-4. It contains strong I-4 aspects, notably the concern with achievement. However, a number of the I-4 responses are redundant in that they involve use of "rewarding" and "enriching." Therefore, there does not seem to be enough variety of content to justify an I-4 TPR.

TPR

I-3/4

ITEM RATINGS AND TPR FOR PRACTICE PROTOCOL 17

ITEM RATINGS

1. I-3, UC	13. I-3, 9	25. I-4, UC
2. I-3/4, UC	14. I-3, UC	26. I-3, 13
3. I-3/4, UC	15. I-4, UC	27. I-3, 3
4. I-3, 18	16. I-3, 3	28. I-4, 3
5. I-3, 10	17. I-3, 2	29. I-3, 6
6. I-3/4, UC	18. I-3, 6	30. I-3/4, UC
7. I-3, 4	19. I-3/4, 10	31. I-3/4, 12
8. I-2, 1	20. I-3, 5	32. Δ, 3
9. I-4, 8	21. I-3/4, 6	33. I-3/4, 13
10. I-3, 2	22. I-3/4, 4	34. I-3/4, 1
11. I-3, 16	23. I-3, 15	35. Δ, 5
12. I-3/4, 1	24. I-3, 7	36. I-4, 2

EXPLANATION OF RATINGS

1. Combines I-3, 4 and I-3, 8.
2. This might be called I-4, UC because it is the opposite of I-4, 7, but since it denies the complexity, we call it I-3/4, UC.
3. A negative version of I-3/4, 3.
5. This could also be I-3, 7.
6. Similar to I-3, 15, but more explicit than that category and not as good as I-4, 4.
9. This could also be I-4, 9.

13. This is not as tautological as I-2, 1.
14. Concrete reference similar to I-3, 3.
15. This response shows role conception.
25. We interpret this response as showing awareness of her social appearance and self-criticism.
28. This could also be I-4, 4.
30. Very much like I-3/4, 7.

DERIVING TPR

	Item Ratings							
	2	Δ	Δ/3	3	3/4	4	4/5	5	6
Distribution	1	2	0	17	11	5
Ogive	1	3	3	20	31	36

According to the ogive rules, the TPR is I-3/4. There are responses here that are similar to ones on low protocols, but the variety and originality of responses indicate a rating above I-3. No responses occur that are strongly suggestive of an I-4 TPR.

TPR

I-3/4

ITEM RATINGS AND TPR FOR PRACTICE PROTOCOL 18

ITEM RATINGS

1. I-3, 7	13. Δ, 8	25. I-3, UC
2. I-2, 2	14. I-3, 1	26. I-3, 9
3. I-3, 7	15. I-2, 2	27. I-3, 4
4. I-3/4, UC	16. I-3, 1	28. I-3/4, 13
5. I-3/4, 4	17. I-3, 3	29. I-3, 5
6. I-3, 3	18. I-3, UC	30. I-3, 4
7. I-3, 1	19. I-3, 2	31. I-3/4, 3
8. I-3, 2	20. I-3, 17	32. Δ, 1
9. I-3, 1	21. Δ/3, 2	33. I-3, 9
10. I-3, 2	22. Δ/3, 1	34. Δ/3, 1
11. Δ, 1	23. I-3, 1	35. Δ/3, 1
12. I-3, 10	24. I-3, 13	36. I-3/4, 8

EXPLANATION OF RATINGS

4. There is a concern for her mother, which raises it above I-3, 18.
6. Similar to I-3/4, 4, but more banal and neutral.

18. Similar to the response at I-3, UC and also to I-3/4, 4.
25. "Responsibility" by itself is vague.
28. Similar also to the first unclassified example at I-3/4.

DERIVING TPR

				Item Ratings					
	2	Δ	Δ/3	3	3/4	4	4/5	5	6
Distribution	2	3	4	22	5				
Ogive	2	5	9	31	36				

According to the ogive rules, the TPR is no higher than Delta/3 and perhaps as low as Delta. However, the responses rated I-2 and Delta are not of sufficient strength (that is, not convincing enough from a theoretical view) to justify a Delta rating; thus, Delta/3 is the chosen rating.

TPR

Delta/3

ITEM RATINGS AND TPR FOR PRACTICE PROTOCOL 19

ITEM RATINGS

1. I-4/5, 5	13. I-4/5, 1	25. I-4/5, UC
2. I-3/4, 6	14. I-5, UC	26. I-4/5, UC
3. I-5, 1	15. I-4, 13	27. I-4/5, UC
4. I-3/4, 6	16. I-4/5, 1	28. I-4, UC
5. I-4/5, UC	17. I-4/5, UC	29. I-3/4, UC
6. I-3/4, UC	18. I-3/4, 10	30. I-4, 8
7. I-4/5, 1	19. I-4, 5	31. I-4, 13
8. I-4, 6	20. I-3, 1	32. I-4, 5
9. I-4, 13	21. I-4/5, 4	33. I-3/4, 10
10. I-4, 1	22. I-4/5, 2	34. I-4/5, UC
11. I-3, 1	23. I-4, 12	35. I-3, 3
12. I-4, UC	24. I-4/5, 1	36. I-3/4, 1

EXPLANATION OF RATINGS

5. "Sharing" implies relation and mutuality.
6. Similar to Delta, 2 and Delta, 3, but "believe" and "hope" raise it to I-3/4.
10. This could also be I-4, 13.
12. This is a combination of I-4, 1 and I-4, 3, which, however, does not raise the level of complexity.

14. This is similar to I-4/5, 3, but is rated higher because of the complexity of feelings, distance, objectivity, and time perspective.

17. There are distance, objectivity, evaluation.

19. This is similar to I-4, 6, with the added role-taking perspective.

21. Though only one pole of the dichotomy is mentioned, this response is closer to I-4/5, 4 than to I-4, 7.

22. This could also be scored I-4/5, 6.

25. This seems to be higher than I-4, 12 because it suggests some psychological causation, but it does not have the interpersonal concern found in I-5, 2.

26. Similar to I-4/5, 1.

28. This does not fit exactly I-4, 4, but is similar to it.

29. Emphasis on concrete action is similar to I-3, 10 and I-3, 11; the notion of propensity appears at I-4, 7, but in relation to more abstract traits.

32. This response does not contain two I-4 ideas, as required for placement in I-4/5, 3.

34. Though each idea, separately, is not higher than I-4, the complexity of the combination raises this response to I-4/5.

DERIVING TPR

	2	Δ	Δ/3	3	3/4	4	4/5	5	6
					Item Ratings				
Distribution				3	7	11	13	2	
Ogive				3	10	21	34	36	

This protocol is distinguished by the conceptual complexity manifested in the uniting of a variety of ideas within single responses. Themes more fully developed at I-5, such as autonomy, individuality, and unique role conception, begin to appear here. High value is placed on interpersonal relations. Additionally, one sees qualifications, long time perspective, distance from self and capacity for role-taking.

TPR

I-4/5

ITEM RATINGS AND TPR FOR PRACTICE PROTOCOL 20

ITEM RATINGS

1. I-3, 1	4. I-3, UC	7. I-3, 6
2. Δ/3, 1	5. I-3, 1	8. I-3, 10
3. I-3, 6	6. I-3, 2	9. Δ, 1

10. I-3, 8	19. I-2, 1	28. Δ, UC
11. I-2, 1	20. I-3, 13	29. I-3, 2
12. I-3, 19	21. Δ/3, 2	30. Δ, 4
13. I-2, 2	22. Δ, UC	31. Δ, UC
14. I-3, 8	23. I-3, 3	32. I-3/4, 4
15. I-3, UC	24. I-3, 2	33. I-3, UC
16. Δ, 2	25. Δ, 4	34. I-3, 1
17. I-3, 9	26. I-2, UC	35. Δ/3, 1
18. I-3, 7	27. I-3, UC	36. I-3, UC

EXPLANATION OF RATINGS

4. The meaning is ambiguous. It could be interpreted as referring to the mother's affective reaction and scored I-3/4.
26. This is similar to I-3, 1 and to I-2, 2. We score down in this case because the idea seems somewhat inappropriate and undifferentiated.
27. This suggests a global concern for approval, which is an I-3 characteristic.
28. Watchfulness.
31. Hostility to the tester.
33. This rating is by default, since the meaning is ambiguous.

DERIVING TPR

Item Ratings

	2	Δ	Δ/3	3	3/4	4	4/5	5	6
Distribution	4	7	3	21	1				
Ogive	4	11	14	35	36				

By the ogive rules, this protocol could not be higher than Delta. Low elements include repetitious use of words such as fine, you, praised, and a physiological view of causation, responses that are compatible with either an I-2 or Delta rating. Responses to Items 6 and 15 contraindicate an I-2 rating. The protocol has a tone of self-protection and hostility.

TPR

Delta

Procedures for Preparing Written Responses for Research Purposes

There are a few words in use on this project to which we have attached some special meanings that may differ from common usage. The definitions offered here are our usages.*

* Assembling these procedures was primarily the work of Radah Schmidt.

228

1. Protocol. The test as completed by the subject (hereafter, S).

2. Item. The individual parts of the test, sometimes used interchangeably with stem.

3. Stem. The part of the sentence that is given S to complete.

4. Response. The completion S adds to the stem, whether it completes a sentence, does not complete a sentence, or is several sentences.

5. Sample. A group of protocols that are treated as a unit. We use the term in two ways: A group of tests collected from the same source, or a group of tests selected for study. Within a study, those from the same source may be referred to as a subsample.

6. TPR, or Total Protocol Rating. The score assigned on the basis of the whole test, as opposed to ratings of items.

7. Roster. This retains its usual meaning of list, but, more specifically, is a list of the subjects gathered from the same source, or, alternatively, those used in the same study. In either case we include in the roster demographic information (age, race, and similar factors) and TPRs, added when a study is completed.

8. Coding. Substituting a code number for S's name.

PREPARATION FOR TYPING

Coding: We have a twofold purpose in coding: (1) to protect the privacy of the S and (2) to protect the raters from information about S which might influence their ratings. Both purposes require that all identifying information be treated as absolutely confidential, and that records which connect Ss to their tests should be handled by someone who is not doing the rating.

Coding that is more elaborate than the situation requires is uneconomical of time and temper. For samples that are to be rated separately rather than incorporated into a larger sample it is usually sufficient to use straight numbering in combination with a code word or initials to identify the sample. The year and month of starting the study can serve in addition to or instead of a code name.

When protocols are collected from a number of sources, and where it is necessary to disguise the origin of each protocol, they are coded first on a master index. After tests have been selected from the master index and assembled into a study sample they are then, for the convenience of the raters, renumbered consecutively. The study sample number is always preceded by the name of the study.

Master Index: To set up a master index from which protocols may be selected for separate studies:

1. Select a block of numbers, anticipating as closely as possible the number of protocols to be collected. (We have been using blocks of 500.)

2. Using lined paper, make up index, leaving columns for S's name, name of sample, date of testing, and a space for remarks.

3. After names have been checked against card index for previous testing, enter S's name in master index and record the number on both pages of the protocol. Scatter the Ss from each testing throughout the entire block of numbers, preferably using a table of random numbers. If a previous test has been recorded for any of the Ss, note this under "remarks" with a cross reference to previous test.

Use separate indices for males and females.

Card Index: The card index serves two purposes: it is a check against retests and a convenient means of sorting information.

A card is made for each protocol. Thus a person who had taken the test twice would have two cards on file. For each test, record the S's name, age, race, education (as it appears on the roster), marital status, the source from which it was obtained, and the code number. Space is provided to record the study in which the test is used, the number assigned to it in the study, and the score.

Rosters: Identify each roster as to the source of sample, date of testing and name of person doing testing. Example:

Washington University Introductory Psychology Students
Tested (date)   by (name)

Then, using column headings across top of page, record the following information:

1. Code number
2. S's name
3. Race
4. Age
5. Marital status (Single, Married, Separated, Divorced, Widowed)
6. Education (number of years of formal academic training completed)

If the sample includes data from more than one source (or more than one testing date), record source (or date) for each S.

We have established these guides to interpretation:

If S has described marital status as "good," "bad," "Yes," and so on, accept this as meaning subject is married.

Disregard nonacademic training such as trade school, beauty school, business school. Nurses' training, however, should be noted as we consider it equivalent to some college training.

For Ss beyond normal school age, assume that stated educational level indicates completion: "college" equals college graduate, "grade school" means eight grades completed.

School age Ss tested during the school year are recorded at the stated level, but those tested during the summer months usually refer to their status in the coming year; therefore, a seventeen year old, tested in June, who describes herself as a senior is recorded as having completed eleven grades.

The education of some Ss must be classified as unknown: a woman who writes "4" and whose protocol evidences a high degree of literacy cannot be assigned with certainty to four years grade school, high school, or college. Sometimes a followup telephone call can supply such missing information.

The following divisions are used when Ss are sorted into educational categories:

Part grade school = less than eight years.

Grade school = eight years.

Part high school = more than eight, less than twelve years.

High school = twelve years.

Part college = nurses' training, or less than four years regular college training, or some combination of the two.

College = graduation from any regular four-year academic institution. (We have included college seniors in their last few months.)

College + = any education beyond bachelor's degree, with the exception of strictly vocational training. Thus, R.N. + B.S. would qualify, but B.A. + secretarial training would not.

Deletions: Deletions from the protocols must be made on the basis of the requirements of each study, but we have routinely deleted all precise references to age, education, occupation, and race. Most responses from which material has been deleted can be kept from falling into the unratable category. Thus the following response can be salvaged:

I am—a 30 yr. old school teacher

I am—[deleted age and occupation]

or:

The thing I like about myself is—that my skin is brown

The thing I like about myself is—that my skin is [deleted reference to race]

Unless the particular study requires more rigorous pruning, the following responses would be allowed to stand as written:

Sometimes she wished that—she could live her teens over again

I am—proud of having completed my education

All changes are marked on the original in red pencil so as to distinguish S's response from researcher's instructions to typist.

GENERAL INSTRUCTIONS FOR TYPING
SENTENCE COMPLETIONS

Make a First Copy and Two Carbons: The second carbon copy is filed as a permanent record; the original typed copy and first carbon are working copies for the raters.

Copy Exactly What the Subject Has Written: Reproduce spelling and punctuation just as you see it, but avoid confusion between actual misspellings and peculiarities of handwriting. Where the difference is not clear, examine the entire protocol and then use your own judgment. A person who generally spells well probably does not write "con" for "can," even though an "a" may look like "o." A response such as "is a Good Mother" should be capitalized as it appears, but it is not necessary to type "I would be veRy soRRy" from a protocol which has been printed.

Many subjects omit the final period of each response; others are inconsistent or make ambiguous marks. We usually omit it arbitrarily, and that has been done throughout most of the present volume. Protocols 19 and 20 in Appendix D retain the final period and show inconsistent usage by those two subjects.

Include Words That Have Been Crossed Out: These words are typed with a line of dashes through them, whether they appear in the stem or the response. If S has changed the stem it should be typed:

When I am with a ~~man~~ boy—I feel feminine.

Erasures: If still legible, an erasure is typed in brackets with the notation that it is an erasure:

[erased—and stupid]

Parentheses: Parentheses are reserved for parenthetical expression in the actual response; brackets indicate any notes added by the typist:

The thing I like about myself is—that I (usually) am very happy about being a [deleted occupation]

TYPING TOTAL PROTOCOLS

Before typing, protocols should be coded, recorded on rosters and card file, and marked for deletions.

Type each page of the test on a separate page.

Place code number in upper left corner of both pages.

Ignoring the identifying information at the beginning of the test, drop down to the body of the test and type each sentence, separating the stem from the response with a dash:

1. Raising a family—is hard work
2. Most men think that women—are bad drivers

If S has failed to write a response, type the stem and hyphen.

Double space between items, but single space between lines of a response running over one line.

Every typed protocol should be proofread at least once. In proofreading one should devise a system of keeping track, so that when a protocol needs to be retyped, it will also be proofread again. Neat corrections of typing errors are acceptable, but bookkeeping is necessary to ensure that all carbons are corrected. As each typed protocol is checked with the original, mark each one in bottom right hand corner with initials of proofreader, as each page is done. When proofreading of a sample of protocols has been completed, the following should be recorded on roster: total protocols proofread. Also record date and initials of proofreaders on appropriate roster.

TYPING RESPONSES TO EACH ITEM

Use original handwritten protocols for copy.

At the top of each page, type name of study, item number and stem; for example:

Sealed Sample—Item #1:   Raising a family—

Without repeating the stem, use single spacing and type protocol number and the response:

1. is hard work
2. is rewarding

It is sometimes necessary to reorder the protocols so that the responses do not appear in the same order for each item. That is, all responses numbered 1 should not be from the same protocol. For each sample devise some simple system of reordering, such as reversing the order for every third item, or substituting the first hundred for the second hundred in the even numbered items, and so on. The general rules are:

1. Keep it simple.
2. Keep a careful record on file.
3. Keep it a secret from the raters.

Careful proofreading is again required, as well as bookkeeping accounts of the proofreading. When completed, record on roster: (Item lists proofread.) Recording the date and initials of proofreaders is advisable on rosters. This may also be done on the item lists.

Appendix F

Some Probabilistic
Considerations
Concerning Extreme
Ratings

Probabilistic considerations govern the decision to award extreme ratings, particularly I-2, Delta, and I-5. Each response to an item is taken as a sign of the subject's I-level. Thus in using the distribution or ogive of item ratings to arrive at a total protocol rating (TPR), the distribution is considered a set of signs. The reasoning of Meehl and Rosen (1955)

234

concerning the use of Bayes' theorem to justify inference from psychometric signs applies here.

Consider, for example, that the condition to be identified is being an I-2, against the alternative, to simplify the formulation, of being any higher I-level. The proportion of I-2 subjects in the population is the base rate, denoted by P; the proportion of those having any higher rating is Q. The base rate will of course depend on the particular population under study, but for the present exercise let us consider it fixed at .05. The proportion of I-2 subjects exhibiting a given sign, that is, giving a response in an I-2 category, is the valid positive rate, denoted p_1. The proportion of higher Ss exhibiting the same sign is the false positive rate, p_2.

A sign is, in a sense, valid so long as $p_1 > p_2$. Meehl and Rosen show, however, that one makes fewer mistakes saying that no one has a rare condition, here being I-2, than saying all who show the sign have it, unless the following inequality holds:

(1) $$P/Q > p_2/p_1.$$

How sure one is that subject is I-2 on the basis of that sign alone is given by:

(2) $$H_p = Pp_1/(Pp_1 + Qp_2).$$

Suppose there is a category of response for an item such that, if it is used as sole basis for classifying an individual as I-2, the valid positive rate would be approximately .5, the false positive rate approximately .05. Then $P/Q = .05/.95$ is about .05, while $p_2/p_1 = .05/.5 = .1$. Since the inequality in (1) is not satisfied, we are worse off using this category of response as a single sign than simply saying there are no I-2s. Our confidence in a diagnosis of I-2 status based on the single sign, according to (2),

$$H_p = .025/ (.025 + .0475),$$

is approximately 1/3.

Meehl and Rosen deprecate the use of more than one such sign as merely softening the impact of the requirements of Bayes' theorem, but they are too pessimistic. One must assume that among the I-2s two such items are statistically independent; a similar independence is assumed among those at higher levels, that is, those not I-2. This assumption does not state there is no correlation among items over the total range of cases, but only that the correlation between two such items depends only on whether S is an I-2 or not.

Consider the joint use of two such items as sign of being an I-2 subject. The ratio of P/Q remains .05, but, using the multiplication theorem for probabilities,

$$p_2'/p_1' = .0025/.25 = .01.$$

Thus the inequality in (1) is satisfied, and one does better saying that cases with both such responses are I-2 than saying that no one is. How sure one is that the subject is I-2 on the basis of two such signs is

$$H_p' = .0125/(.0125 + .0024) = .84.$$

If there are three such items, the probability of an I-2 exhibiting three diagnostic responses is .125; the false positive rate is .000125. Thus,

$$p_2''/p_1'' = .001, \text{ and}$$
$$H_p'' = .00625/(.00625 + .000119) = .98.$$

The presence of three I-2 responses no more univocal than the one under consideration can be considered reasonably clear evidence for I-2 status.

Suppose that of the thirty-six items, twenty have I-2 categories as good as the one considered here. The problem is to set the cutting score for ogives classed as I-2 so that almost all I-2s will be identified and almost no others will be classed I-2. The binominal theorem applies, with mean equal to np, standard deviation equal to $\sqrt{npq}$, where n is the number of items for which there is a scorable I-2 response, here twenty, and $q = 1 - p$.

We have assumed that for the I-2 population $p = p_1 = .5$. Thus the mean number of diagnostic responses will equal ten with a standard deviation of $\sqrt{5}$. For the non-I-2 group, $p = p_2 = .05$. The mean number of I-2 responses will be 1 with a standard deviation of about 1. A cutting point between three and four I-2 responses misclassifies only about 1 per cent of each group.

The absence of base rates from the latter formulation is illusory. The number of misclassifications is proportional to the rate of error times the base rate. Since there are many more who are not I-2 than who are, one could justify taking the cutting point between four and five I-2 responses. This would increase slightly the number of I-2s missed but decrease the total number of errors.

Obviously the items of our test do not constitute true Bernoulli trials. The valid positive rate and the false positive rate vary from item to item. A value of p_1 much greater than .5 seems unlikely to be achieved, but some items do have a value of p_2 much less than .05. While these variations affect the parameters of the problem, they do not affect the logic, and one could in principle refine the statistical model to take such facts into account. The assumption of "local independence" is more problematic. Concerning persons who are in some sense not really I-2 subjects, is it fair to assume that the ones who give I-2 responses to one item are no more likely than the others to give I-2 responses to different items? An intuitive appreciation of this difficulty has led us to look for qualitatively different signs in awarding extreme ratings, particularly high ones. The assumption of local independence is more plausible with respect to qualitatively different signs than with respect to two or more instances of a given kind of sign.

APPENDIX G

Abbreviations

I-level = ego level
Δ = Delta = an ego level interpolated between I-2 and I-3
N = number of cases
S = subject
SC = sentence completion
TAT = Thematic Apperception Test
TPR = total protocol rating
$\overline{\text{TPR}}$ = criterion TPR
UC = unclassified

REFERENCES

Adler, A. *The Individual Psychology of Alfred Adler*. H. L. Ansbacher and R. R. Ansbacher (Eds.) New York: Basic Books, 1956.

Arnold, M. *Story Sequence Analysis*. New York: Columbia University Press, 1962.

Cronbach, L. J. "Coefficient Alpha and the Internal Structure of Tests." *Psychometrika*, 1951, *16*, 297–334.

Dewey, J., and Tufts, J. H. *Ethics*. New York: Holt, 1908.

Fingarette, H. *The Self in Transformation*. New York: Basic Books, 1963.

Harvey, O. J., Hunt, D. E., and Schroder, H. M. *Conceptual Systems and Personality Organization*. New York: Wiley, 1961.

Isaacs, K. S. "Relatability, a Proposed Construct and an Approach to Its Validation." Unpublished doctoral dissertation, University of Chicago, 1956.

239

Kohlberg, L. "Development of Moral Character and Moral Ideology." In M. Hoffman and L. W. Hoffman (Eds.), *Review of Child Development Research*. Vol. 1. New York: Russell Sage Foundation, 1964. Pp. 383–431.

Loevinger, J. "Effect of Distortions of Measurement on Item Selection." *Educational and Psychological Measurement*, 1954, *14*, 441–448.

Loevinger, J. "The Meaning and Measurement of Ego Development." *American Psychologist*, 1966, *21*, 195–206.

Loevinger, J. "Theories of Ego Development." In L. Breger (Ed.), *Clinical-Cognitive Psychology: Models and Integrations*. Englewood Cliffs, N.J.: Prentice-Hall, 1969. Pp. 83–135.

Maslow, A. H. *Motivation and Personality*. New York: Harper, 1954.

Meehl, P. E., and Rosen, A. "Antecedent Probability and the Efficiency of Psychometric Signs, Patterns, or Cutting Scores." *Psychological Bulletin*, 1955, *52*, 194–216.

Peck, R. F., and Havighurst, R. J. *The Psychology of Character Development*. New York: Wiley, 1960.

Piaget, J. *The Moral Judgment of the Child*. London: Kegan Paul, 1932.

Rotter, J. B., and Rafferty, J. E. *Manual for the Rotter Incomplete Sentences Blank, College Form*. New York: Psychological Corporation, 1950.

Sullivan, C., Grant, M. Q., and Grant, J. D. "The Development of Interpersonal Maturity: Applications to Delinquency." *Psychiatry*, 1957, *20*, 373–385.

Sullivan, H. S. *The Interpersonal Theory of Psychiatry*. New York: Norton, 1953.

Thomson, G. H. *The Factorial Analysis of Human Ability*. New York: Houghton Mifflin, 1939.

Index

A

Achievement motive, 6, 75, 78, 90, 101
Adjustment: as bias in rating, 122–124; and ego development, 21, 125; importance of first ego level to, 4; relation of to ego level, 7, 22
ADLER, A., 2, 7
Affects, 58, 74, 82, 104, 132
Age-contingent scoring, 122
Age differences, 50–51, 122
Aggressive feelings, 58, 67, 74
Alpha coefficient, 44, 48, 49
Anxiety, 7, 8
Anxiety-gating theory, relation of to ego stability, 7–8
ARNOLD, M., 20

Autistic phase. *See* Presocial phase
Automatic compromise of TPR, 23, 35
Autonomous stage, 6; manifestations of, 98–106; nonpsychometric signs of, 132; relation of to interpersonal integration scale, 16

B

BALDWIN, J. M., 2
Behavior: diversity of, 9; as sign of ego level, 12
Behaviorism, 2, 120
Bias in rating, 117, 120–125
BLASI, A., 53
Bootstrap operation. **See** Empirical verification paradigm

C

Categories, 18; discrimination among, 21; formation of, 22, 24; I-level placement in, 24–25; as indication of popularity, 113; nondiscriminating, 19, 64; purpose of, 21–22; revision of in decoding, 23–25; use of in rating, 112–113

Categorized manual: comparison of with prepublication manual, 37; construction of, 31; description of, 18; in empirical studies, 22, 25

Character development: Peck's concept of, 3; relation of to ego development, 3

Children, 6, 7, 17, 32, 59

Clichés: avoided in manual, 21; of helping professions, 121–122; lower level given to in rating, 12, 55, 93, 108; as sign of conformist stage, 66

Clinical insight, 12–13. See also Psychometrics

Cognitive complexity. See Conceptual complexity

Cognitive preoccupations, 3, 5

Composite trained rater, 37, 41; as criterion, 42, 45–47

Compound response, 114–115; contrasted with pseudo-compound, 115; rating of, 114–117

Compromising differences, 35, 41

Conceptual complexity, 3–6, 75–76, 80, 88–89, 107, 132; as clue to ego level, 115–116; in compound responses, 115–116; relation of to verbal fluency, 51

Conceptual confusion, 4, 56

Conceptual simplicity, 4, 65

Conflict, inner, 6, 69, 94–95, 99, 106, 132

Conformist stage, 4–5; manifestations of, 64–70; relation of to adjustment, 7; relation of to interpersonal integration scale, 16

Conscience, 84

Conscientious stage, 5–6; manifestations of, 76–88; nonpsychomet-

ric signs of, 131–132; relation of to interpersonal integration scale, 16

Construct validity, 21; studies of in sentence completion test, 49–53

Context effects: in rating protocols, 112; removal of in scoring items, 22–23

Core functioning: as concept of Sullivan, Grant, and Grant, 15; relation of to scoring paradigm, 128

CRONBACH, L. J., 44

D

DARWIN, C., 2

Decoding, 23; in revision of categories, 23–24

Delta as level of interpersonal relatability, 16. See also Self-protective stage

Demographic variables: as bias in rating, 120; in conformist thinking, 4, 70; of samples, 26, 38

Dependence, 6, 57, 69, 88, 92, 101

DEWEY, J., 2

Distortion factor in measurement, 51–52

E

Ego: Adler's concept of, 7; as frame of reference, 7–8; not Freud's term, 1; origin of concept of, 1–3. See also Psychoanalysis; Regression

Egocentricity, 57, 95, 133

Eigen values, 48

Emotion. See Affects

Empirical verification paradigm, 22–26

Errors: of raters, 9, 12, 19; of subjects, 55, 121

Evasive responses, 64, 133

Exemplar manual, 18

F

Factor score, sum of item ratings as, 127

Factor structure of sentence completion test, 48–49
FINGARETTE, H., 7, 8
Format, history of, 18–19
Fragmentary responses, 118–119
FREUD, S., 1, 2

G

GRANT, J. D., 3, 15, 16
GRANT, M. Q. See WARREN, M.
Guilt, 5, 79

H

HARVEY, O. J., 3
Holism, 3
HOTELLING, H., 48
Humor, 97, 122; existential, 105–106; hostile, 20, 63, 133
HUNT, D., 3, 53, 127

I

I-2. See Impulsive stage
I-2/Δ as compromise TPR, 133
I-3. See Conformist stage
I-3/4. See Self-conscious transition
I-4. See Conscientious stage
I-4/5. See Transition
I-5. See Autonomous stage
I-6. See Integrated stage
Idealization, 63, 65, 81
Ideals, 5, 80, 106, 133
Identity, 102, 108–109, 121
I-level: behavioral signs of, 8–9; as code term, 16–17; intervals of, 17, 45; of interpersonal integration, 16; in manual construction, 18; nonpsychometric signs of, 131–132; transitions in, 16–17
Impressionistic I-level, 52, 131
Impulse control, 3, 82, 133; sexual, 58, 62, 133
Impulsive stage, 4; manifestations of, 56–58; nonpsychometric signs of, 132–133; relation of to interpersonal integration scale, 16
Independence. See Dependence

Individuality, 6, 7, 88, 93, 101
Inner life, 5, 68, 81, 94–95, 107, 122. See also Conflict
Instinctual drives, 2
Integrated stage, 6–7; manifestations of, 106–109; nonpsychometric signs of, 132; relation of to adjustment, 7
Intellectual development: importance of first ego level to, 3–4; relation of to ego development, 2, 9
Intelligence: as bias in ratings, 120–121; relation of to ego level, 52–53
Interpersonal integration: core function of, 15; relation of to ego development, 3
Interpersonal relatability, 3
Interpersonal relations, 3, 68, 74, 83–84, 90–91, 121
Interrater reliability, 41–47
Intuitive ratings, 52, 131
IQ. See Intelligence
ISAACS, K., 3, 16, 126–127
Item manuals: construction of, 16, 26–27; use of in rating, 55, 111–113

K

KOHLBERG, L., 3, 53, 127

L

Literary quality of responses, 122
LOEVINGER, J., 2, 3, 51
LUCAS, R., 49–50

M

Manipulation, 4, 16, 59
Manual construction, rules of, 19–22
MASLOW, A., 7
MEAD, G. H., 2
Meaning, 3, 20, 111, 113; search for, 7
MEEHL, P. E., 234–236
Milestone sequence, 15
Moralization of judgment, 3

N

Nonpsychometric signs of ego level, 41, 131–133

O

Ogive: automatic score of, 52; basis for rules of, 128; composite rater score of, 46–47; and rules for deriving TPRs, 128–130; use of in rating, 41, 130
Omissions, scoring of, 20, 64, 118–119
Opportunism. *See* Self-protective stage

P

Parents, 6, 59, 60, 81
Pathology, 22; as bias in rating, 122–124, 132
PECK, R., 3
PIAGET, J., 3, 127
Polar continuum, 15
Prepublication manual, 21; comparison of with (a) categorized manual, 35–37, (b) present manual, 21–22; example of decoding in, 23–24; samples used for, 26–33; studies with, 37–53
Presocial phase, 4
Projective technique, 8, 9
Psychoanalysis, 1–3, 21, 128; ego psychology of, 2, 7; psychic energy in, 3
Psychological causality, 5, 56, 85, 91–92, 103–104, 132
Psychometrics, 9, 19, 51; compared with clinical approach, 12–13, 127–128; and quantification strategy, 15–18
Psychosexual development: importance of first ego level to, 4; relation of to ego development, 2, 9
Psychotherapy, effect of on sentence completion test, 124

Q

Quantification strategy in measuring ego level, 15–18

R

Raters: best, 35; reliability of, 41–47; self-trained, 37; self-training program for, 111–113; in studies of prepublication manual, 37–38
Rating: bias in, 117, 120–125; psychometric attitude toward, 111–112; tacit component of, 111
Rating procedures: for criterion TPRs, 45; intuitive, 52, 131; ogive rules in, 128–130; recording ratings in, 119–120; for single responses, 113–119; for total protocols, 131–133
Rationalized manual, 18–19; in verification paradigm, 22
Regression: ego, 123–124; in service of ego, 127
Richness of protocol, 55, 98, 131
Role: conception, 21, 55, 86, 102, 121, 132; conventional sex, 4, 66; feminine, 21, 73; reconciliation, 108
Rorschach test, 15
ROSEN, A., 234–236
ROTTER, J., 15, 49
Rotter Incomplete Sentence Blank, 15, 18, 49

S

Samples: December 1967, 27–28, 32–33, 38–41; Form 9–62, 27–30, 32, 40; preliminary, 27, 29–31; for prepublication manual, 26–33; professional, 27–32; sealed, 27–28, 32, 38–41; single-women, 27–31; in studies of prepublication manual, 38–41; supplementary, 27–31; Toronto, 27–28, 32, 38–41
SCHRODER, H., 3
Scoring paradigm: and core functioning, 127–130; highest level of, 126–127; mean item rating in, 127; modal item rating in, 127
Selective inattention, 7, 125
Self-actualizing persons, 7
Self-concept, 3, 82; as pawn, 61, 78

Self-conscious transition, 5; manifestations of, 70–76

Self-criticism, 5, 72, 82, 125

Self-fulfillment. *See* Self-realization

Self-protective stage, 4; manifestations of, 59–64; nonpsychometric signs of, 133; relation of to adjustment, 7; relation of to interpersonal integration scale, 16; similarity of to Delta level of relatability, 16

Self-realization, 6, 84, 93, 101, 106, 108, 121, 132

Self-rejection, 5, 58

Self-trained raters, 37

Self-system, 3; and ego stability, 7–8; relation of to style of life, 7

Sex, 69, 86, 105, 106, 119, 124. See *also* Psychosexual development; Impulse control; Role

Sex differences, 51

Social acceptability, 5, 65

Social desirability, 5, 65

Socioeconomic status: biasing effect of, 120–121; and ego development, 9

Stereotypes, 100

Stereotypy, 56, 77

Style of life, 7

SULLIVAN, C., 3, 15, 16

SULLIVAN, E. V., 32, 50–51

SULLIVAN, H. S., 2–3, 7–8; and concept of "malevolent transformation," 59

Symbiotic phase, 4

T

Thematic Apperception Test, 15, 127

THOMSON, G. H., 48

Toleration for ambiguity, 98

Total protocol rating (TPR): criterion, 35, 44–45; procedure, 131–133; use of in manual revision, 26

Transition: concept of, 17–18; from conscientious to autonomous stage, 6, 88–97; from self-protective to conformist stage, 64. *See also* Self-conscious transition

TUFTS, J., 2

U

Unclassified response, procedure for rating, 117–118

Unique responses, 55, 117, 123, 125, 132

V

Verbal fluency. *See* Word count

W

WARREN, M., 3, 15, 16

WORD, V. I., 35

Word count, 20; as bias in rating, 121; relation of to ego level, 35–36, 51–52

Z

Zero-sum game, 4